A SHERLOCK HOLMES GRAPHIC NOVEL

The HOUND of the BASKERVILLES

A SHERLOCK HOLMES GRAPHIC NOVEL

The HOUND of the BASKERVILLES

ADAPTED FROM THE ORIGINAL NOVEL BY
SIR ARTHUR CONAN DOYLE
ILLUSTRATED BY
I.N.J. CULBARD
TEXT ADAPTED BY
IAN EDGINTON

SELF MADE HERO

First published 2009 by SelfMadeHero
139–141 Pancras Road
London NW1 1UN
www.selfmadehero.com

Copyright © 2009 SelfMadeHero
This edition printed in 2017

Adapted by Ian Edginton
Art by I.N.J. Culbard
Layout by Andy Huckle

Publishing Director: Emma Hayley
Sales & Marketing Manager: Sam Humphrey
Editorial & Production Manager: Guillaume Rater
UK Publicist: Paul Smith
US Publicist: Maya Bradford
Designer: Txabi Jones
Textual Consultant: Nick de Somogyi
With thanks to: Catherine Cooke, John Corbett
and Jane Laporte

Dedications
For Katy and Joseph and Benjamin and my dear Mamma.
With enormous thanks to my dear friend Colin – I.N.J. Culbard

For my son Seth and the trio of lovely ladies in my life: my wife,
Jane, and daughters, Constance and Corinthia – Ian Edginton

A CIP record for this book is available from the British Library

ISBN 978-1-910593-32-5

10 9 8 7 6 5 4 3 2 1

Printed and bound in Slovenia

FOREWORD

THE FOOTPRINTS OF A GIGANTIC HOUND...

Sherlock Holmes wasn't supposed to be in this book.

When Conan Doyle set to work in March of 1901, he simply wanted to write what he called "a real creeper". In a note to his mother, he proposed a title, *The Hound of the Baskervilles*, but there was no mention of his famous detective. As the novel progressed, however, Conan Doyle found that he needed a strong central figure to hold the plot together. "Why should I invent such a character," he said, "when I have him already in the form of Holmes?"

There was one problem: Sherlock Holmes was supposed to be dead. Eight years earlier, in a story called "The Final Problem", Holmes had been dragged to his death by the notorious Professor Moriarty at Switzerland's Reichenbach Falls. "I have been much blamed for doing that gentleman to death," wrote the weary author, "but I hold that it was not murder, but justifiable homicide in self-defence, since, if I had not killed him, he would certainly have killed me."

Now, however, as *The Hound of the Baskervilles* took shape, Conan Doyle relented and brought the detective back for a curtain call. "I have nearly finished 'Sherlock'," he told his mother as the manuscript neared completion, "and I hope he will live up to his reputation."

He needn't have worried. On the morning of publication in *The Strand* magazine, home of the original Holmes tales, a long line of expectant readers stood waiting for copies, and bribes were offered for advance peeks. The subsequent book edition became a massive bestseller, and would go on to become one of the most popular novels of the 20th century.

Not surprisingly, this success brought pressure for more Sherlock Holmes stories. Conan Doyle had made it clear that *The Hound* was nothing more than a previously untold tale, predating the fatal encounter with Professor Moriarty. Soon, however, the American magazine *Collier's Weekly* offered a staggering sum of money for a series of new adventures featuring a fully resurrected Holmes. Bowing to the inevitable, Conan Doyle signalled his acceptance with a laconic postcard: "Very well. A.C.D." All that remained was to figure out how the detective had survived his apparent death at the Reichenbach Falls.

But that's a different story...

— Daniel Stashower
author of the Edgar Award-winning
Teller of Tales: The Life of Arthur Conan Doyle

MR.
SHERLOCK
HOLMES
LONDON, 1889.
BAKER
STREET .W.
RATHBONE'S
BROOKER'S FISHPASTE
BROOKER'S FISHPASTE
SAILOR ARRESTED
221B

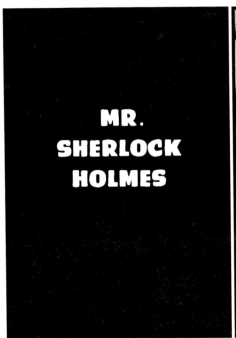

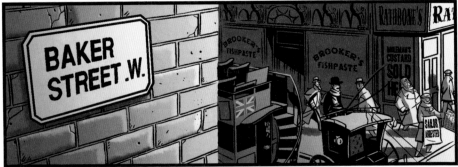

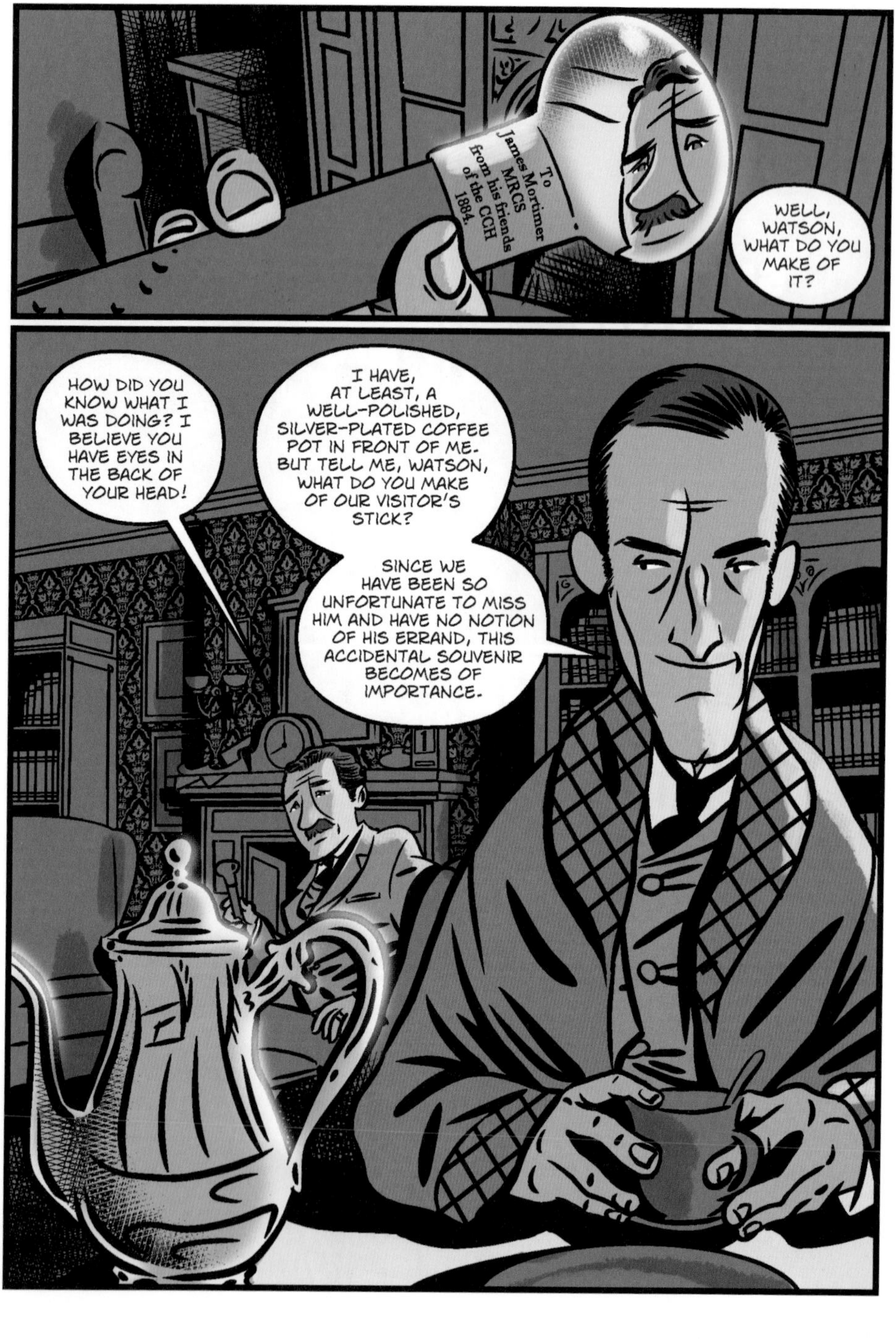
To
James Mortimer
MRCS
from his friends
of the CCH
1884.
WELL, WATSON, WHAT DO YOU MAKE OF IT?
HOW DID YOU KNOW WHAT I WAS DOING? I BELIEVE YOU HAVE EYES IN THE BACK OF YOUR HEAD!
I HAVE, AT LEAST, A WELL-POLISHED, SILVER-PLATED COFFEE POT IN FRONT OF ME. BUT TELL ME, WATSON, WHAT DO YOU MAKE OF OUR VISITOR'S STICK?
SINCE WE HAVE BEEN SO UNFORTUNATE TO MISS HIM AND HAVE NO NOTION OF HIS ERRAND, THIS ACCIDENTAL SOUVENIR BECOMES OF IMPORTANCE.

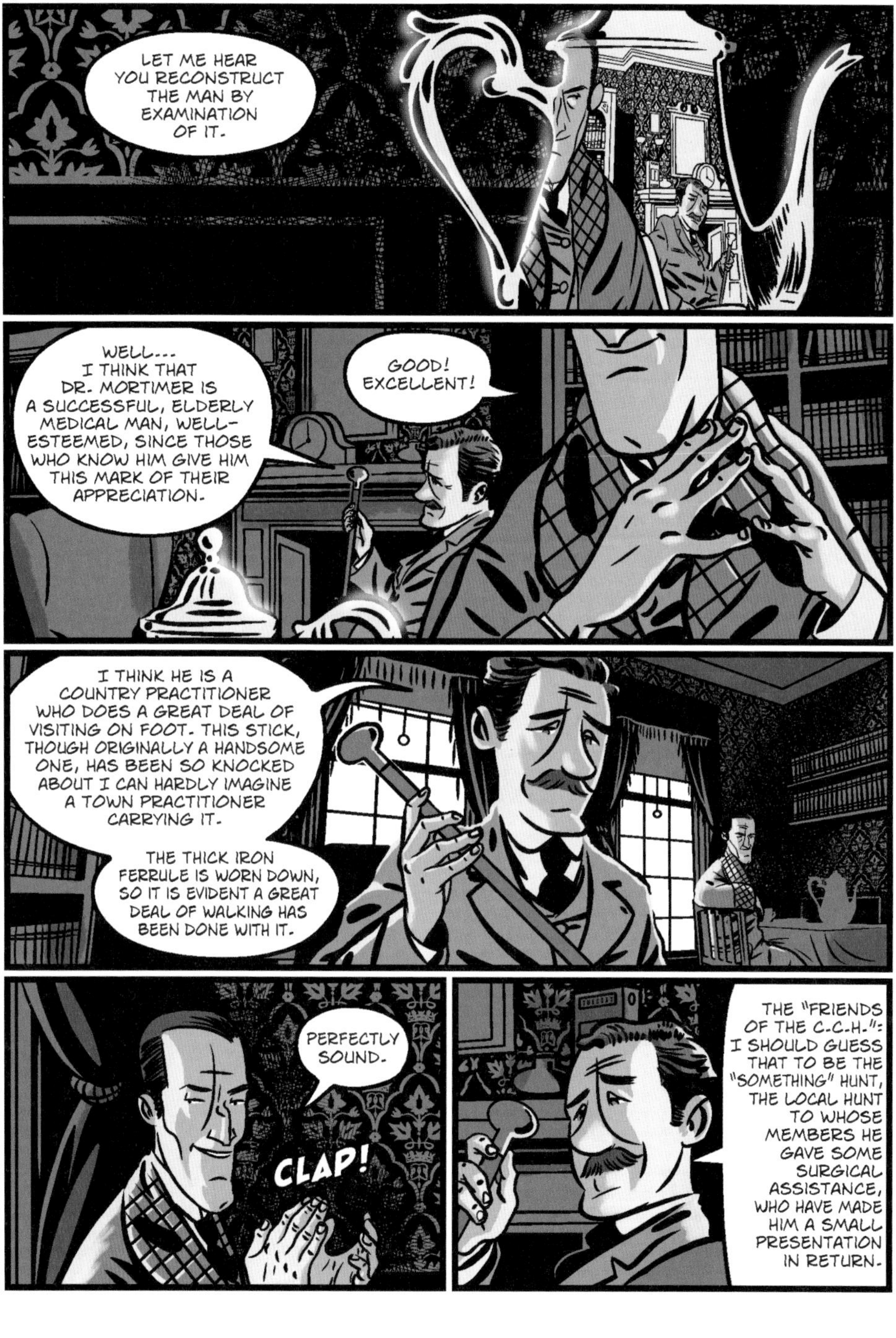
LET ME HEAR YOU RECONSTRUCT THE MAN BY EXAMINATION OF IT.
WELL... I THINK THAT DR. MORTIMER IS A SUCCESSFUL, ELDERLY MEDICAL MAN, WELL-ESTEEMED, SINCE THOSE WHO KNOW HIM GIVE HIM THIS MARK OF THEIR APPRECIATION.
GOOD! EXCELLENT!
I THINK HE IS A COUNTRY PRACTITIONER WHO DOES A GREAT DEAL OF VISITING ON FOOT. THIS STICK, THOUGH ORIGINALLY A HANDSOME ONE, HAS BEEN SO KNOCKED ABOUT I CAN HARDLY IMAGINE A TOWN PRACTITIONER CARRYING IT.
THE THICK IRON FERRULE IS WORN DOWN, SO IT IS EVIDENT A GREAT DEAL OF WALKING HAS BEEN DONE WITH IT.
PERFECTLY SOUND.
CLAP!
THE "FRIENDS OF THE C.C.H.": I SHOULD GUESS THAT TO BE THE "SOMETHING" HUNT, THE LOCAL HUNT TO WHOSE MEMBERS HE GAVE SOME SURGICAL ASSISTANCE, WHO HAVE MADE HIM A SMALL PRESENTATION IN RETURN.

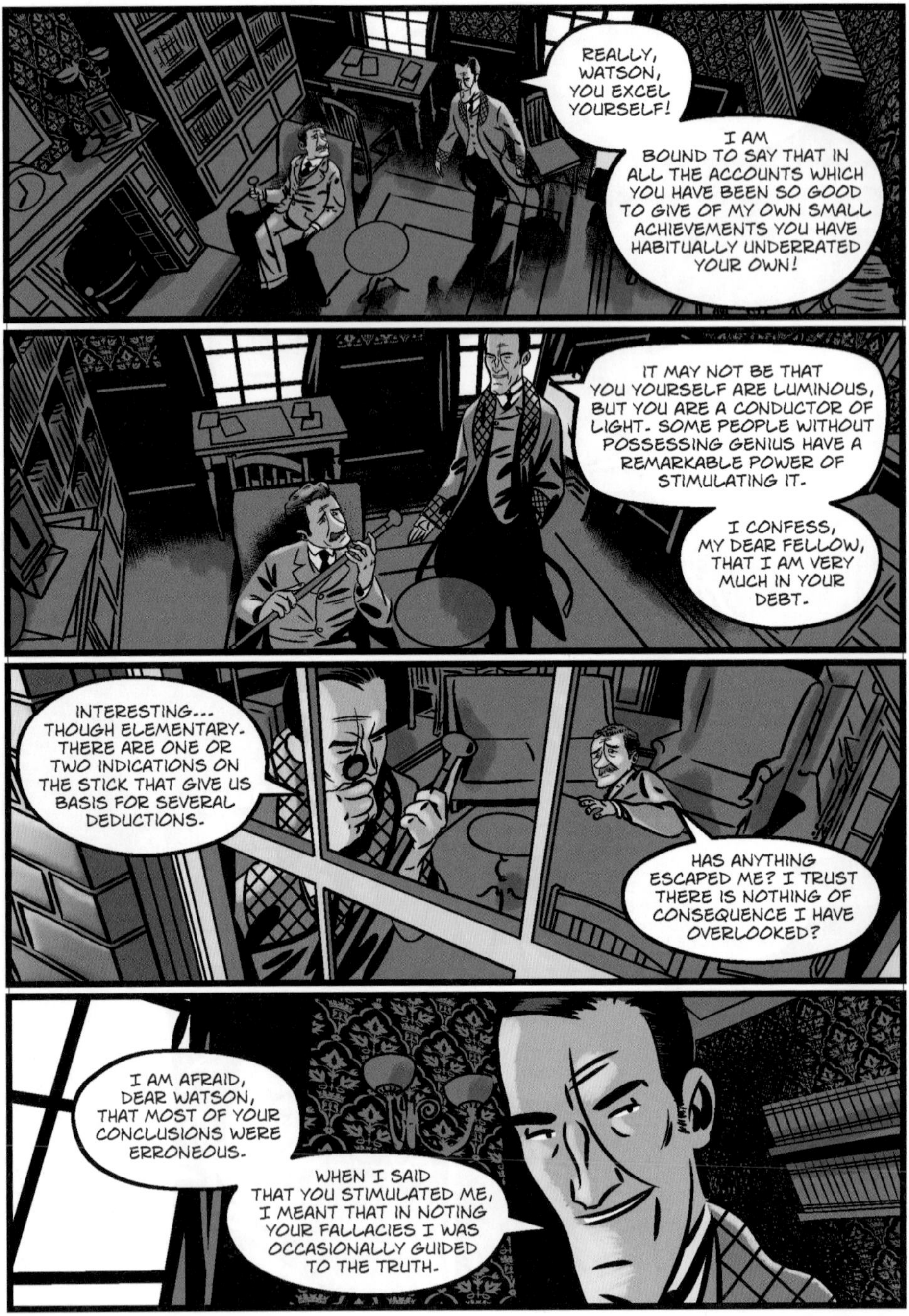
REALLY, WATSON, YOU EXCEL YOURSELF!
I AM BOUND TO SAY THAT IN ALL THE ACCOUNTS WHICH YOU HAVE BEEN SO GOOD TO GIVE OF MY OWN SMALL ACHIEVEMENTS YOU HAVE HABITUALLY UNDERRATED YOUR OWN!
IT MAY NOT BE THAT YOU YOURSELF ARE LUMINOUS, BUT YOU ARE A CONDUCTOR OF LIGHT. SOME PEOPLE WITHOUT POSSESSING GENIUS HAVE A REMARKABLE POWER OF STIMULATING IT.
I CONFESS, MY DEAR FELLOW, THAT I AM VERY MUCH IN YOUR DEBT.
INTERESTING... THOUGH ELEMENTARY. THERE ARE ONE OR TWO INDICATIONS ON THE STICK THAT GIVE US BASIS FOR SEVERAL DEDUCTIONS.
HAS ANYTHING ESCAPED ME? I TRUST THERE IS NOTHING OF CONSEQUENCE I HAVE OVERLOOKED?
I AM AFRAID, DEAR WATSON, THAT MOST OF YOUR CONCLUSIONS WERE ERRONEOUS.
WHEN I SAID THAT YOU STIMULATED ME, I MEANT THAT IN NOTING YOUR FALLACIES I WAS OCCASIONALLY GUIDED TO THE TRUTH.

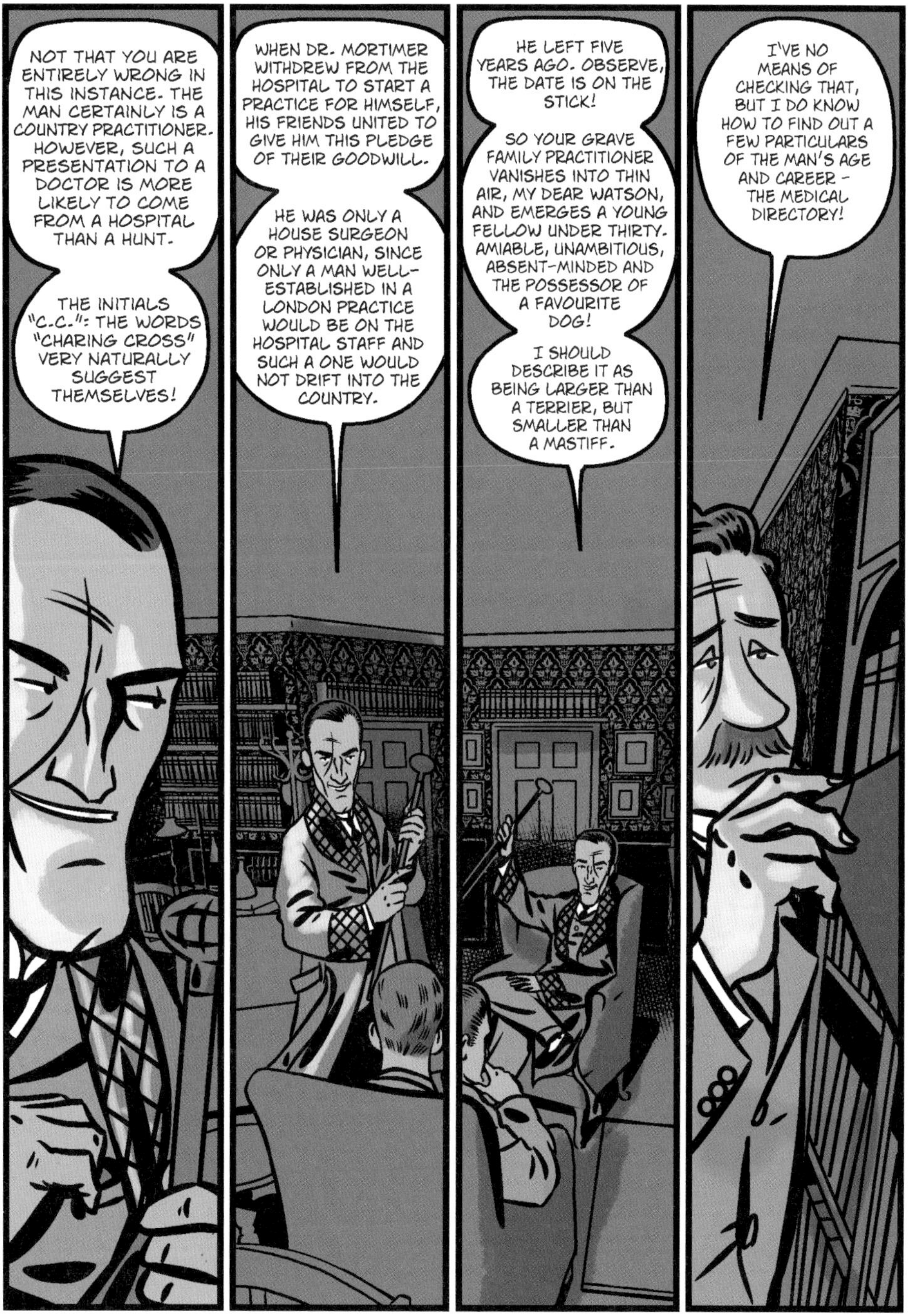
NOT THAT YOU ARE ENTIRELY WRONG IN THIS INSTANCE. THE MAN CERTAINLY IS A COUNTRY PRACTITIONER. HOWEVER, SUCH A PRESENTATION TO A DOCTOR IS MORE LIKELY TO COME FROM A HOSPITAL THAN A HUNT.
THE INITIALS "C.C.": THE WORDS "CHARING CROSS" VERY NATURALLY SUGGEST THEMSELVES!
WHEN DR. MORTIMER WITHDREW FROM THE HOSPITAL TO START A PRACTICE FOR HIMSELF, HIS FRIENDS UNITED TO GIVE HIM THIS PLEDGE OF THEIR GOODWILL.
HE WAS ONLY A HOUSE SURGEON OR PHYSICIAN, SINCE ONLY A MAN WELL-ESTABLISHED IN A LONDON PRACTICE WOULD BE ON THE HOSPITAL STAFF AND SUCH A ONE WOULD NOT DRIFT INTO THE COUNTRY.
HE LEFT FIVE YEARS AGO. OBSERVE, THE DATE IS ON THE STICK!
SO YOUR GRAVE FAMILY PRACTITIONER VANISHES INTO THIN AIR, MY DEAR WATSON, AND EMERGES A YOUNG FELLOW UNDER THIRTY. AMIABLE, UNAMBITIOUS, ABSENT-MINDED AND THE POSSESSOR OF A FAVOURITE DOG!
I SHOULD DESCRIBE IT AS BEING LARGER THAN A TERRIER, BUT SMALLER THAN A MASTIFF.
I'VE NO MEANS OF CHECKING THAT, BUT I DO KNOW HOW TO FIND OUT A FEW PARTICULARS OF THE MAN'S AGE AND CAREER - THE MEDICAL DIRECTORY!

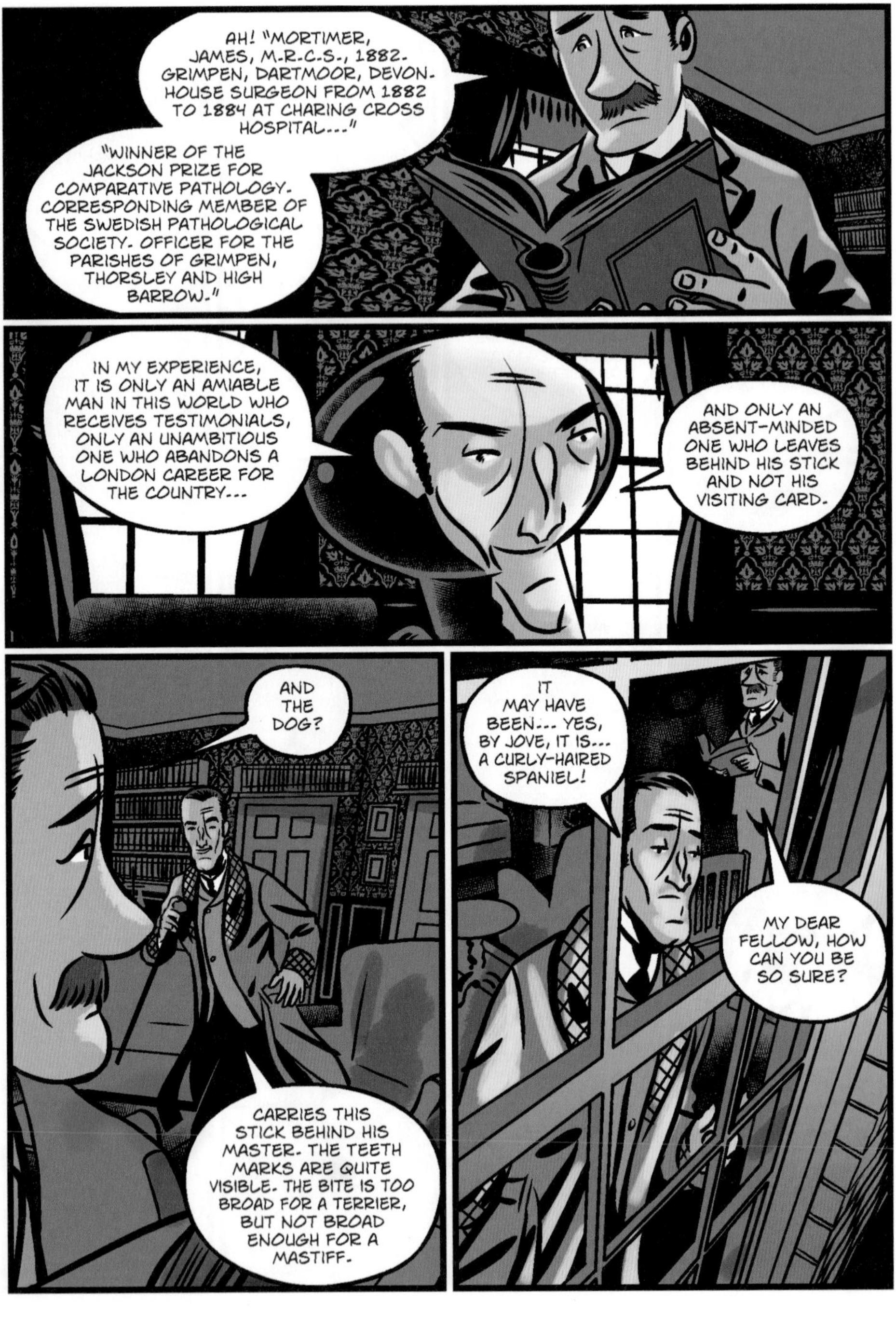
AH! "MORTIMER, JAMES, M.R.C.S., 1882. GRIMPEN, DARTMOOR, DEVON. HOUSE SURGEON FROM 1882 TO 1884 AT CHARING CROSS HOSPITAL..."
"WINNER OF THE JACKSON PRIZE FOR COMPARATIVE PATHOLOGY. CORRESPONDING MEMBER OF THE SWEDISH PATHOLOGICAL SOCIETY. OFFICER FOR THE PARISHES OF GRIMPEN, THORSLEY AND HIGH BARROW."
IN MY EXPERIENCE, IT IS ONLY AN AMIABLE MAN IN THIS WORLD WHO RECEIVES TESTIMONIALS, ONLY AN UNAMBITIOUS ONE WHO ABANDONS A LONDON CAREER FOR THE COUNTRY...
AND ONLY AN ABSENT-MINDED ONE WHO LEAVES BEHIND HIS STICK AND NOT HIS VISITING CARD.
AND THE DOG?
CARRIES THIS STICK BEHIND HIS MASTER. THE TEETH MARKS ARE QUITE VISIBLE. THE BITE IS TOO BROAD FOR A TERRIER, BUT NOT BROAD ENOUGH FOR A MASTIFF.
IT MAY HAVE BEEN... YES, BY JOVE, IT IS... A CURLY-HAIRED SPANIEL!
MY DEAR FELLOW, HOW CAN YOU BE SO SURE?

"FOR THE VERY SIMPLE REASON I CAN SEE THE DOG HIMSELF ON OUR VERY DOORSTEP..."

TRRRRIINGGG!

AND THERE IS THE RING OF ITS OWNER!

DO NOT MOVE, WATSON! HE IS A PROFESSIONAL BROTHER OF YOURS; YOUR PRESENCE MAY BE OF ASSISTANCE TO ME!

NOW IS THE DRAMATIC MOMENT OF FATE, WHEN YOU HEAR A STEP UPON THE STAIR AND KNOW NOT WHETHER FOR GOOD OR ILL!

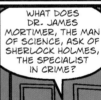

WHAT DOES DR. JAMES MORTIMER, THE MAN OF SCIENCE, ASK OF SHERLOCK HOLMES, THE SPECIALIST IN CRIME?

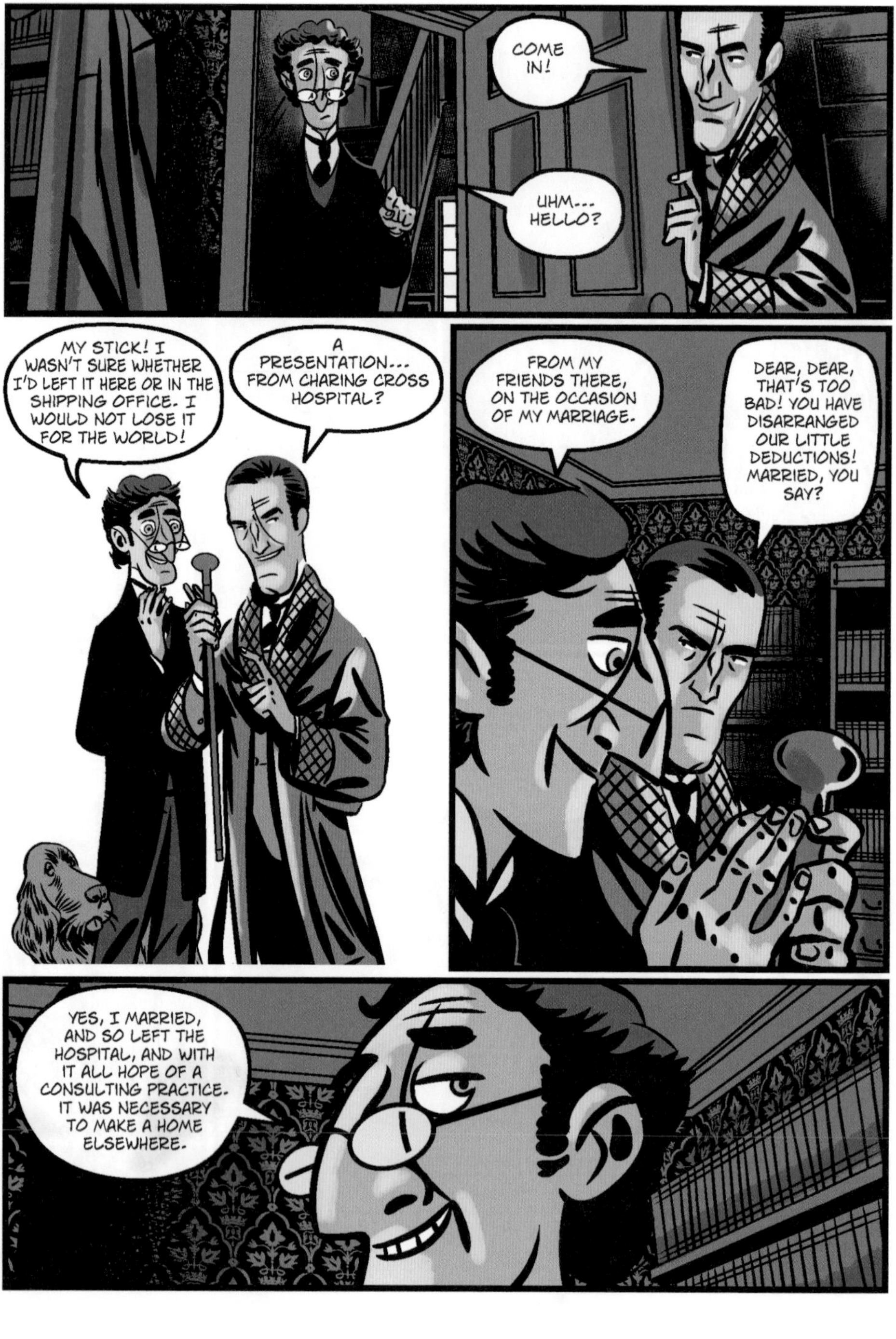
COME IN!
UHM... HELLO?
MY STICK! I WASN'T SURE WHETHER I'D LEFT IT HERE OR IN THE SHIPPING OFFICE. I WOULD NOT LOSE IT FOR THE WORLD!
A PRESENTATION... FROM CHARING CROSS HOSPITAL?
FROM MY FRIENDS THERE, ON THE OCCASION OF MY MARRIAGE.
DEAR, DEAR, THAT'S TOO BAD! YOU HAVE DISARRANGED OUR LITTLE DEDUCTIONS! MARRIED, YOU SAY?
YES, I MARRIED, AND SO LEFT THE HOSPITAL, AND WITH IT ALL HOPE OF A CONSULTING PRACTICE. IT WAS NECESSARY TO MAKE A HOME ELSEWHERE.

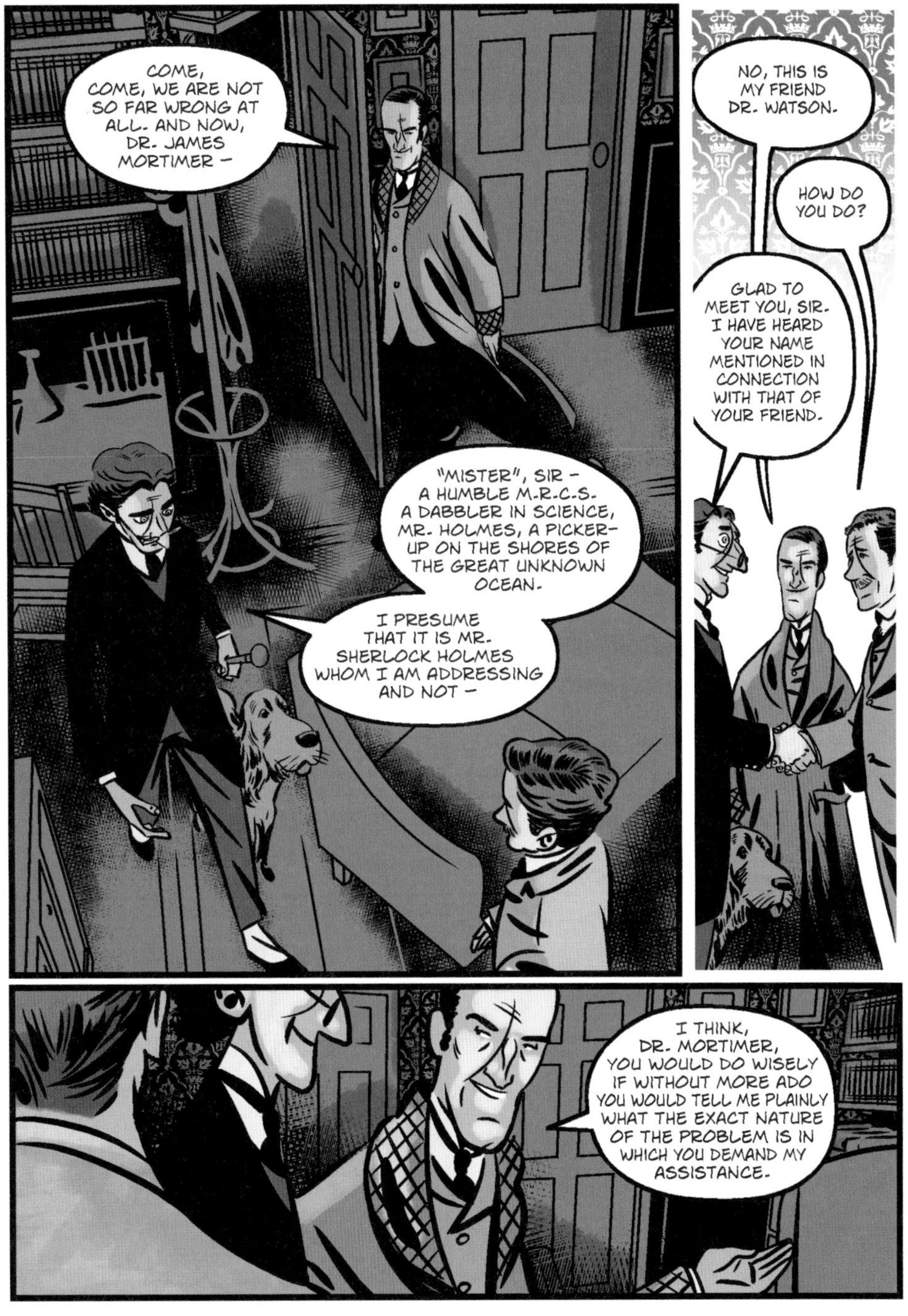
COME, COME, WE ARE NOT SO FAR WRONG AT ALL. AND NOW, DR. JAMES MORTIMER –
"MISTER", SIR – A HUMBLE M.R.C.S. A DABBLER IN SCIENCE, MR. HOLMES, A PICKER-UP ON THE SHORES OF THE GREAT UNKNOWN OCEAN.
I PRESUME THAT IT IS MR. SHERLOCK HOLMES WHOM I AM ADDRESSING AND NOT –
NO, THIS IS MY FRIEND DR. WATSON.
HOW DO YOU DO?
GLAD TO MEET YOU, SIR. I HAVE HEARD YOUR NAME MENTIONED IN CONNECTION WITH THAT OF YOUR FRIEND.
I THINK, DR. MORTIMER, YOU WOULD DO WISELY IF WITHOUT MORE ADO YOU WOULD TELL ME PLAINLY WHAT THE EXACT NATURE OF THE PROBLEM IS IN WHICH YOU DEMAND MY ASSISTANCE.

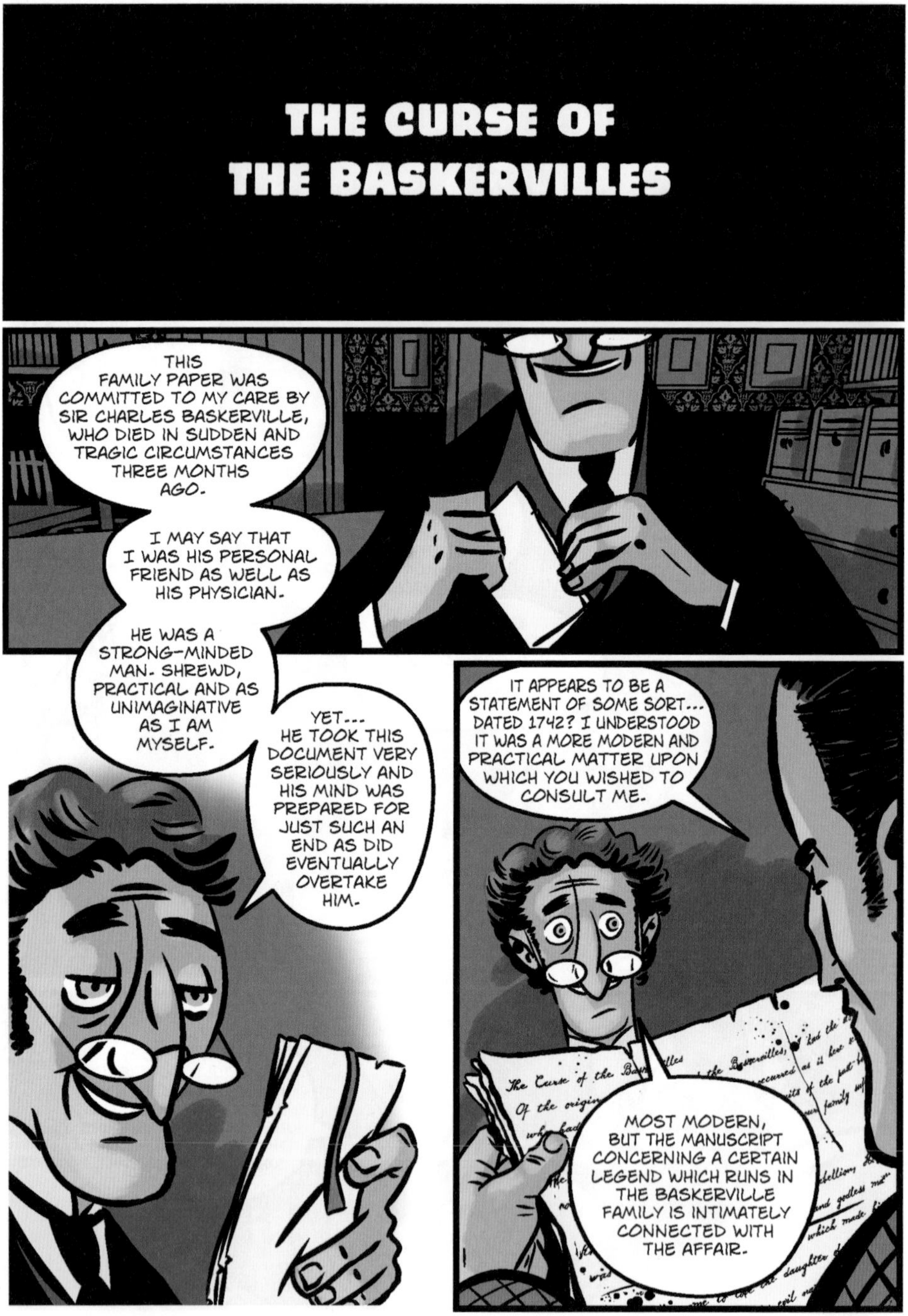
THE CURSE OF THE BASKERVILLES
THIS FAMILY PAPER WAS COMMITTED TO MY CARE BY SIR CHARLES BASKERVILLE, WHO DIED IN SUDDEN AND TRAGIC CIRCUMSTANCES THREE MONTHS AGO.
I MAY SAY THAT I WAS HIS PERSONAL FRIEND AS WELL AS HIS PHYSICIAN.
HE WAS A STRONG-MINDED MAN. SHREWD, PRACTICAL AND AS UNIMAGINATIVE AS I AM MYSELF.
YET... HE TOOK THIS DOCUMENT VERY SERIOUSLY AND HIS MIND WAS PREPARED FOR JUST SUCH AN END AS DID EVENTUALLY OVERTAKE HIM.
IT APPEARS TO BE A STATEMENT OF SOME SORT... DATED 1742? I UNDERSTOOD IT WAS A MORE MODERN AND PRACTICAL MATTER UPON WHICH YOU WISHED TO CONSULT ME.
MOST MODERN, BUT THE MANUSCRIPT CONCERNING A CERTAIN LEGEND WHICH RUNS IN THE BASKERVILLE FAMILY IS INTIMATELY CONNECTED WITH THE AFFAIR.

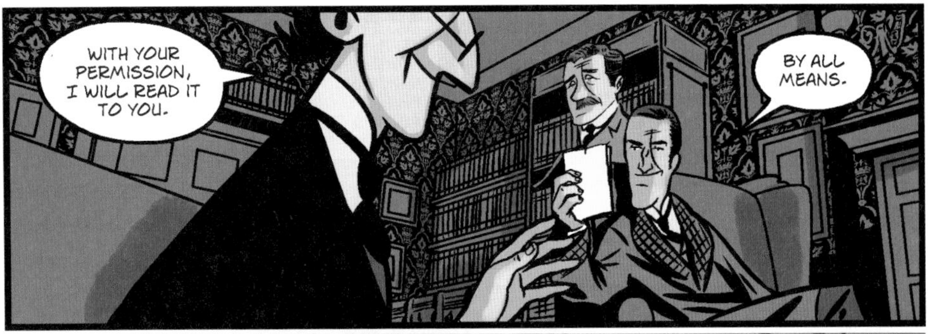
WITH YOUR PERMISSION, I WILL READ IT TO YOU.
BY ALL MEANS.

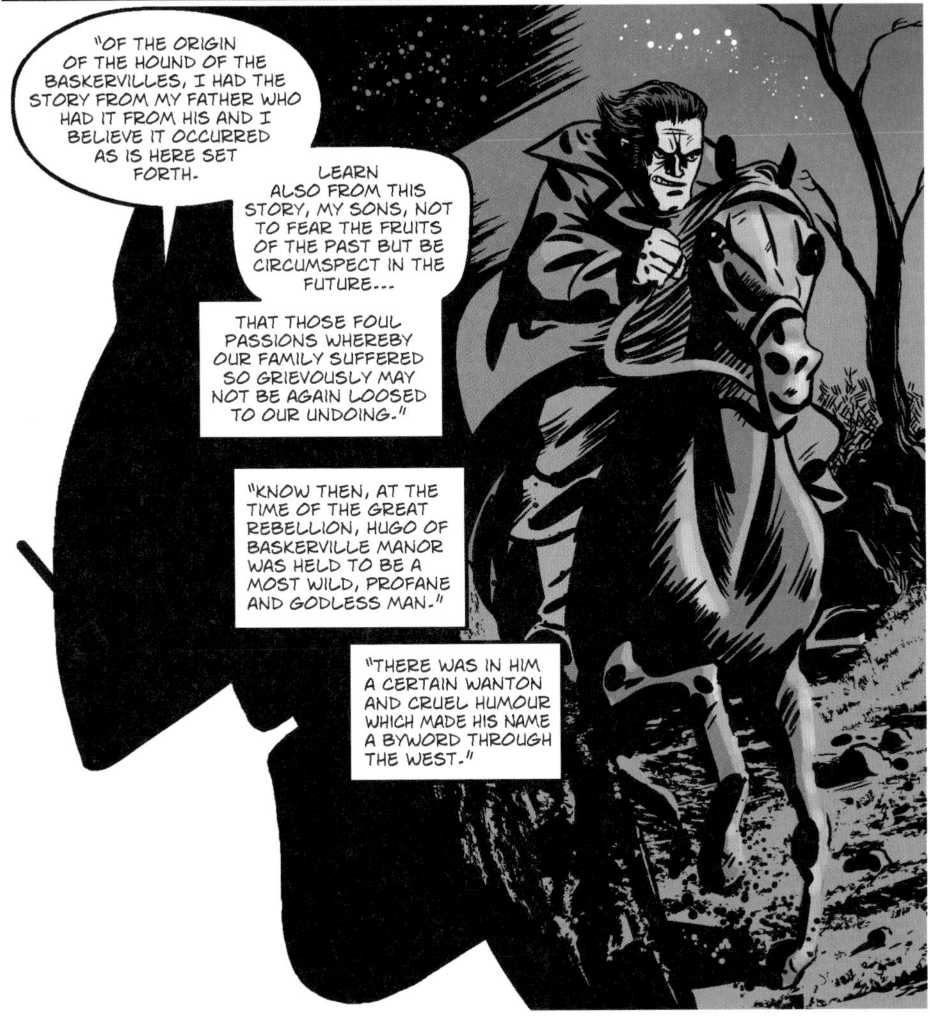
"OF THE ORIGIN OF THE HOUND OF THE BASKERVILLES, I HAD THE STORY FROM MY FATHER WHO HAD IT FROM HIS AND I BELIEVE IT OCCURRED AS IS HERE SET FORTH.
LEARN ALSO FROM THIS STORY, MY SONS, NOT TO FEAR THE FRUITS OF THE PAST BUT BE CIRCUMSPECT IN THE FUTURE...
THAT THOSE FOUL PASSIONS WHEREBY OUR FAMILY SUFFERED SO GRIEVOUSLY MAY NOT BE AGAIN LOOSED TO OUR UNDOING."
"KNOW THEN, AT THE TIME OF THE GREAT REBELLION, HUGO OF BASKERVILLE MANOR WAS HELD TO BE A MOST WILD, PROFANE AND GODLESS MAN."
"THERE WAS IN HIM A CERTAIN WANTON AND CRUEL HUMOUR WHICH MADE HIS NAME A BYWORD THROUGH THE WEST."

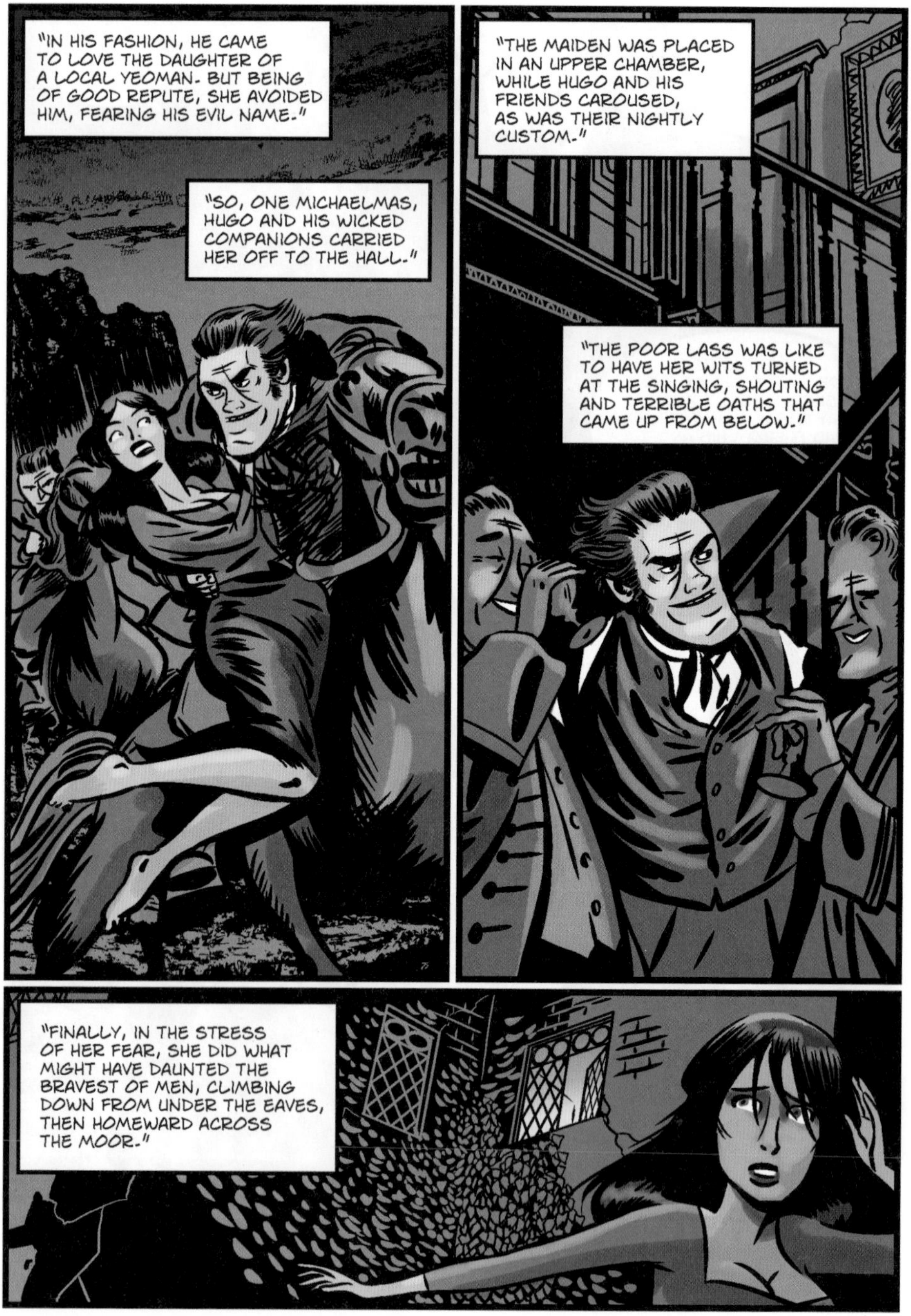
"IN HIS FASHION, HE CAME TO LOVE THE DAUGHTER OF A LOCAL YEOMAN. BUT BEING OF GOOD REPUTE, SHE AVOIDED HIM, FEARING HIS EVIL NAME."
"SO, ONE MICHAELMAS, HUGO AND HIS WICKED COMPANIONS CARRIED HER OFF TO THE HALL."
"THE MAIDEN WAS PLACED IN AN UPPER CHAMBER, WHILE HUGO AND HIS FRIENDS CAROUSED, AS WAS THEIR NIGHTLY CUSTOM."
"THE POOR LASS WAS LIKE TO HAVE HER WITS TURNED AT THE SINGING, SHOUTING AND TERRIBLE OATHS THAT CAME UP FROM BELOW."
"FINALLY, IN THE STRESS OF HER FEAR, SHE DID WHAT MIGHT HAVE DAUNTED THE BRAVEST OF MEN, CLIMBING DOWN FROM UNDER THE EAVES, THEN HOMEWARD ACROSS THE MOOR."

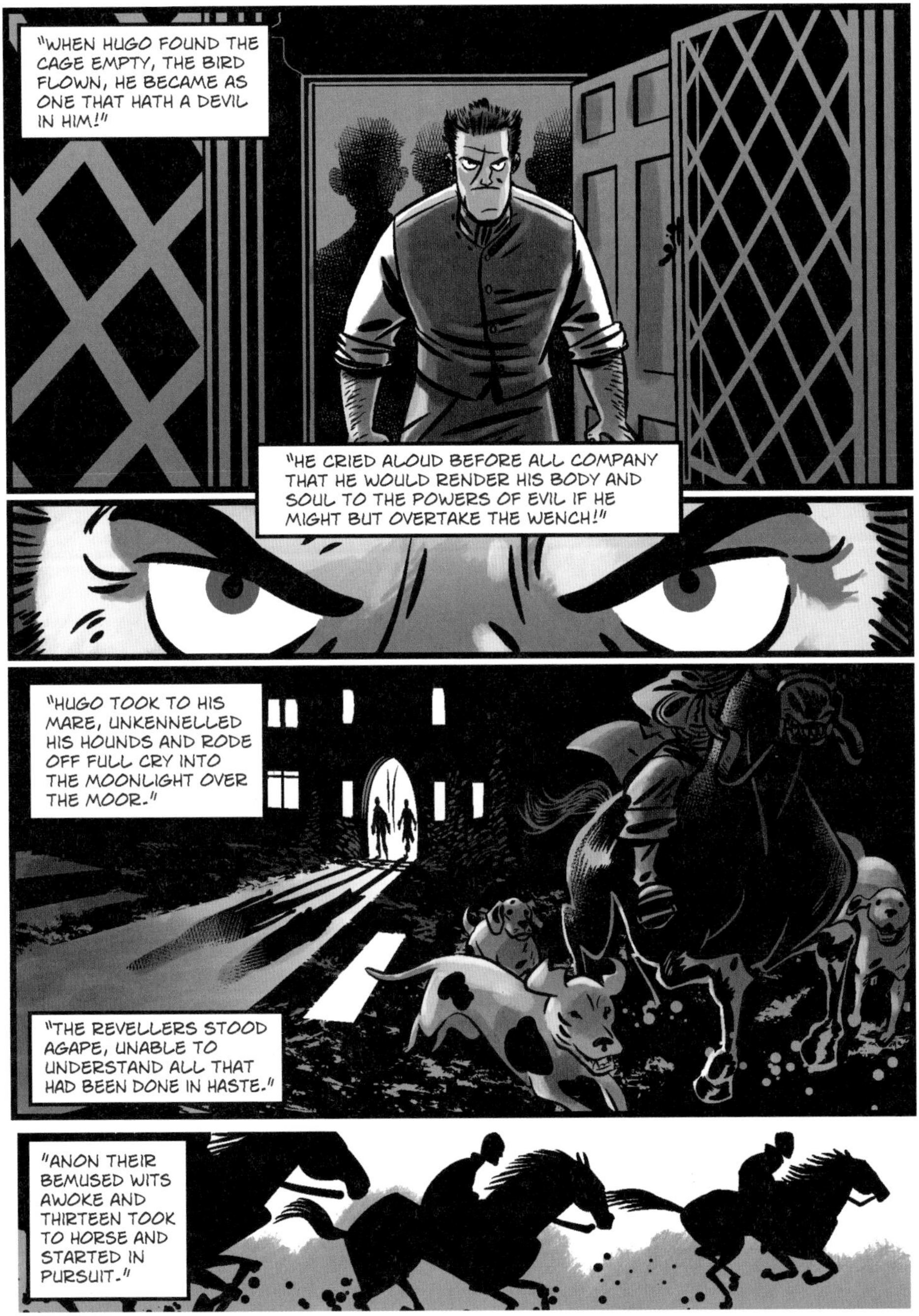
"WHEN HUGO FOUND THE CAGE EMPTY, THE BIRD FLOWN, HE BECAME AS ONE THAT HATH A DEVIL IN HIM!"
"HE CRIED ALOUD BEFORE ALL COMPANY THAT HE WOULD RENDER HIS BODY AND SOUL TO THE POWERS OF EVIL IF HE MIGHT BUT OVERTAKE THE WENCH!"
"HUGO TOOK TO HIS MARE, UNKENNELLED HIS HOUNDS AND RODE OFF FULL CRY INTO THE MOONLIGHT OVER THE MOOR."
"THE REVELLERS STOOD AGAPE, UNABLE TO UNDERSTAND ALL THAT HAD BEEN DONE IN HASTE."
"ANON THEIR BEMUSED WITS AWOKE AND THIRTEEN TOOK TO HORSE AND STARTED IN PURSUIT."

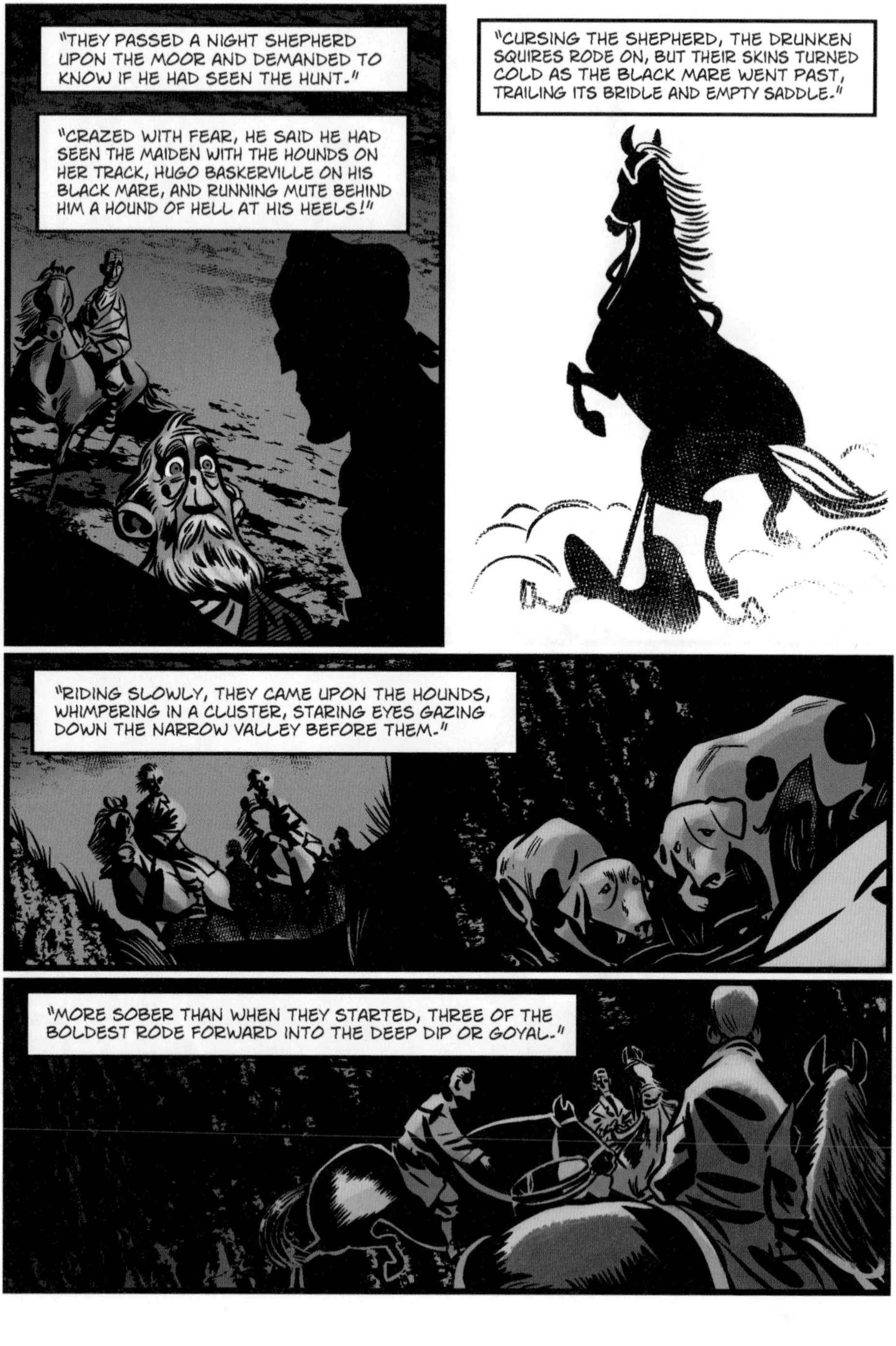
"THEY PASSED A NIGHT SHEPHERD UPON THE MOOR AND DEMANDED TO KNOW IF HE HAD SEEN THE HUNT."
"CRAZED WITH FEAR, HE SAID HE HAD SEEN THE MAIDEN WITH THE HOUNDS ON HER TRACK, HUGO BASKERVILLE ON HIS BLACK MARE, AND RUNNING MUTE BEHIND HIM A HOUND OF HELL AT HIS HEELS!"
"CURSING THE SHEPHERD, THE DRUNKEN SQUIRES RODE ON, BUT THEIR SKINS TURNED COLD AS THE BLACK MARE WENT PAST, TRAILING ITS BRIDLE AND EMPTY SADDLE."
"RIDING SLOWLY, THEY CAME UPON THE HOUNDS, WHIMPERING IN A CLUSTER, STARING EYES GAZING DOWN THE NARROW VALLEY BEFORE THEM."
"MORE SOBER THAN WHEN THEY STARTED, THREE OF THE BOLDEST RODE FORWARD INTO THE DEEP DIP OR GOYAL."

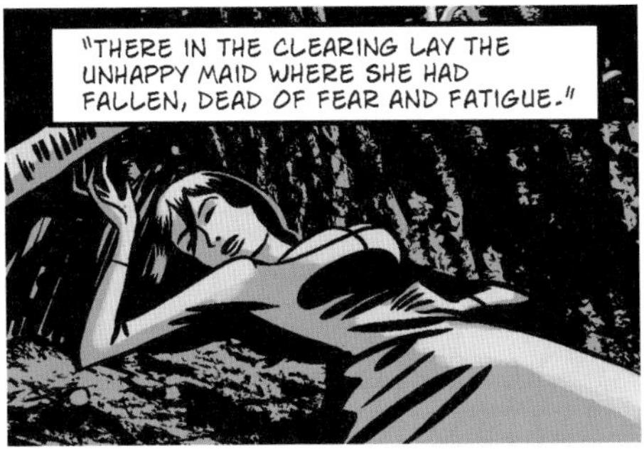
"THERE IN THE CLEARING LAY THE UNHAPPY MAID WHERE SHE HAD FALLEN, DEAD OF FEAR AND FATIGUE."

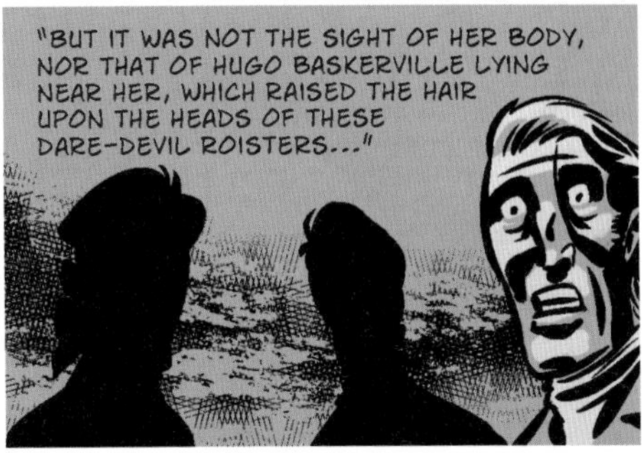
"BUT IT WAS NOT THE SIGHT OF HER BODY, NOR THAT OF HUGO BASKERVILLE LYING NEAR HER, WHICH RAISED THE HAIR UPON THE HEADS OF THESE DARE-DEVIL ROISTERS..."

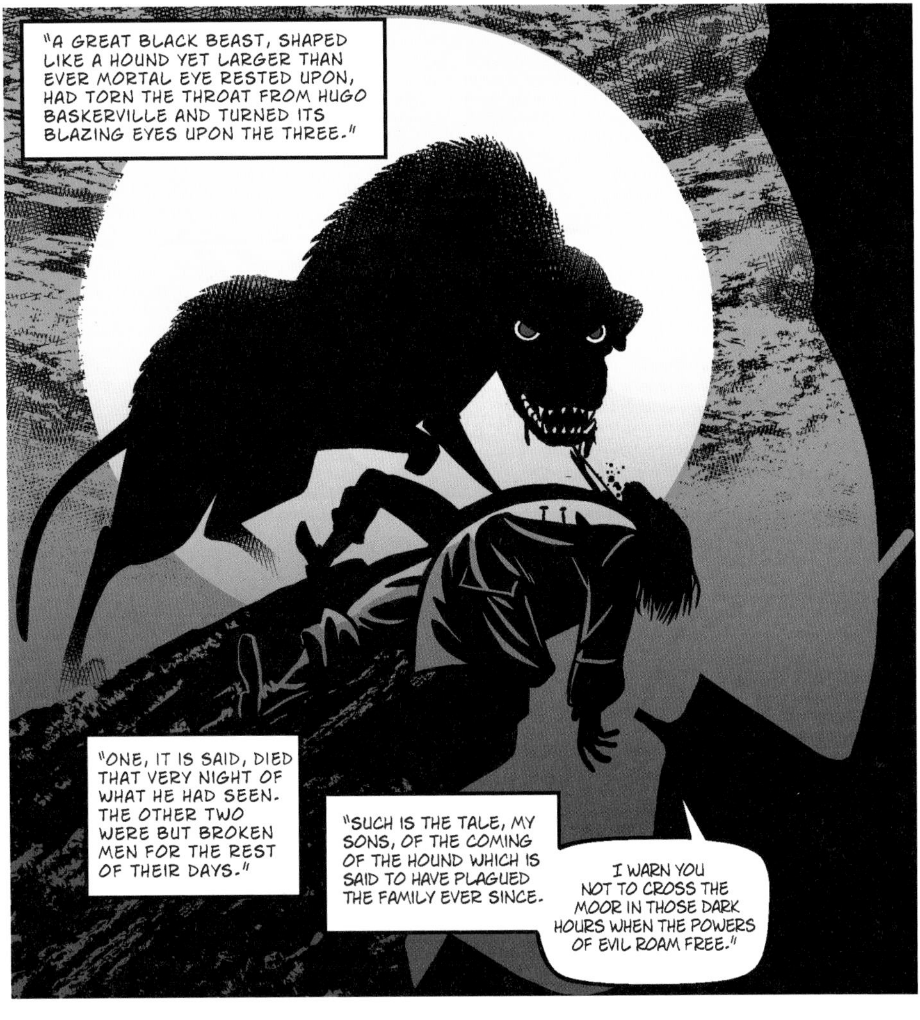
"A GREAT BLACK BEAST, SHAPED LIKE A HOUND YET LARGER THAN EVER MORTAL EYE RESTED UPON, HAD TORN THE THROAT FROM HUGO BASKERVILLE AND TURNED ITS BLAZING EYES UPON THE THREE."
"ONE, IT IS SAID, DIED THAT VERY NIGHT OF WHAT HE HAD SEEN. THE OTHER TWO WERE BUT BROKEN MEN FOR THE REST OF THEIR DAYS."
"SUCH IS THE TALE, MY SONS, OF THE COMING OF THE HOUND WHICH IS SAID TO HAVE PLAGUED THE FAMILY EVER SINCE.
I WARN YOU NOT TO CROSS THE MOOR IN THOSE DARK HOURS WHEN THE POWERS OF EVIL ROAM FREE."

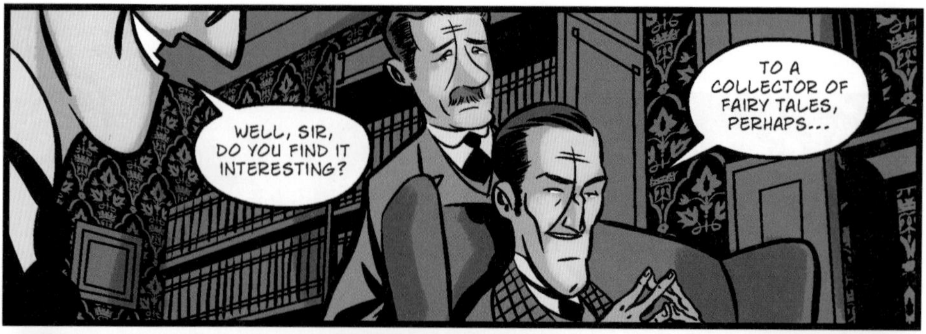
WELL, SIR, DO YOU FIND IT INTERESTING?
TO A COLLECTOR OF FAIRY TALES, PERHAPS...

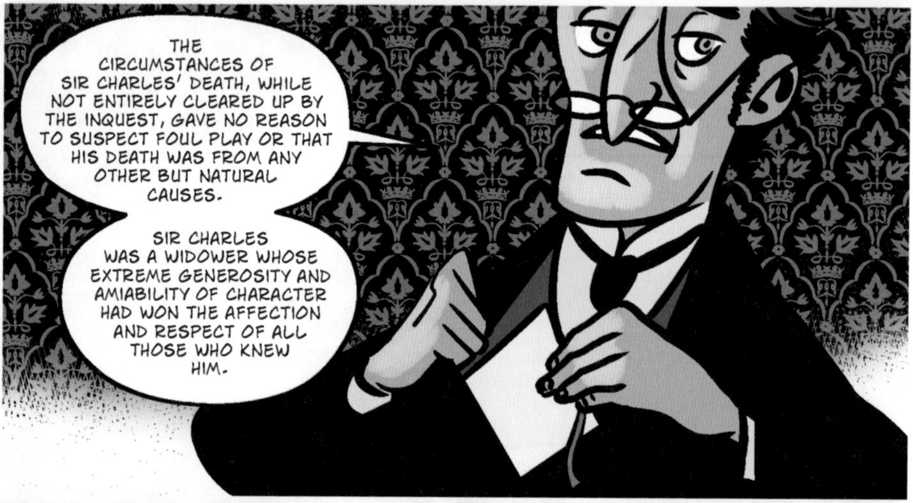
THE CIRCUMSTANCES OF SIR CHARLES' DEATH, WHILE NOT ENTIRELY CLEARED UP BY THE INQUEST, GAVE NO REASON TO SUSPECT FOUL PLAY OR THAT HIS DEATH WAS FROM ANY OTHER BUT NATURAL CAUSES.
SIR CHARLES WAS A WIDOWER WHOSE EXTREME GENEROSITY AND AMIABILITY OF CHARACTER HAD WON THE AFFECTION AND RESPECT OF ALL THOSE WHO KNEW HIM.

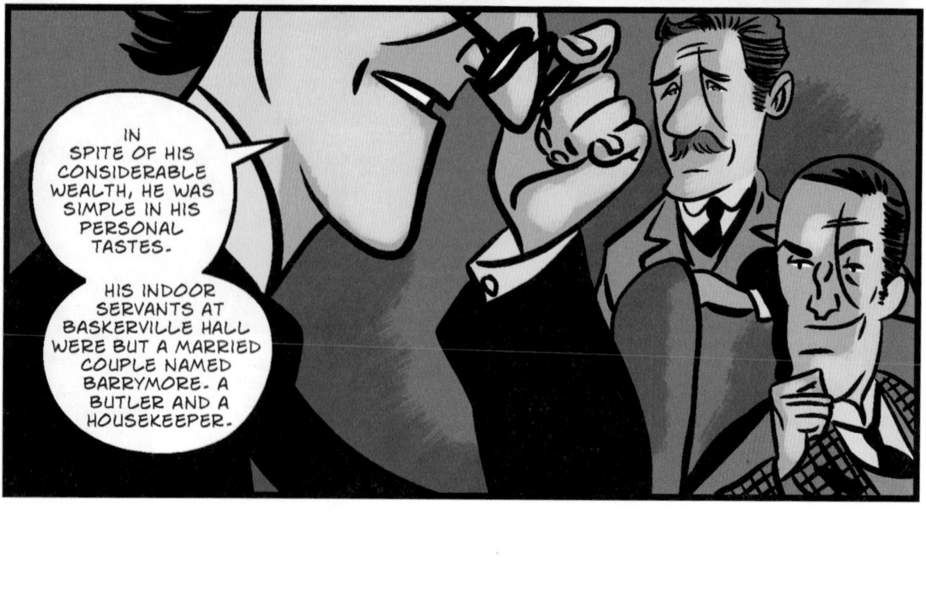
IN SPITE OF HIS CONSIDERABLE WEALTH, HE WAS SIMPLE IN HIS PERSONAL TASTES.
HIS INDOOR SERVANTS AT BASKERVILLE HALL WERE BUT A MARRIED COUPLE NAMED BARRYMORE. A BUTLER AND A HOUSEKEEPER.

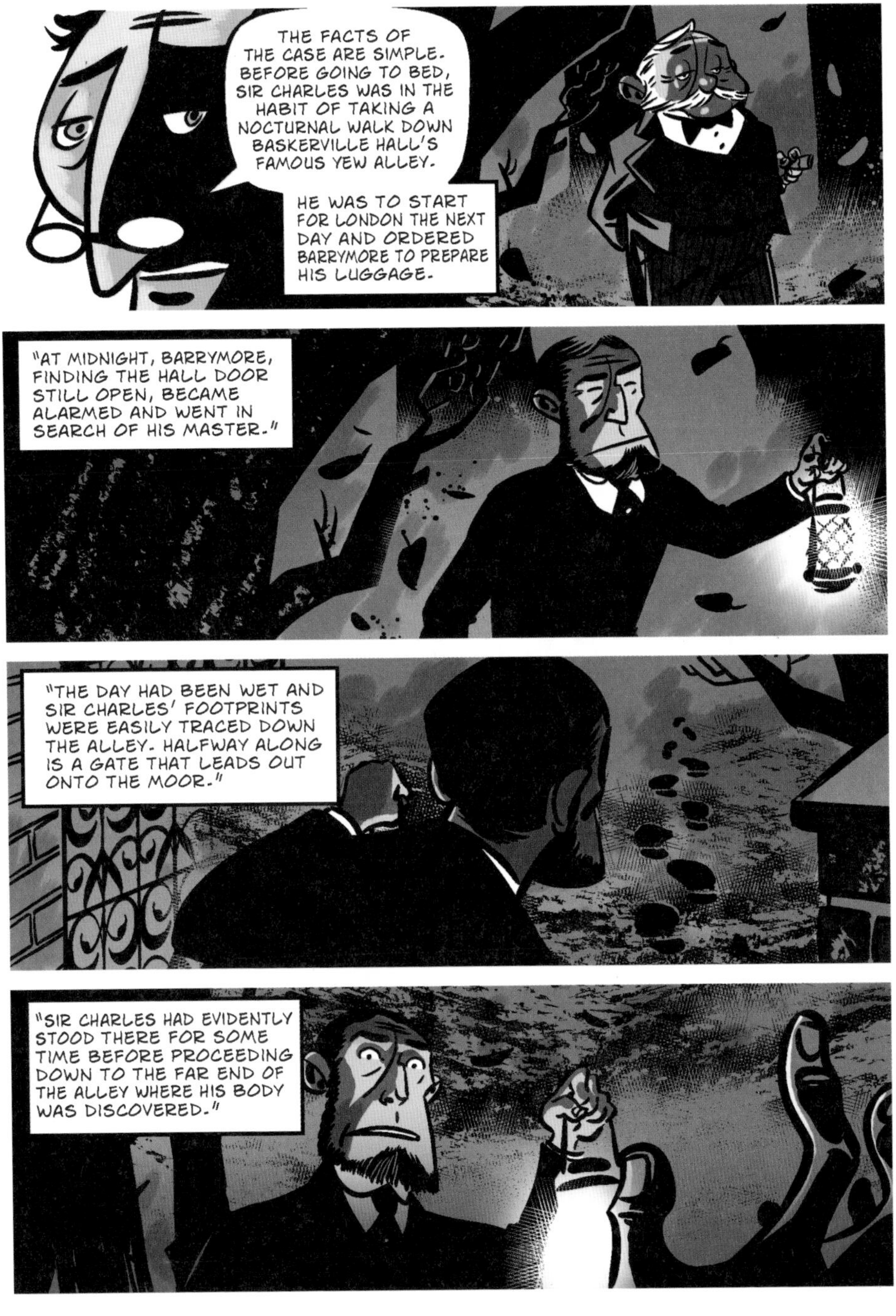
THE FACTS OF THE CASE ARE SIMPLE. BEFORE GOING TO BED, SIR CHARLES WAS IN THE HABIT OF TAKING A NOCTURNAL WALK DOWN BASKERVILLE HALL'S FAMOUS YEW ALLEY.
HE WAS TO START FOR LONDON THE NEXT DAY AND ORDERED BARRYMORE TO PREPARE HIS LUGGAGE.
"AT MIDNIGHT, BARRYMORE, FINDING THE HALL DOOR STILL OPEN, BECAME ALARMED AND WENT IN SEARCH OF HIS MASTER."
"THE DAY HAD BEEN WET AND SIR CHARLES' FOOTPRINTS WERE EASILY TRACED DOWN THE ALLEY. HALFWAY ALONG IS A GATE THAT LEADS OUT ONTO THE MOOR."
"SIR CHARLES HAD EVIDENTLY STOOD THERE FOR SOME TIME BEFORE PROCEEDING DOWN TO THE FAR END OF THE ALLEY WHERE HIS BODY WAS DISCOVERED."

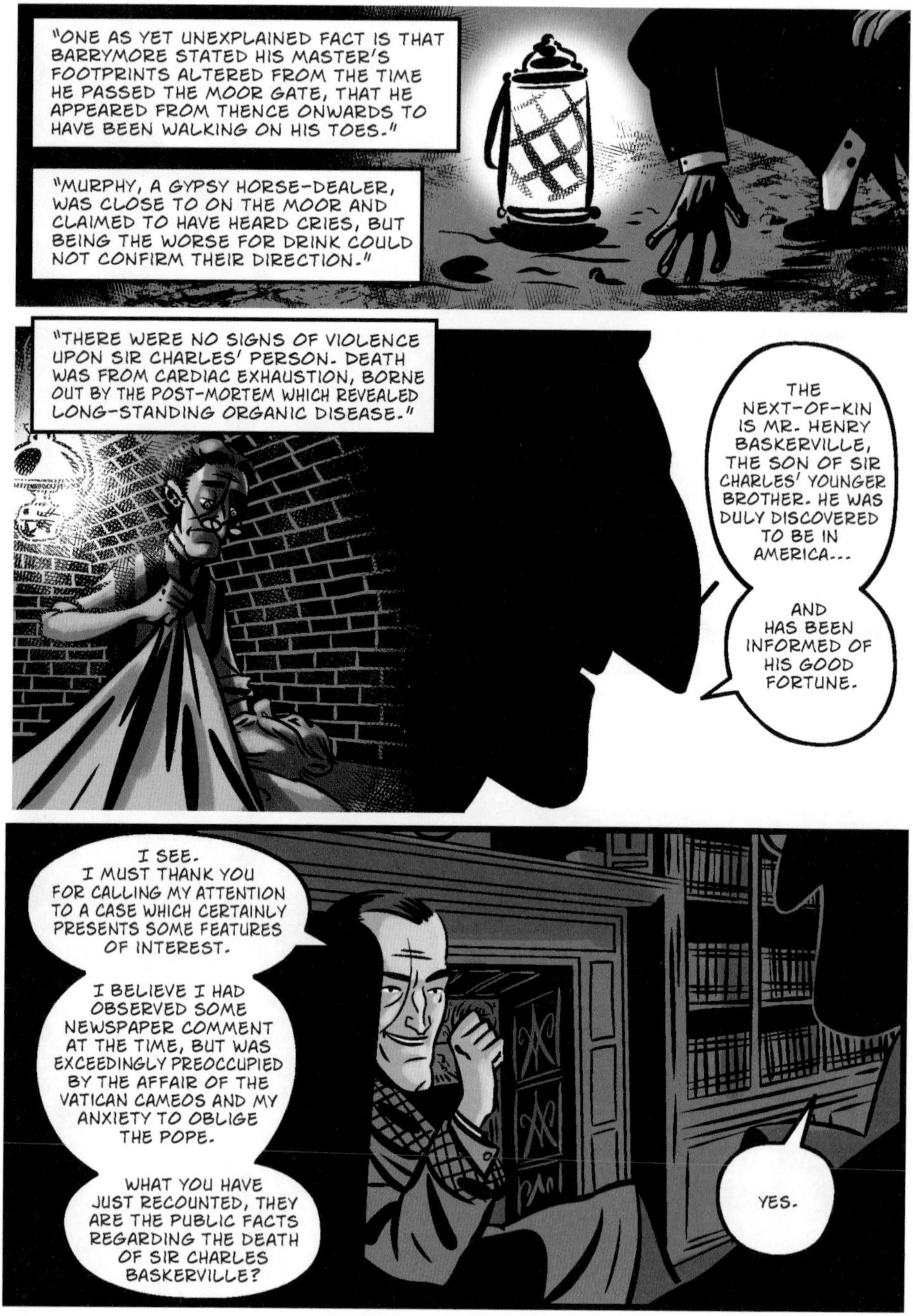
"ONE AS YET UNEXPLAINED FACT IS THAT BARRYMORE STATED HIS MASTER'S FOOTPRINTS ALTERED FROM THE TIME HE PASSED THE MOOR GATE, THAT HE APPEARED FROM THENCE ONWARDS TO HAVE BEEN WALKING ON HIS TOES."
"MURPHY, A GYPSY HORSE-DEALER, WAS CLOSE TO ON THE MOOR AND CLAIMED TO HAVE HEARD CRIES, BUT BEING THE WORSE FOR DRINK COULD NOT CONFIRM THEIR DIRECTION."
"THERE WERE NO SIGNS OF VIOLENCE UPON SIR CHARLES' PERSON. DEATH WAS FROM CARDIAC EXHAUSTION, BORNE OUT BY THE POST-MORTEM WHICH REVEALED LONG-STANDING ORGANIC DISEASE."
THE NEXT-OF-KIN IS MR. HENRY BASKERVILLE, THE SON OF SIR CHARLES' YOUNGER BROTHER. HE WAS DULY DISCOVERED TO BE IN AMERICA...
AND HAS BEEN INFORMED OF HIS GOOD FORTUNE.
I SEE. I MUST THANK YOU FOR CALLING MY ATTENTION TO A CASE WHICH CERTAINLY PRESENTS SOME FEATURES OF INTEREST.
I BELIEVE I HAD OBSERVED SOME NEWSPAPER COMMENT AT THE TIME, BUT WAS EXCEEDINGLY PREOCCUPIED BY THE AFFAIR OF THE VATICAN CAMEOS AND MY ANXIETY TO OBLIGE THE POPE.
WHAT YOU HAVE JUST RECOUNTED, THEY ARE THE PUBLIC FACTS REGARDING THE DEATH OF SIR CHARLES BASKERVILLE?
YES.

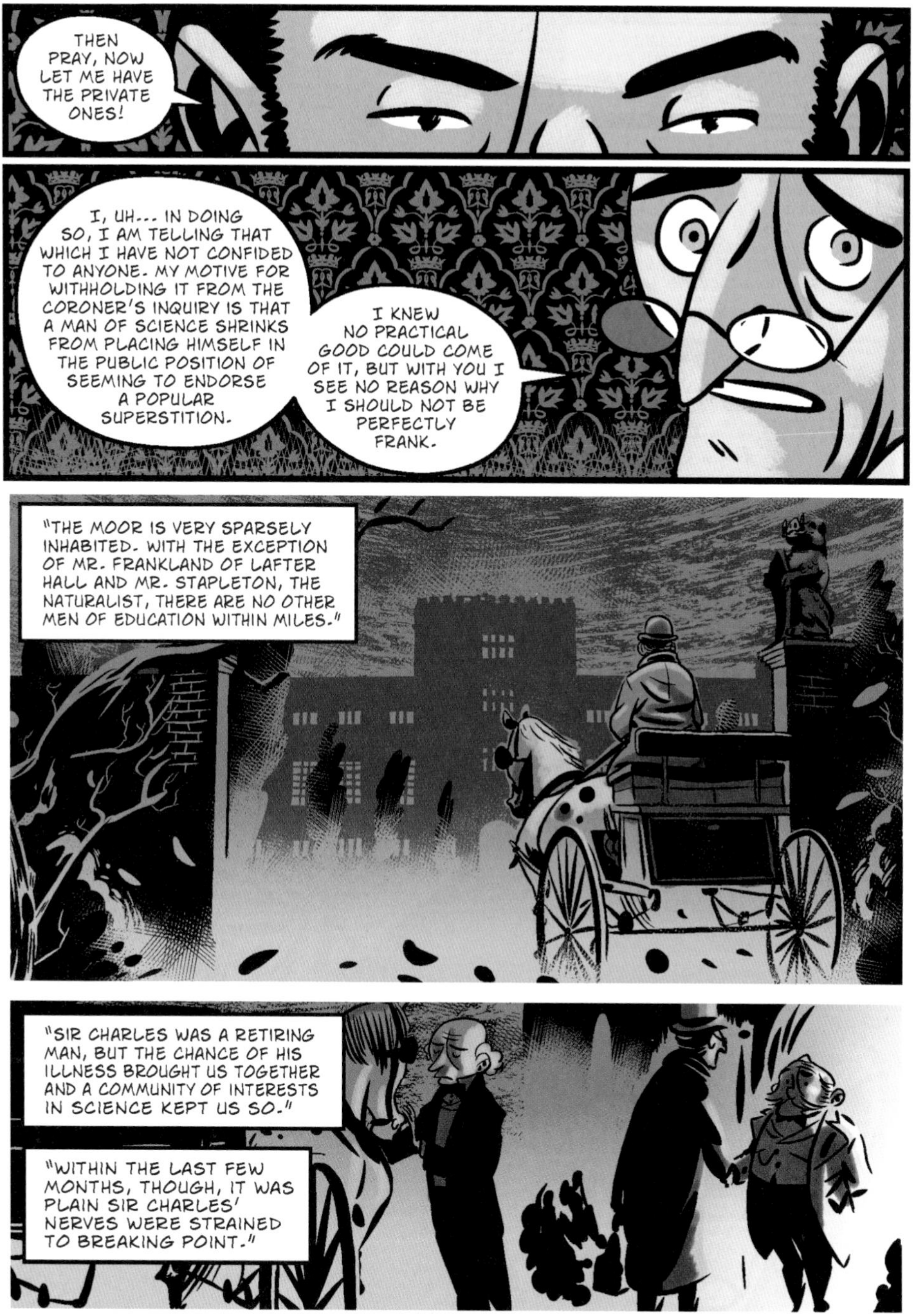
THEN PRAY, NOW LET ME HAVE THE PRIVATE ONES!
I, UH... IN DOING SO, I AM TELLING THAT WHICH I HAVE NOT CONFIDED TO ANYONE. MY MOTIVE FOR WITHHOLDING IT FROM THE CORONER'S INQUIRY IS THAT A MAN OF SCIENCE SHRINKS FROM PLACING HIMSELF IN THE PUBLIC POSITION OF SEEMING TO ENDORSE A POPULAR SUPERSTITION.
I KNEW NO PRACTICAL GOOD COULD COME OF IT, BUT WITH YOU I SEE NO REASON WHY I SHOULD NOT BE PERFECTLY FRANK.
"THE MOOR IS VERY SPARSELY INHABITED. WITH THE EXCEPTION OF MR. FRANKLAND OF LAFTER HALL AND MR. STAPLETON, THE NATURALIST, THERE ARE NO OTHER MEN OF EDUCATION WITHIN MILES."
"SIR CHARLES WAS A RETIRING MAN, BUT THE CHANCE OF HIS ILLNESS BROUGHT US TOGETHER AND A COMMUNITY OF INTERESTS IN SCIENCE KEPT US SO."
"WITHIN THE LAST FEW MONTHS, THOUGH, IT WAS PLAIN SIR CHARLES' NERVES WERE STRAINED TO BREAKING POINT."

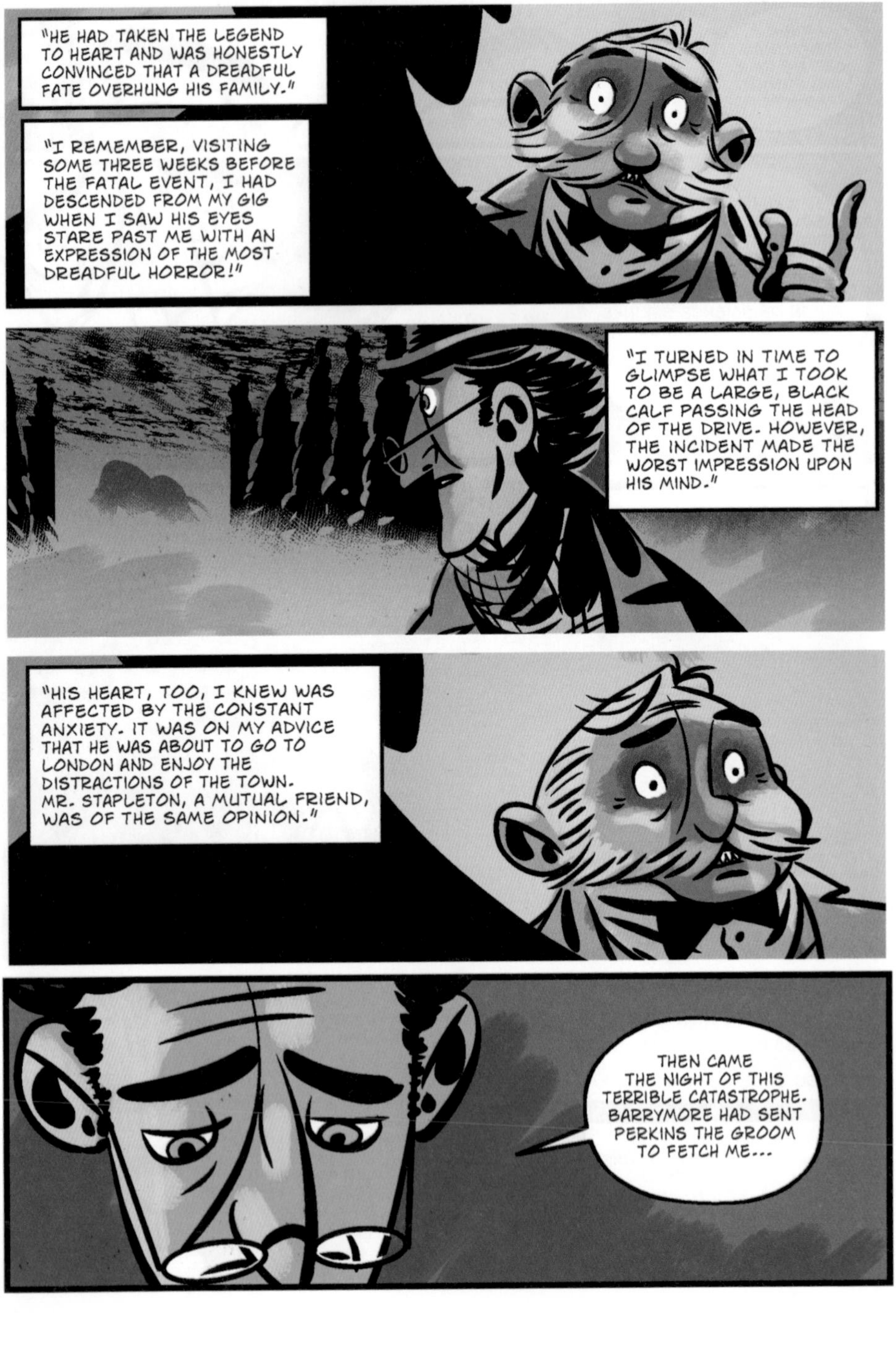
"HE HAD TAKEN THE LEGEND TO HEART AND WAS HONESTLY CONVINCED THAT A DREADFUL FATE OVERHUNG HIS FAMILY."
"I REMEMBER, VISITING SOME THREE WEEKS BEFORE THE FATAL EVENT, I HAD DESCENDED FROM MY GIG WHEN I SAW HIS EYES STARE PAST ME WITH AN EXPRESSION OF THE MOST DREADFUL HORROR!"
"I TURNED IN TIME TO GLIMPSE WHAT I TOOK TO BE A LARGE, BLACK CALF PASSING THE HEAD OF THE DRIVE. HOWEVER, THE INCIDENT MADE THE WORST IMPRESSION UPON HIS MIND."
"HIS HEART, TOO, I KNEW WAS AFFECTED BY THE CONSTANT ANXIETY. IT WAS ON MY ADVICE THAT HE WAS ABOUT TO GO TO LONDON AND ENJOY THE DISTRACTIONS OF THE TOWN. MR. STAPLETON, A MUTUAL FRIEND, WAS OF THE SAME OPINION."
THEN CAME THE NIGHT OF THIS TERRIBLE CATASTROPHE. BARRYMORE HAD SENT PERKINS THE GROOM TO FETCH ME...

"I REACHED THE HALL WITHIN THE HOUR. I CHECKED AND CORROBORATED THE FACTS. I FOLLOWED THE FOOTSTEPS DOWN THE YEW ALLEY, SAW WHERE SIR CHARLES PAUSED AT THE MOOR GATE AND THENCE BEYOND."

"SIR CHARLES' FEATURES WERE CONVULSED TO SUCH AN EXTENT I COULD HARDLY HAVE SWORN TO HIS IDENTITY. THERE WAS NO PHYSICAL INJURY OF ANY KIND, BUT ONE FALSE STATEMENT WAS MADE BY BARRYMORE AT THE INQUEST."

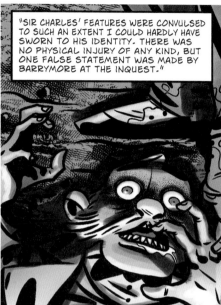

HE SAID HE DID NOT OBSERVE ANY TRACES UPON THE GROUND AROUND THE BODY... BUT I DID. FRESH AND CLEAR!

FOOTPRINTS! A MAN OR WOMAN'S?

"MR. HOLMES, THEY WERE THE FOOTPRINTS OF A GIGANTIC HOUND!"

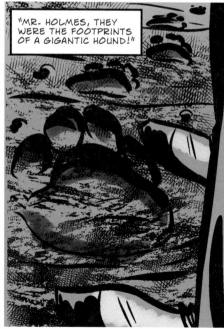

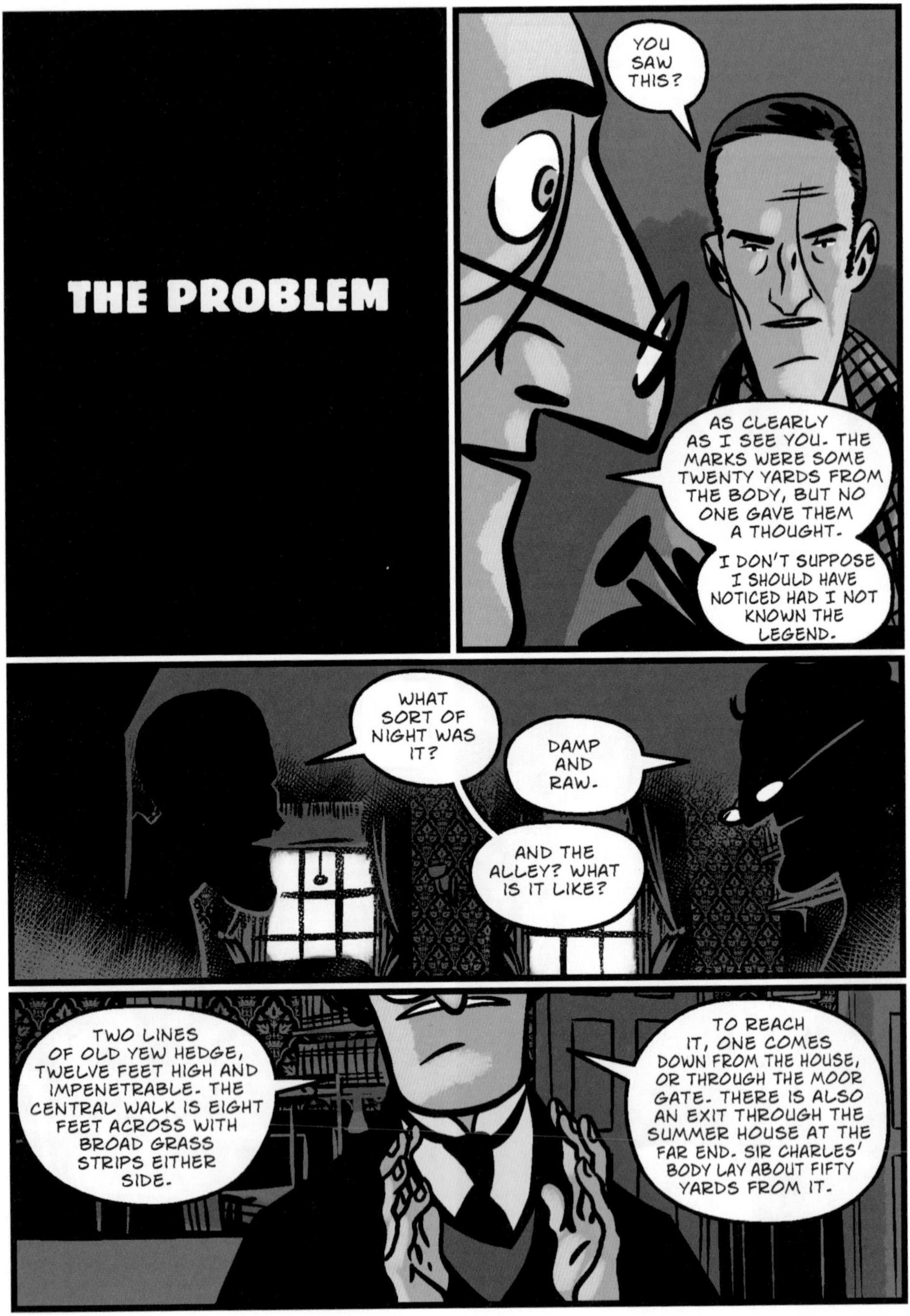
THE PROBLEM
YOU SAW THIS?
AS CLEARLY AS I SEE YOU. THE MARKS WERE SOME TWENTY YARDS FROM THE BODY, BUT NO ONE GAVE THEM A THOUGHT.
I DON'T SUPPOSE I SHOULD HAVE NOTICED HAD I NOT KNOWN THE LEGEND.
WHAT SORT OF NIGHT WAS IT?
DAMP AND RAW.
AND THE ALLEY? WHAT IS IT LIKE?
TWO LINES OF OLD YEW HEDGE, TWELVE FEET HIGH AND IMPENETRABLE. THE CENTRAL WALK IS EIGHT FEET ACROSS WITH BROAD GRASS STRIPS EITHER SIDE.
TO REACH IT, ONE COMES DOWN FROM THE HOUSE, OR THROUGH THE MOOR GATE. THERE IS ALSO AN EXIT THROUGH THE SUMMER HOUSE AT THE FAR END. SIR CHARLES' BODY LAY ABOUT FIFTY YARDS FROM IT.

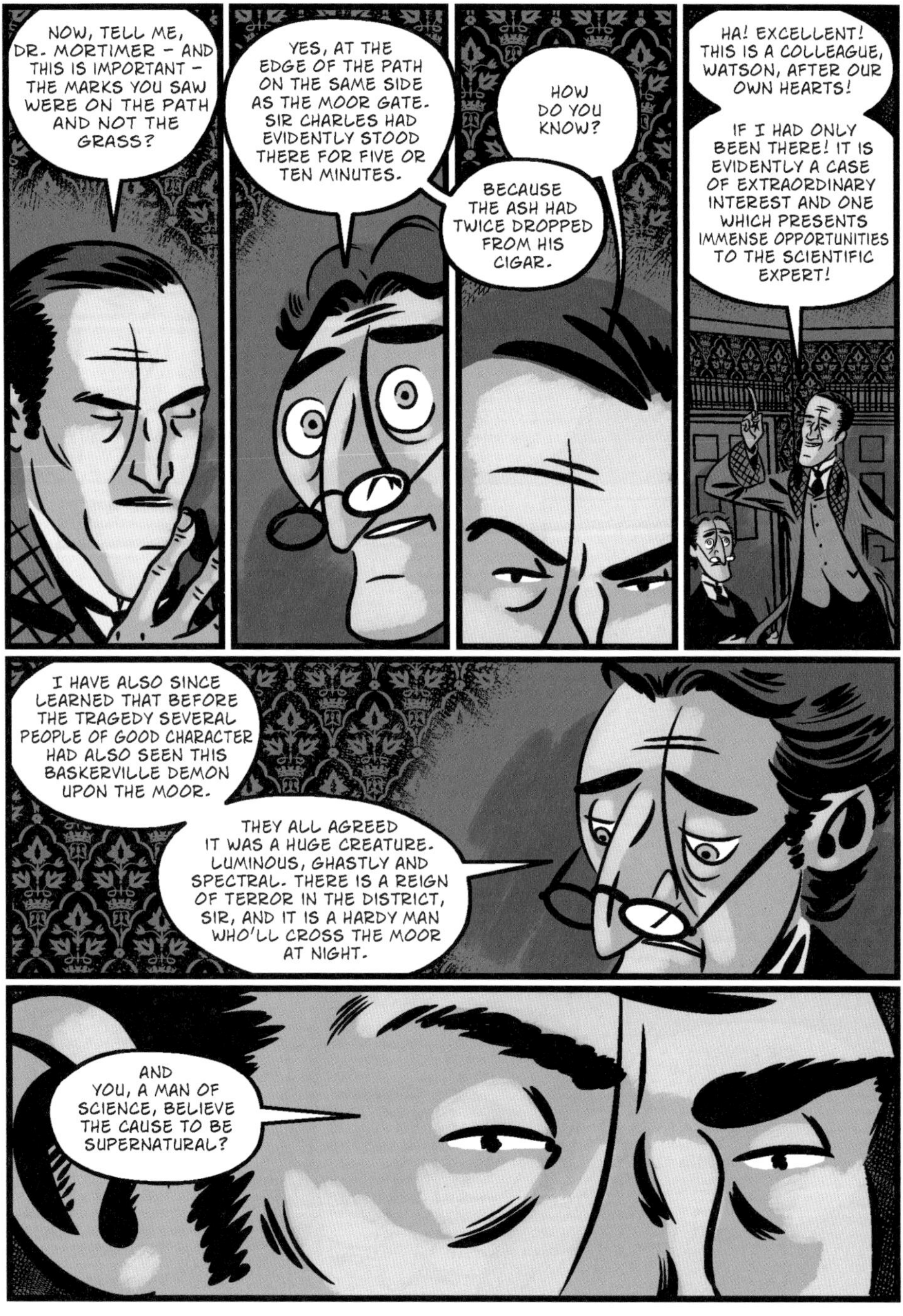
NOW, TELL ME, DR. MORTIMER – AND THIS IS IMPORTANT – THE MARKS YOU SAW WERE ON THE PATH AND NOT THE GRASS?
YES, AT THE EDGE OF THE PATH ON THE SAME SIDE AS THE MOOR GATE. SIR CHARLES HAD EVIDENTLY STOOD THERE FOR FIVE OR TEN MINUTES.
HOW DO YOU KNOW?
BECAUSE THE ASH HAD TWICE DROPPED FROM HIS CIGAR.
HA! EXCELLENT! THIS IS A COLLEAGUE, WATSON, AFTER OUR OWN HEARTS!
IF I HAD ONLY BEEN THERE! IT IS EVIDENTLY A CASE OF EXTRAORDINARY INTEREST AND ONE WHICH PRESENTS IMMENSE OPPORTUNITIES TO THE SCIENTIFIC EXPERT!
I HAVE ALSO SINCE LEARNED THAT BEFORE THE TRAGEDY SEVERAL PEOPLE OF GOOD CHARACTER HAD ALSO SEEN THIS BASKERVILLE DEMON UPON THE MOOR.
THEY ALL AGREED IT WAS A HUGE CREATURE. LUMINOUS, GHASTLY AND SPECTRAL. THERE IS A REIGN OF TERROR IN THE DISTRICT, SIR, AND IT IS A HARDY MAN WHO'LL CROSS THE MOOR AT NIGHT.
AND YOU, A MAN OF SCIENCE, BELIEVE THE CAUSE TO BE SUPERNATURAL?

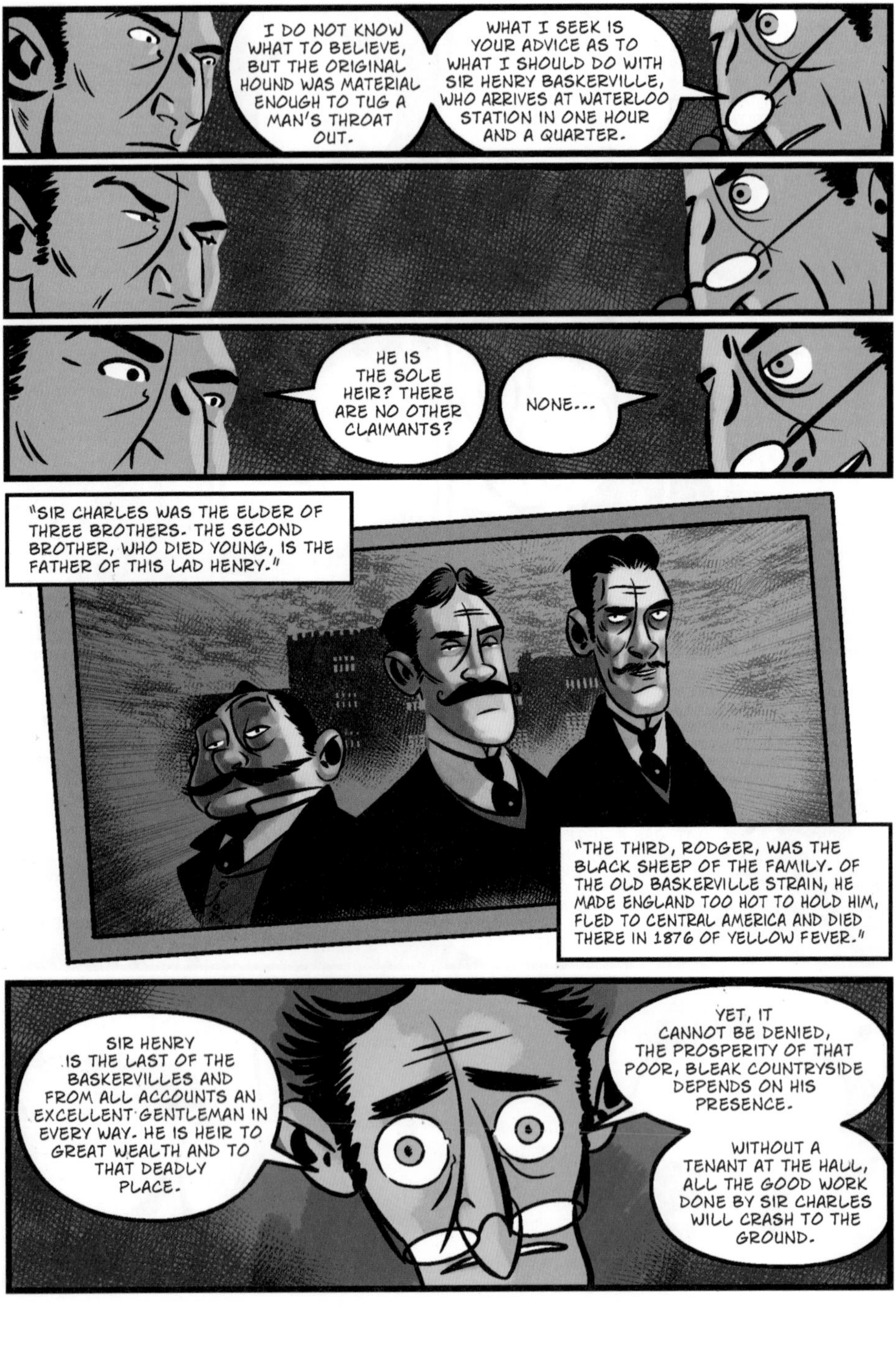
I DO NOT KNOW WHAT TO BELIEVE, BUT THE ORIGINAL HOUND WAS MATERIAL ENOUGH TO TUG A MAN'S THROAT OUT.
WHAT I SEEK IS YOUR ADVICE AS TO WHAT I SHOULD DO WITH SIR HENRY BASKERVILLE, WHO ARRIVES AT WATERLOO STATION IN ONE HOUR AND A QUARTER.
HE IS THE SOLE HEIR? THERE ARE NO OTHER CLAIMANTS?
NONE...
"SIR CHARLES WAS THE ELDER OF THREE BROTHERS. THE SECOND BROTHER, WHO DIED YOUNG, IS THE FATHER OF THIS LAD HENRY."
"THE THIRD, RODGER, WAS THE BLACK SHEEP OF THE FAMILY. OF THE OLD BASKERVILLE STRAIN, HE MADE ENGLAND TOO HOT TO HOLD HIM, FLED TO CENTRAL AMERICA AND DIED THERE IN 1876 OF YELLOW FEVER."
SIR HENRY IS THE LAST OF THE BASKERVILLES AND FROM ALL ACCOUNTS AN EXCELLENT GENTLEMAN IN EVERY WAY. HE IS HEIR TO GREAT WEALTH AND TO THAT DEADLY PLACE.
YET, IT CANNOT BE DENIED, THE PROSPERITY OF THAT POOR, BLEAK COUNTRYSIDE DEPENDS ON HIS PRESENCE.
WITHOUT A TENANT AT THE HALL, ALL THE GOOD WORK DONE BY SIR CHARLES WILL CRASH TO THE GROUND.

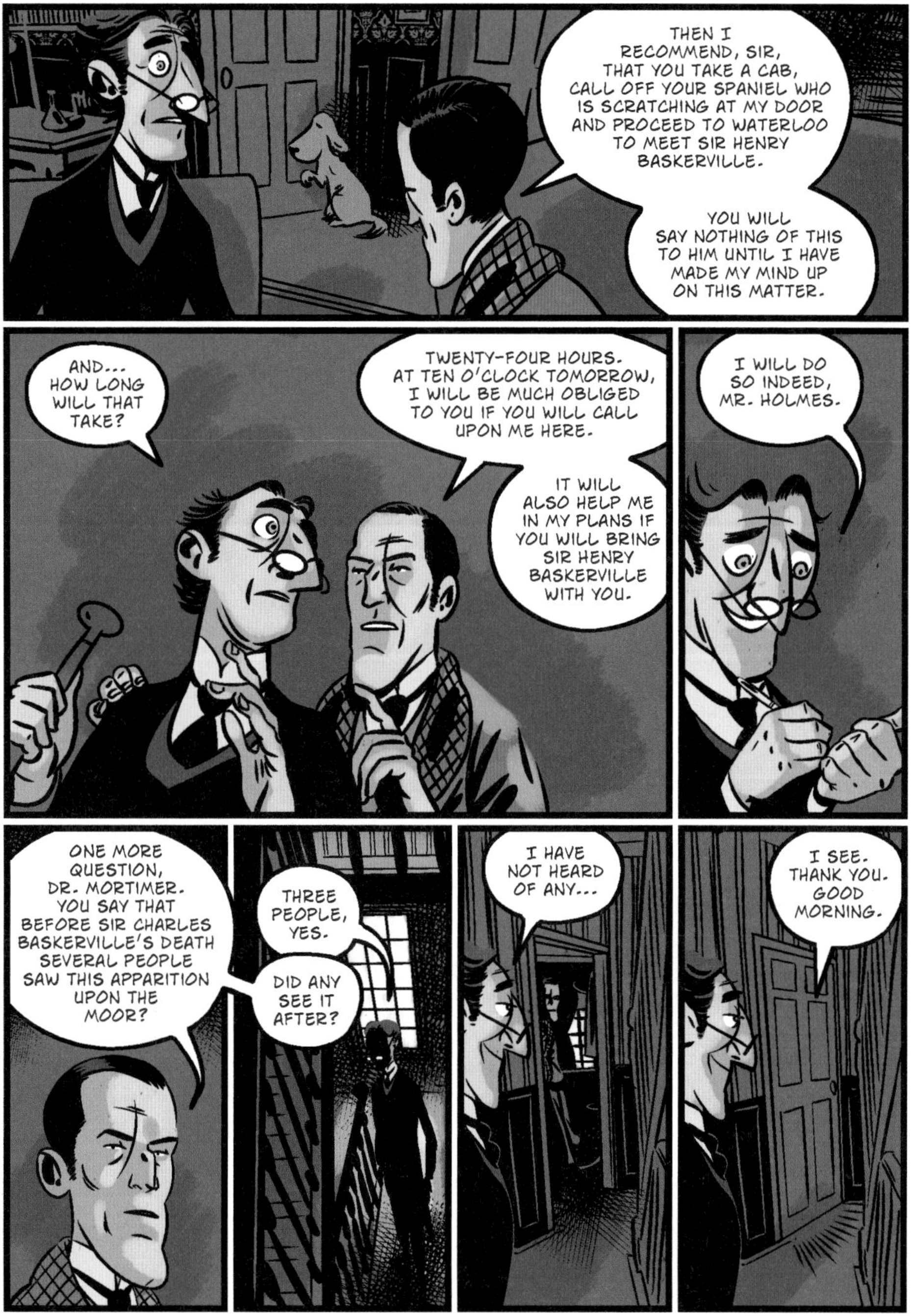
THEN I RECOMMEND, SIR, THAT YOU TAKE A CAB, CALL OFF YOUR SPANIEL WHO IS SCRATCHING AT MY DOOR AND PROCEED TO WATERLOO TO MEET SIR HENRY BASKERVILLE.
YOU WILL SAY NOTHING OF THIS TO HIM UNTIL I HAVE MADE MY MIND UP ON THIS MATTER.
AND... HOW LONG WILL THAT TAKE?
TWENTY-FOUR HOURS. AT TEN O'CLOCK TOMORROW, I WILL BE MUCH OBLIGED TO YOU IF YOU WILL CALL UPON ME HERE.
IT WILL ALSO HELP ME IN MY PLANS IF YOU WILL BRING SIR HENRY BASKERVILLE WITH YOU.
I WILL DO SO INDEED, MR. HOLMES.
ONE MORE QUESTION, DR. MORTIMER. YOU SAY THAT BEFORE SIR CHARLES BASKERVILLE'S DEATH SEVERAL PEOPLE SAW THIS APPARITION UPON THE MOOR?
THREE PEOPLE, YES.
DID ANY SEE IT AFTER?
I HAVE NOT HEARD OF ANY...
I SEE. THANK YOU. GOOD MORNING.

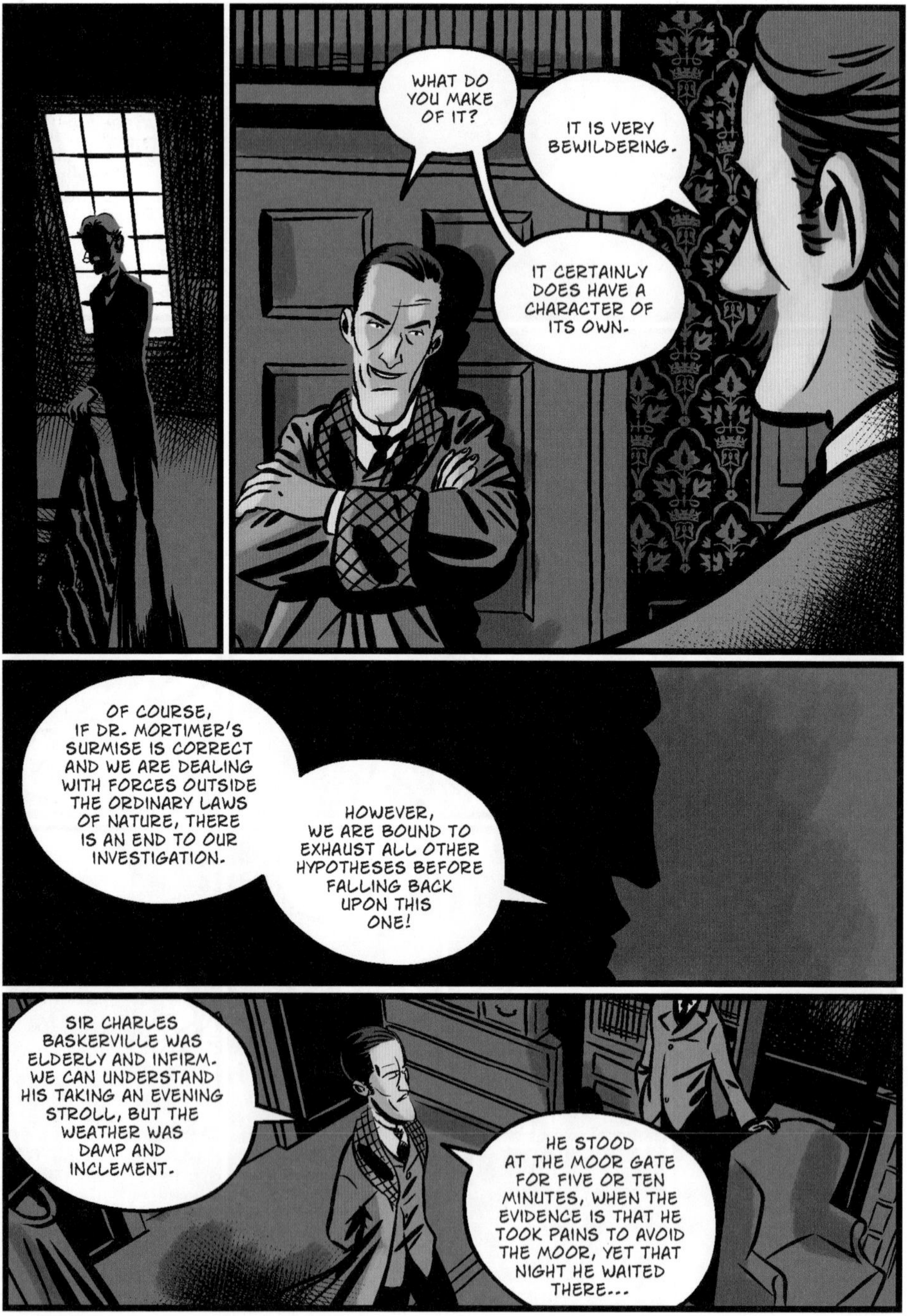
WHAT DO YOU MAKE OF IT?
IT IS VERY BEWILDERING.
IT CERTAINLY DOES HAVE A CHARACTER OF ITS OWN.
OF COURSE, IF DR. MORTIMER'S SURMISE IS CORRECT AND WE ARE DEALING WITH FORCES OUTSIDE THE ORDINARY LAWS OF NATURE, THERE IS AN END TO OUR INVESTIGATION.
HOWEVER, WE ARE BOUND TO EXHAUST ALL OTHER HYPOTHESES BEFORE FALLING BACK UPON THIS ONE!
SIR CHARLES BASKERVILLE WAS ELDERLY AND INFIRM. WE CAN UNDERSTAND HIS TAKING AN EVENING STROLL, BUT THE WEATHER WAS DAMP AND INCLEMENT.
HE STOOD AT THE MOOR GATE FOR FIVE OR TEN MINUTES, WHEN THE EVIDENCE IS THAT HE TOOK PAINS TO AVOID THE MOOR, YET THAT NIGHT HE WAITED THERE...

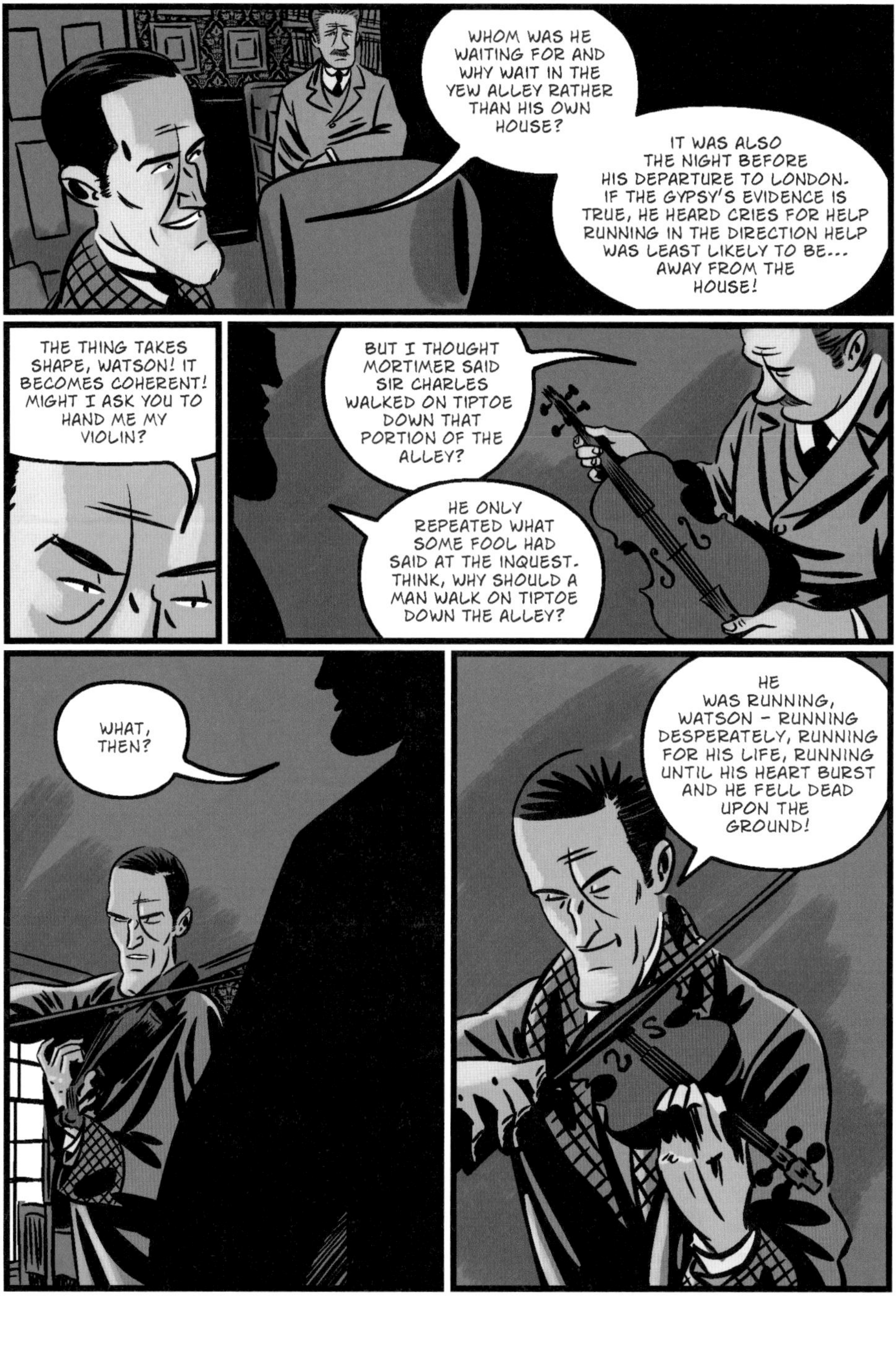
WHOM WAS HE WAITING FOR AND WHY WAIT IN THE YEW ALLEY RATHER THAN HIS OWN HOUSE?
IT WAS ALSO THE NIGHT BEFORE HIS DEPARTURE TO LONDON. IF THE GYPSY'S EVIDENCE IS TRUE, HE HEARD CRIES FOR HELP RUNNING IN THE DIRECTION HELP WAS LEAST LIKELY TO BE... AWAY FROM THE HOUSE!
THE THING TAKES SHAPE, WATSON! IT BECOMES COHERENT! MIGHT I ASK YOU TO HAND ME MY VIOLIN?
BUT I THOUGHT MORTIMER SAID SIR CHARLES WALKED ON TIPTOE DOWN THAT PORTION OF THE ALLEY?
HE ONLY REPEATED WHAT SOME FOOL HAD SAID AT THE INQUEST. THINK, WHY SHOULD A MAN WALK ON TIPTOE DOWN THE ALLEY?
WHAT, THEN?
HE WAS RUNNING, WATSON – RUNNING DESPERATELY, RUNNING FOR HIS LIFE, RUNNING UNTIL HIS HEART BURST AND HE FELL DEAD UPON THE GROUND!

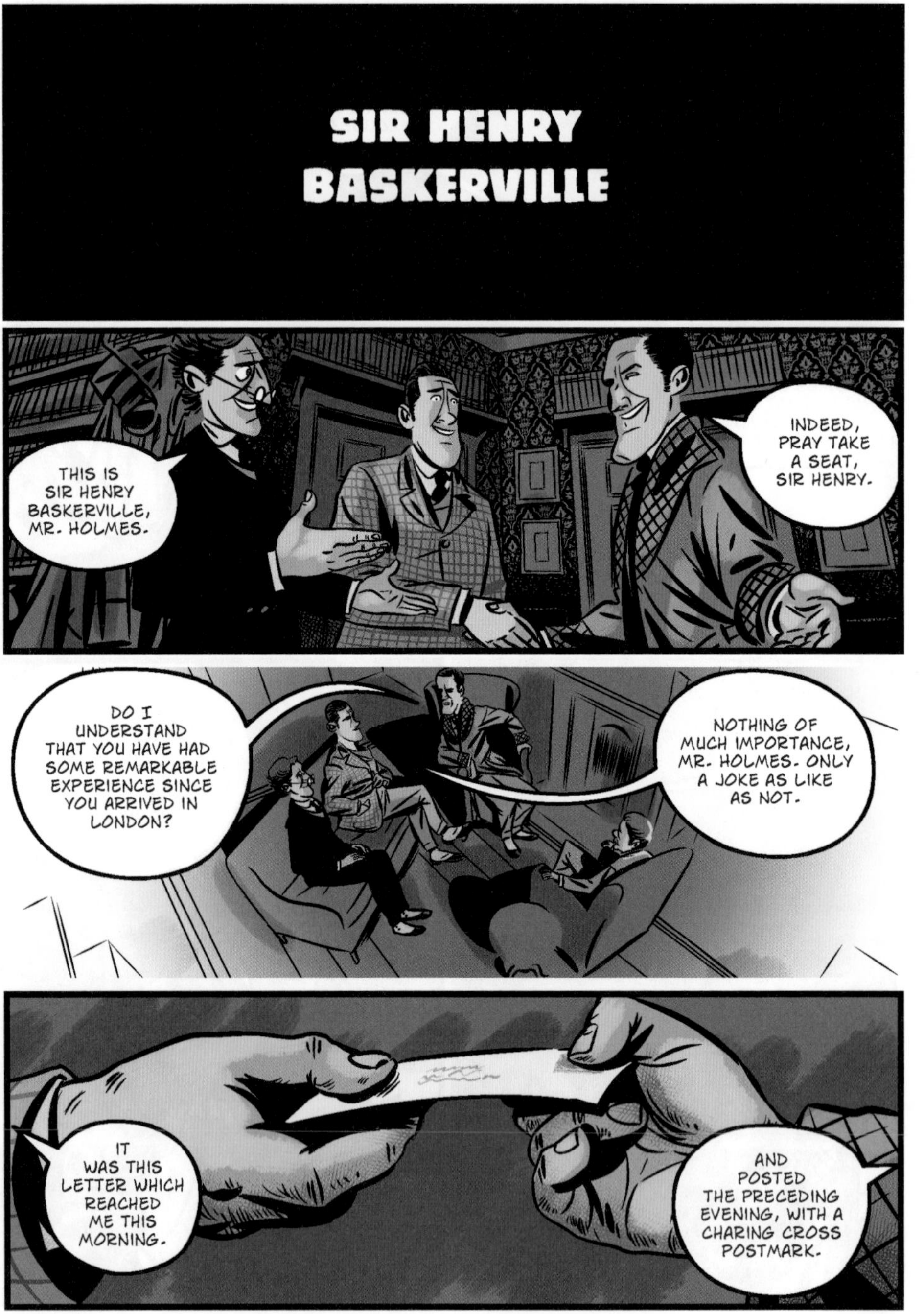
SIR HENRY BASKERVILLE
THIS IS SIR HENRY BASKERVILLE, MR. HOLMES.
INDEED, PRAY TAKE A SEAT, SIR HENRY.
DO I UNDERSTAND THAT YOU HAVE HAD SOME REMARKABLE EXPERIENCE SINCE YOU ARRIVED IN LONDON?
NOTHING OF MUCH IMPORTANCE, MR. HOLMES. ONLY A JOKE AS LIKE AS NOT.
IT WAS THIS LETTER WHICH REACHED ME THIS MORNING.
AND POSTED THE PRECEDING EVENING, WITH A CHARING CROSS POSTMARK.

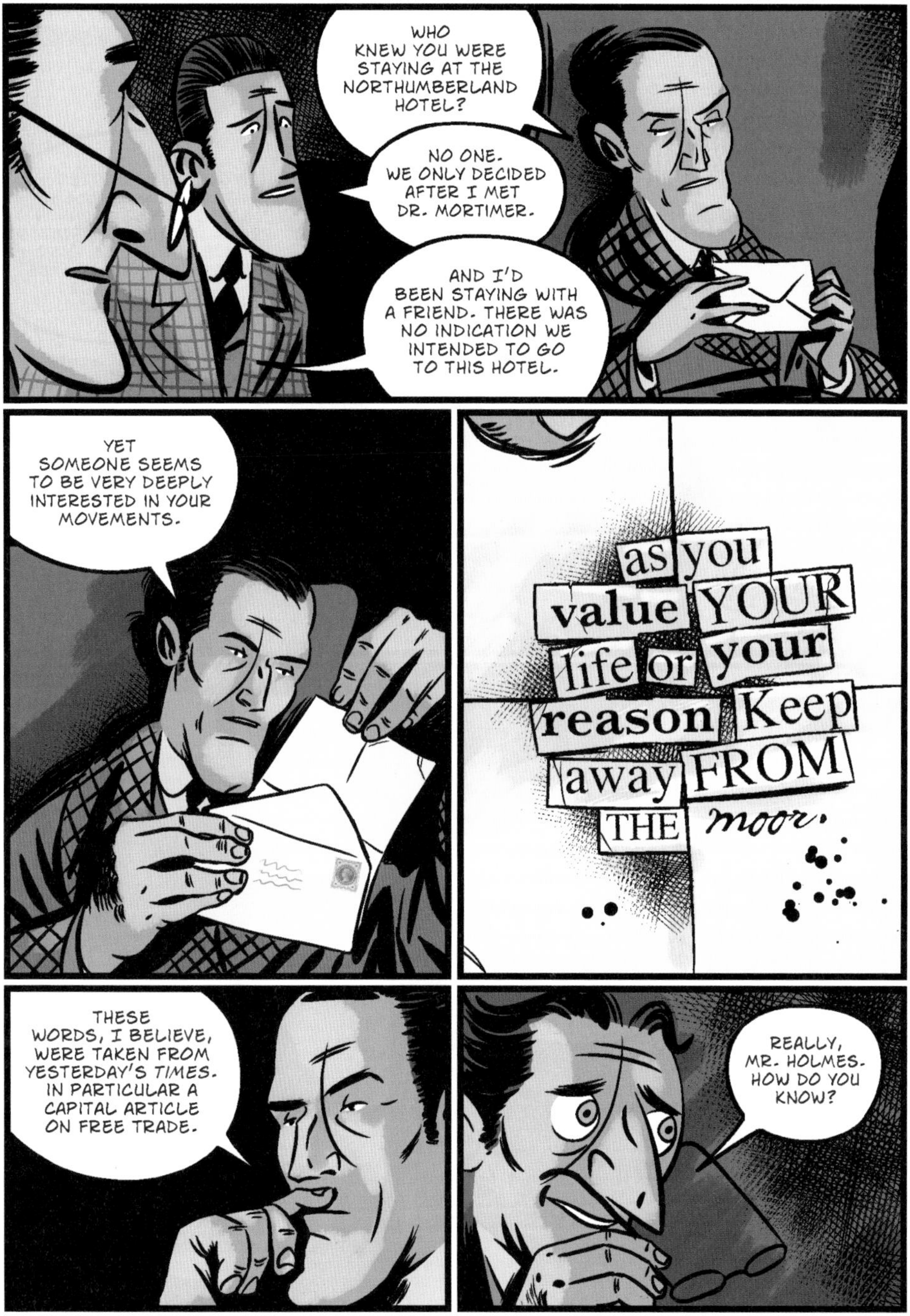
WHO KNEW YOU WERE STAYING AT THE NORTHUMBERLAND HOTEL?
NO ONE. WE ONLY DECIDED AFTER I MET DR. MORTIMER.
AND I'D BEEN STAYING WITH A FRIEND. THERE WAS NO INDICATION WE INTENDED TO GO TO THIS HOTEL.
YET SOMEONE SEEMS TO BE VERY DEEPLY INTERESTED IN YOUR MOVEMENTS.
as you value YOUR life or your reason Keep away FROM THE moor.
THESE WORDS, I BELIEVE, WERE TAKEN FROM YESTERDAY'S *TIMES*. IN PARTICULAR A CAPITAL ARTICLE ON FREE TRADE.
REALLY, MR. HOLMES. HOW DO YOU KNOW?

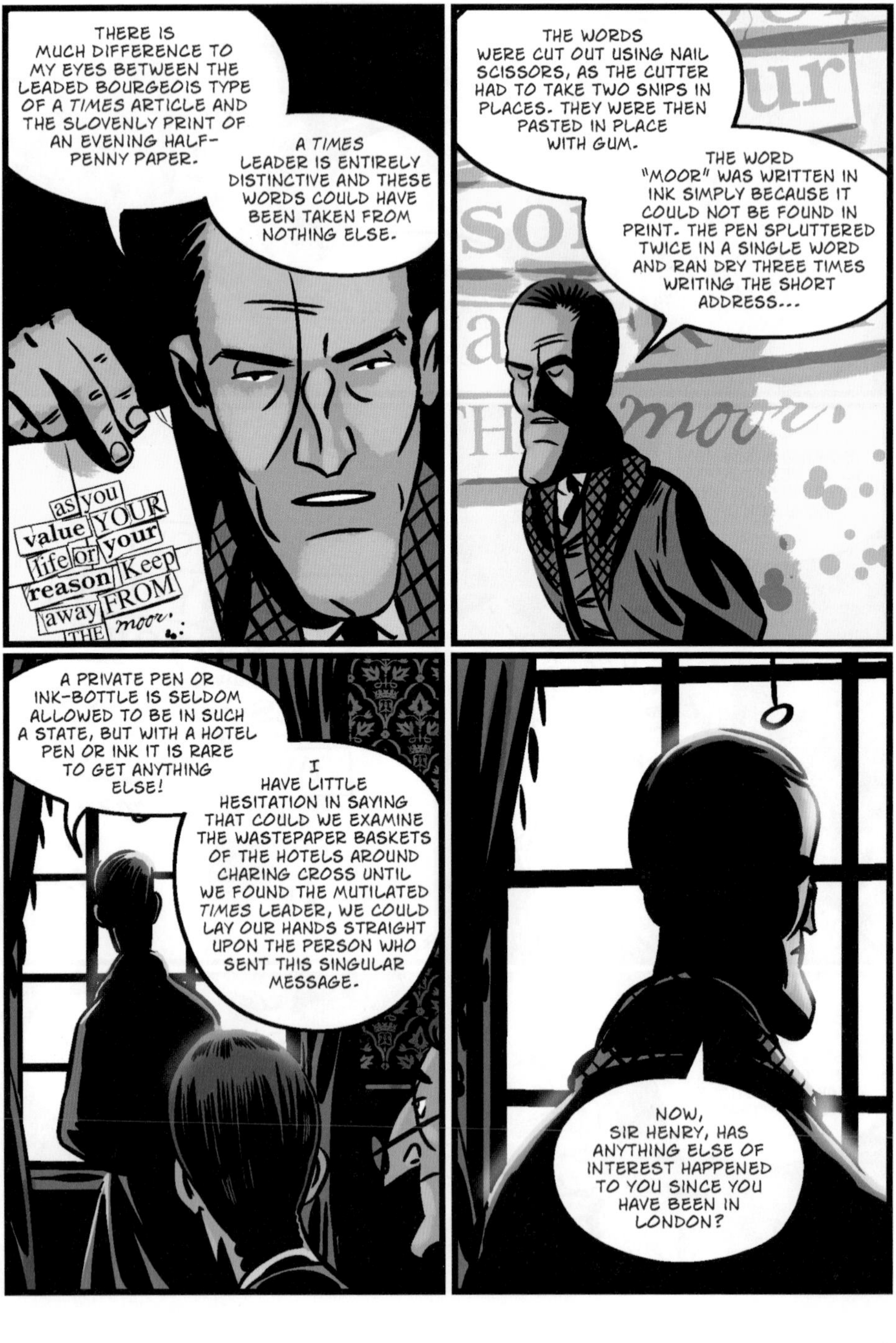
THERE IS MUCH DIFFERENCE TO MY EYES BETWEEN THE LEADED BOURGEOIS TYPE OF A *TIMES* ARTICLE AND THE SLOVENLY PRINT OF AN EVENING HALF-PENNY PAPER.
A *TIMES* LEADER IS ENTIRELY DISTINCTIVE AND THESE WORDS COULD HAVE BEEN TAKEN FROM NOTHING ELSE.
as you value YOUR life or your reason Keep away FROM THE moor.
THE WORDS WERE CUT OUT USING NAIL SCISSORS, AS THE CUTTER HAD TO TAKE TWO SNIPS IN PLACES. THEY WERE THEN PASTED IN PLACE WITH GUM.
THE WORD "MOOR" WAS WRITTEN IN INK SIMPLY BECAUSE IT COULD NOT BE FOUND IN PRINT. THE PEN SPLUTTERED TWICE IN A SINGLE WORD AND RAN DRY THREE TIMES WRITING THE SHORT ADDRESS...
A PRIVATE PEN OR INK-BOTTLE IS SELDOM ALLOWED TO BE IN SUCH A STATE, BUT WITH A HOTEL PEN OR INK IT IS RARE TO GET ANYTHING ELSE!
I HAVE LITTLE HESITATION IN SAYING THAT COULD WE EXAMINE THE WASTEPAPER BASKETS OF THE HOTELS AROUND CHARING CROSS UNTIL WE FOUND THE MUTILATED *TIMES* LEADER, WE COULD LAY OUR HANDS STRAIGHT UPON THE PERSON WHO SENT THIS SINGULAR MESSAGE.
NOW, SIR HENRY, HAS ANYTHING ELSE OF INTEREST HAPPENED TO YOU SINCE YOU HAVE BEEN IN LONDON?

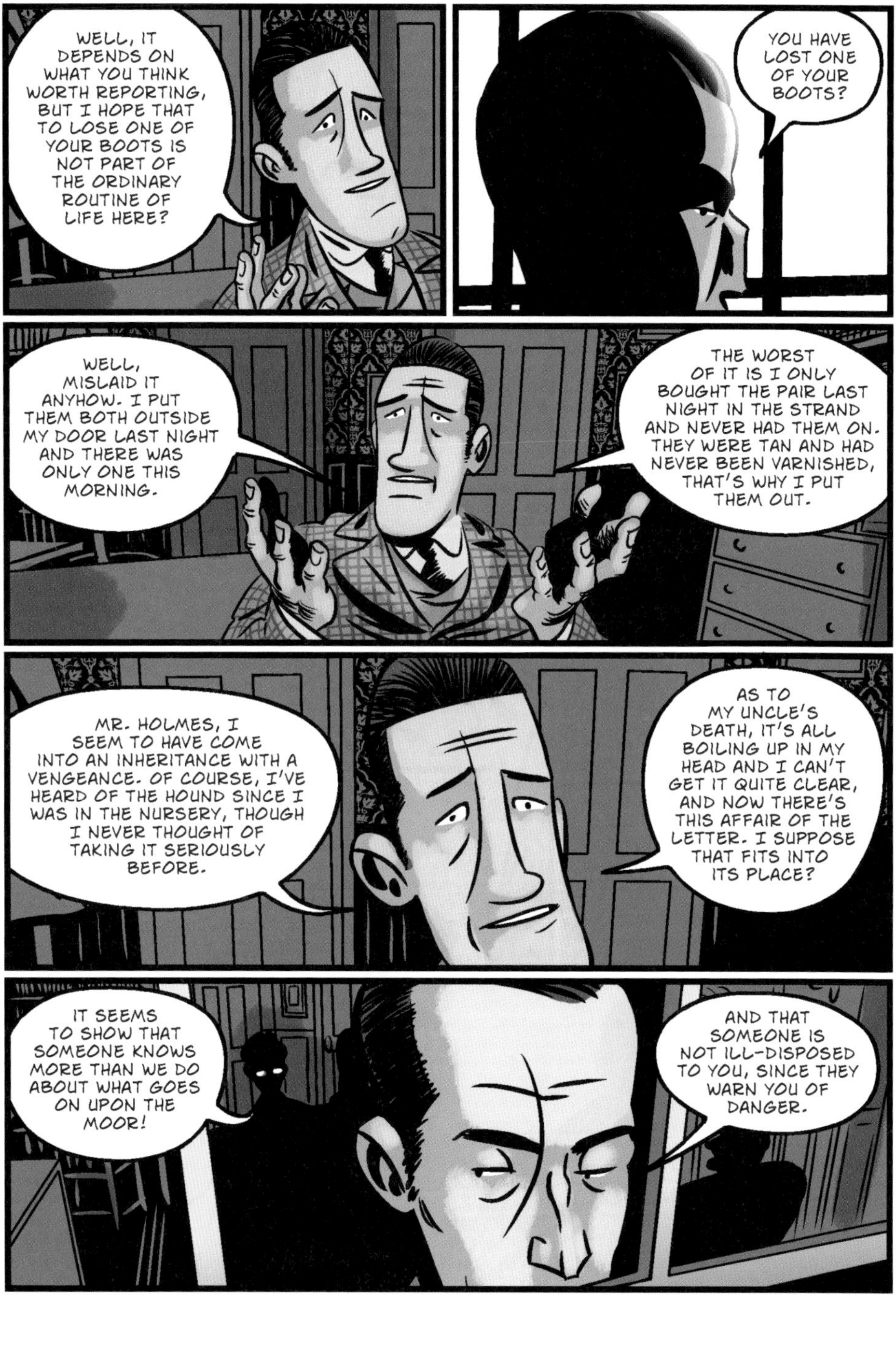
WELL, IT DEPENDS ON WHAT YOU THINK WORTH REPORTING, BUT I HOPE THAT TO LOSE ONE OF YOUR BOOTS IS NOT PART OF THE ORDINARY ROUTINE OF LIFE HERE?
YOU HAVE LOST ONE OF YOUR BOOTS?
WELL, MISLAID IT ANYHOW. I PUT THEM BOTH OUTSIDE MY DOOR LAST NIGHT AND THERE WAS ONLY ONE THIS MORNING.
THE WORST OF IT IS I ONLY BOUGHT THE PAIR LAST NIGHT IN THE STRAND AND NEVER HAD THEM ON. THEY WERE TAN AND HAD NEVER BEEN VARNISHED, THAT'S WHY I PUT THEM OUT.
MR. HOLMES, I SEEM TO HAVE COME INTO AN INHERITANCE WITH A VENGEANCE. OF COURSE, I'VE HEARD OF THE HOUND SINCE I WAS IN THE NURSERY, THOUGH I NEVER THOUGHT OF TAKING IT SERIOUSLY BEFORE.
AS TO MY UNCLE'S DEATH, IT'S ALL BOILING UP IN MY HEAD AND I CAN'T GET IT QUITE CLEAR, AND NOW THERE'S THIS AFFAIR OF THE LETTER. I SUPPOSE THAT FITS INTO ITS PLACE?
IT SEEMS TO SHOW THAT SOMEONE KNOWS MORE THAN WE DO ABOUT WHAT GOES ON UPON THE MOOR!
AND THAT SOMEONE IS NOT ILL-DISPOSED TO YOU, SINCE THEY WARN YOU OF DANGER.

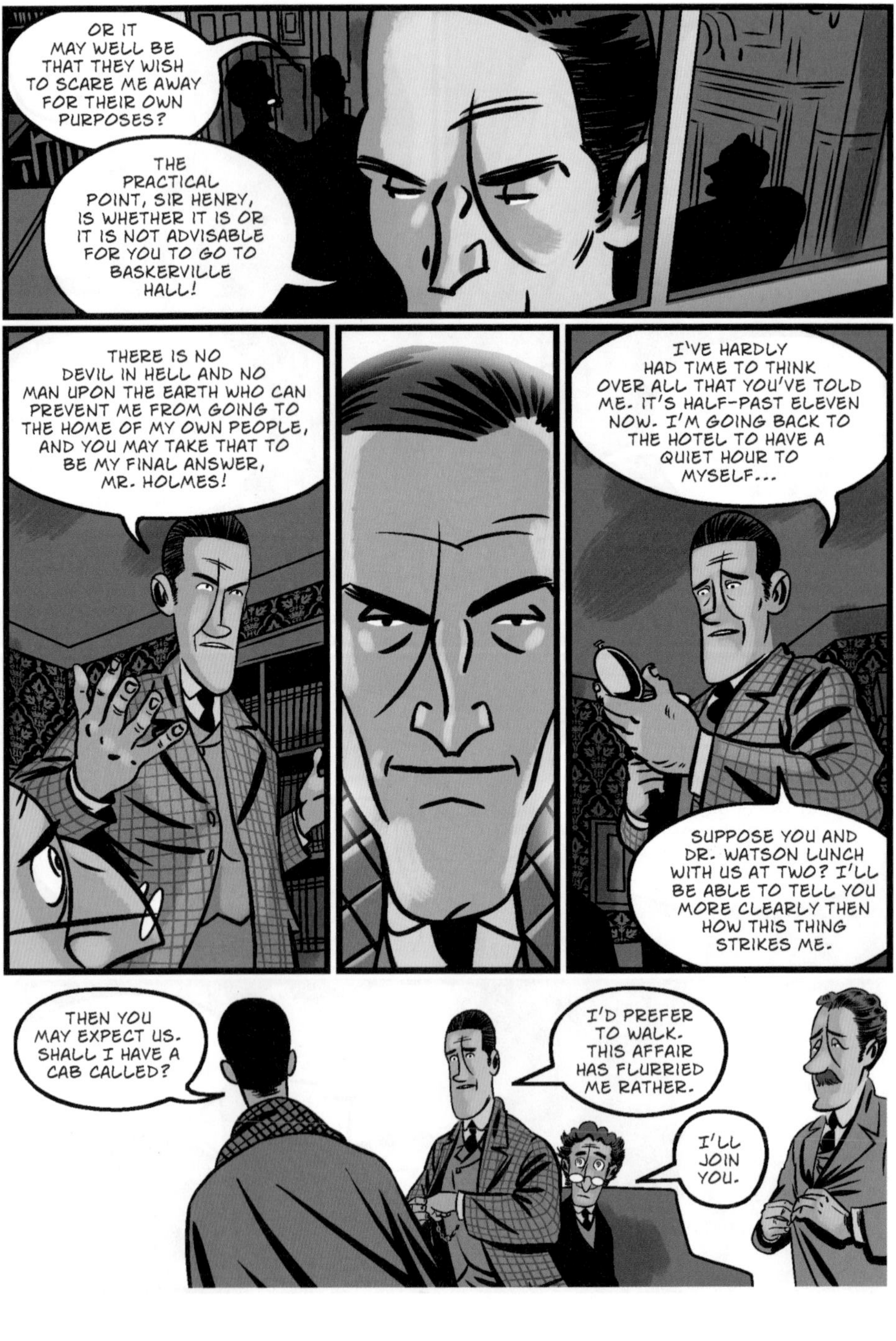
OR IT MAY WELL BE THAT THEY WISH TO SCARE ME AWAY FOR THEIR OWN PURPOSES?
THE PRACTICAL POINT, SIR HENRY, IS WHETHER IT IS OR IT IS NOT ADVISABLE FOR YOU TO GO TO BASKERVILLE HALL!
THERE IS NO DEVIL IN HELL AND NO MAN UPON THE EARTH WHO CAN PREVENT ME FROM GOING TO THE HOME OF MY OWN PEOPLE, AND YOU MAY TAKE THAT TO BE MY FINAL ANSWER, MR. HOLMES!
I'VE HARDLY HAD TIME TO THINK OVER ALL THAT YOU'VE TOLD ME. IT'S HALF-PAST ELEVEN NOW. I'M GOING BACK TO THE HOTEL TO HAVE A QUIET HOUR TO MYSELF...
SUPPOSE YOU AND DR. WATSON LUNCH WITH US AT TWO? I'LL BE ABLE TO TELL YOU MORE CLEARLY THEN HOW THIS THING STRIKES ME.
THEN YOU MAY EXPECT US. SHALL I HAVE A CAB CALLED?
I'D PREFER TO WALK. THIS AFFAIR HAS FLURRIED ME RATHER.
I'LL JOIN YOU.

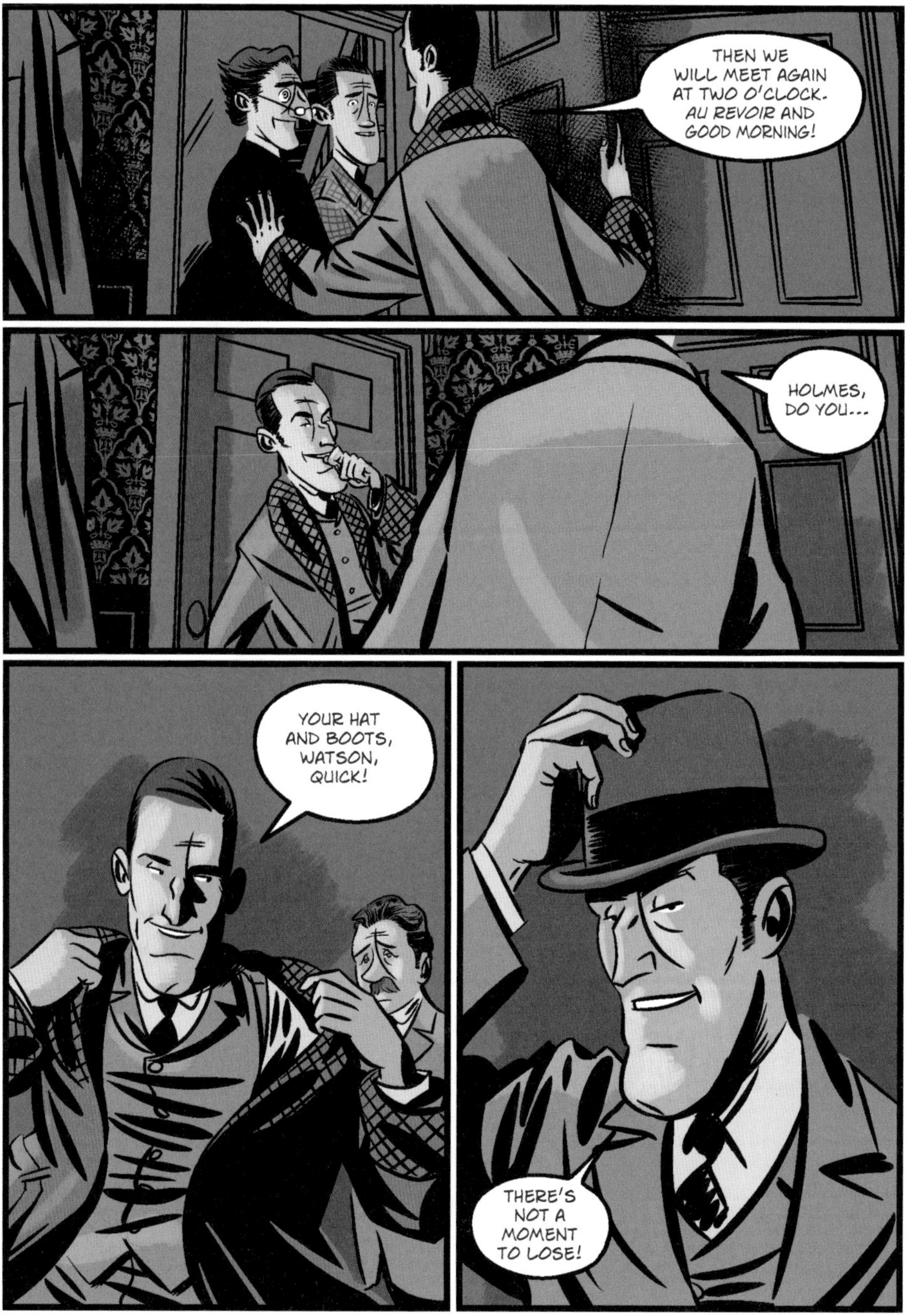
THEN WE WILL MEET AGAIN AT TWO O'CLOCK. AU REVOIR AND GOOD MORNING!
HOLMES, DO YOU...
YOUR HAT AND BOOTS, WATSON, QUICK!
THERE'S NOT A MOMENT TO LOSE!

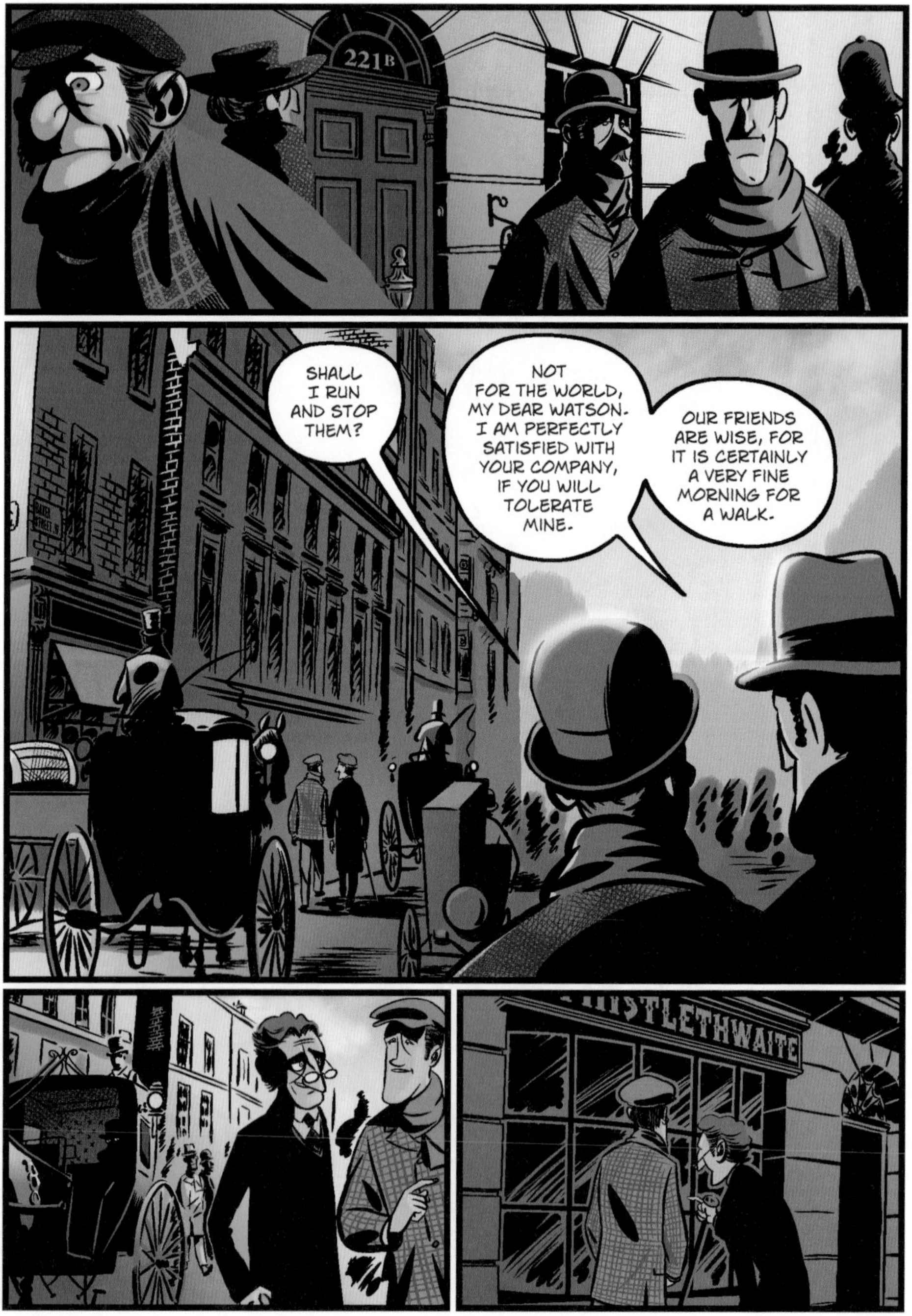
221B
SHALL I RUN AND STOP THEM?
NOT FOR THE WORLD, MY DEAR WATSON. I AM PERFECTLY SATISFIED WITH YOUR COMPANY, IF YOU WILL TOLERATE MINE.
OUR FRIENDS ARE WISE, FOR IT IS CERTAINLY A VERY FINE MORNING FOR A WALK.
HISTLETHWAITE

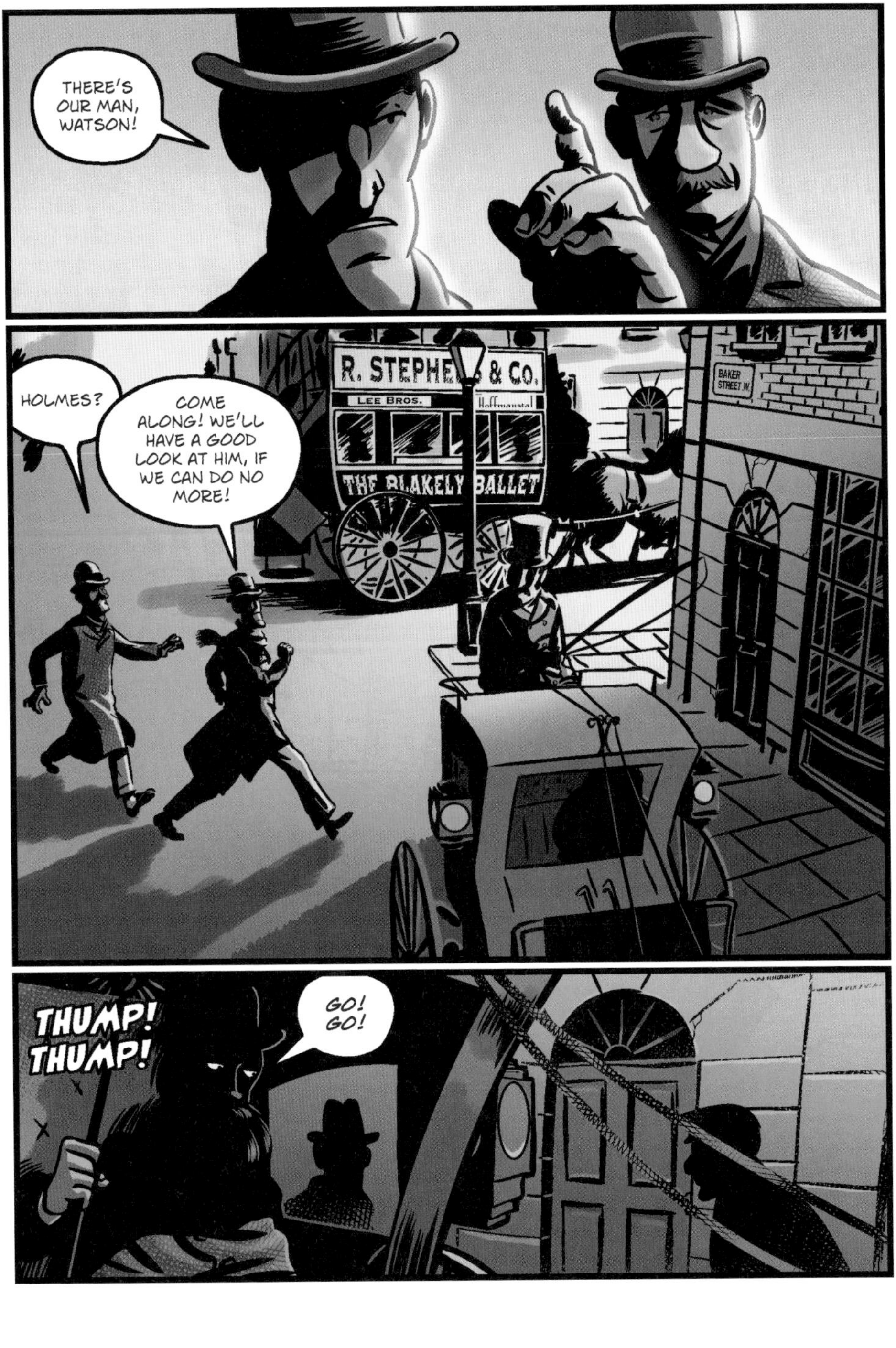
THERE'S OUR MAN, WATSON!
LEE BROS.
THE BLAKELY BALLET
BAKER STREET W.
HOLMES?
COME ALONG! WE'LL HAVE A GOOD LOOK AT HIM, IF WE CAN DO NO MORE!
THUMP! THUMP!
GO! GO!

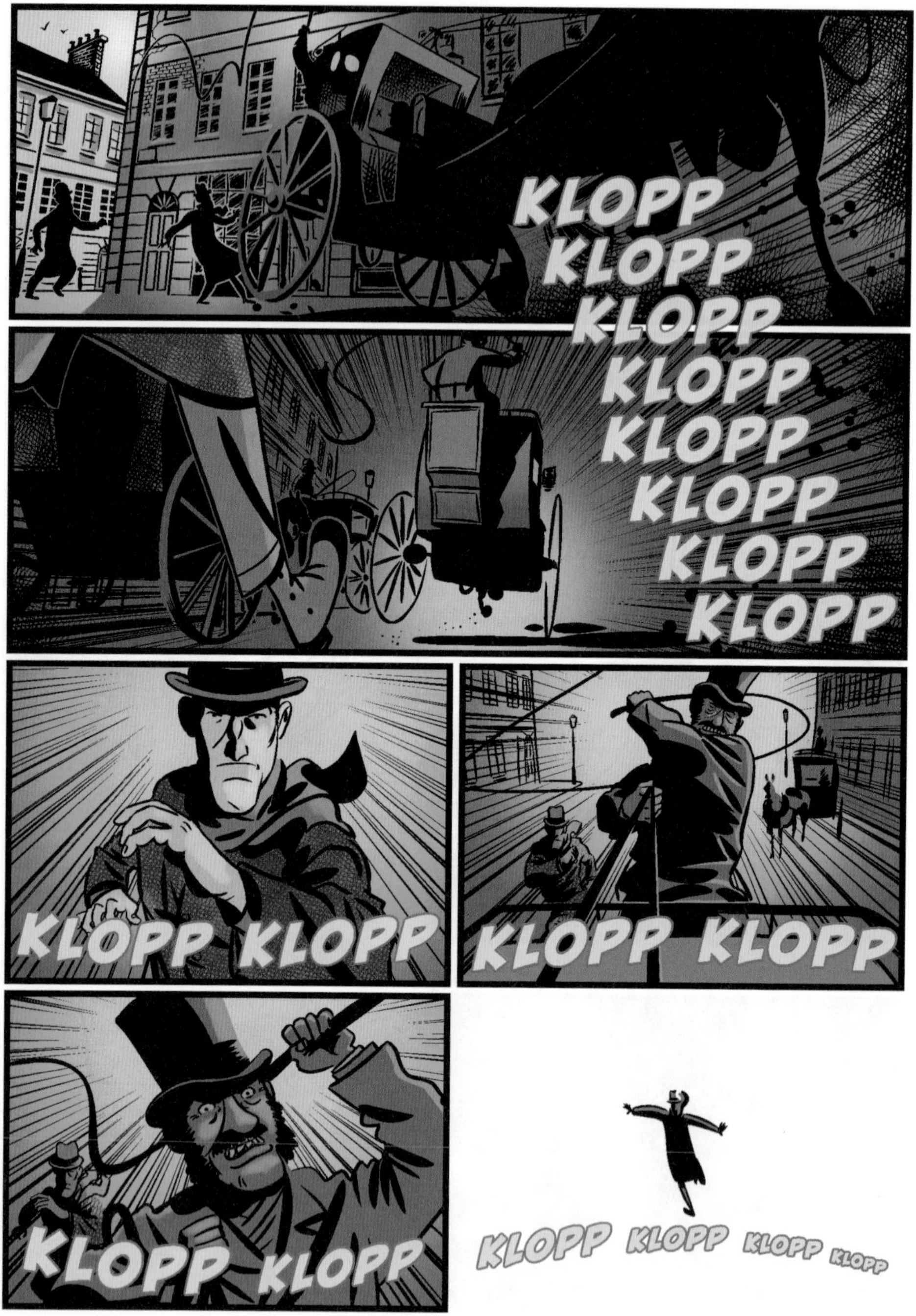
KLOPP
KLOPP
KLOPP
KLOPP
KLOPP
KLOPP
KLOPP
KLOPP
KLOPP KLOPP
KLOPP KLOPP
KLOPP KLOPP
KLOPP KLOPP KLOPP KLOPP

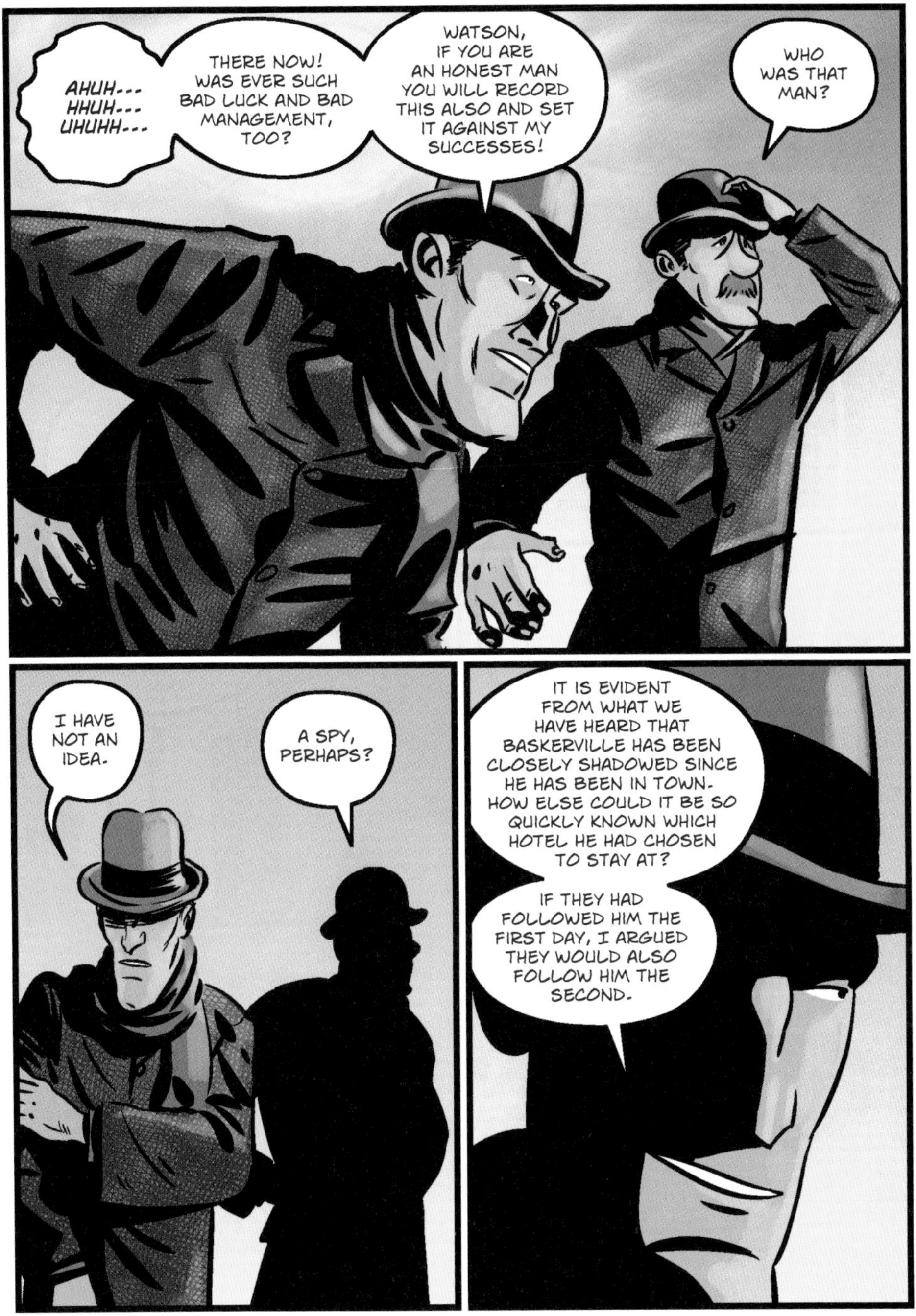
AHUH---
HHUH---
UHUHH---
THERE NOW! WAS EVER SUCH BAD LUCK AND BAD MANAGEMENT, TOO?
WATSON, IF YOU ARE AN HONEST MAN YOU WILL RECORD THIS ALSO AND SET IT AGAINST MY SUCCESSES!
WHO WAS THAT MAN?
I HAVE NOT AN IDEA.
A SPY, PERHAPS?
IT IS EVIDENT FROM WHAT WE HAVE HEARD THAT BASKERVILLE HAS BEEN CLOSELY SHADOWED SINCE HE HAS BEEN IN TOWN. HOW ELSE COULD IT BE SO QUICKLY KNOWN WHICH HOTEL HE HAD CHOSEN TO STAY AT?
IF THEY HAD FOLLOWED HIM THE FIRST DAY, I ARGUED THEY WOULD ALSO FOLLOW HIM THE SECOND.

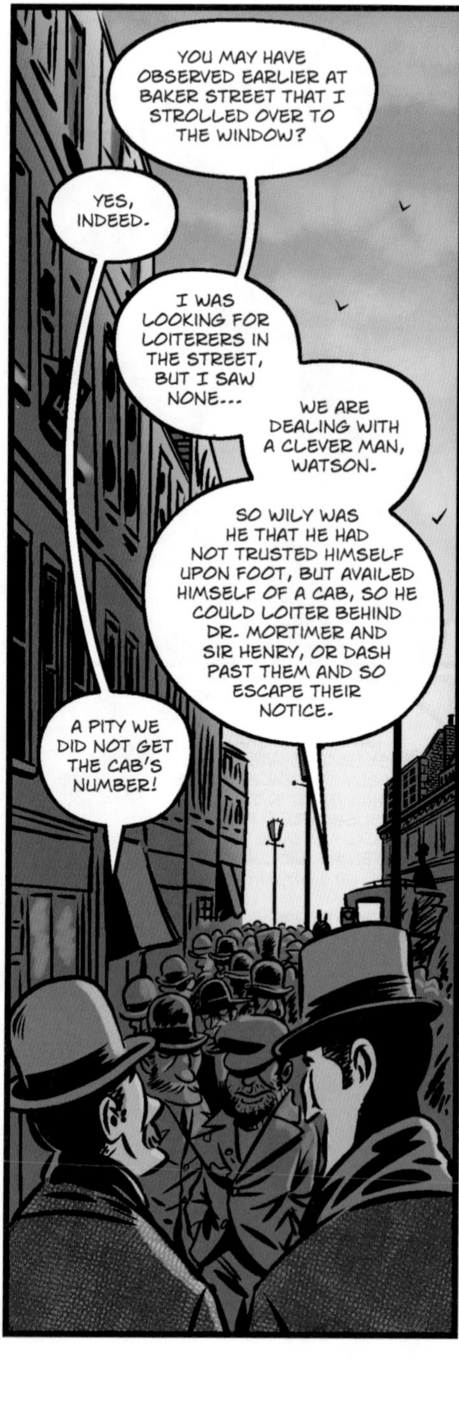
YOU MAY HAVE OBSERVED EARLIER AT BAKER STREET THAT I STROLLED OVER TO THE WINDOW?
YES, INDEED.
I WAS LOOKING FOR LOITERERS IN THE STREET, BUT I SAW NONE...
WE ARE DEALING WITH A CLEVER MAN, WATSON.
SO WILY WAS HE THAT HE HAD NOT TRUSTED HIMSELF UPON FOOT, BUT AVAILED HIMSELF OF A CAB, SO HE COULD LOITER BEHIND DR. MORTIMER AND SIR HENRY, OR DASH PAST THEM AND SO ESCAPE THEIR NOTICE.
A PITY WE DID NOT GET THE CAB'S NUMBER!

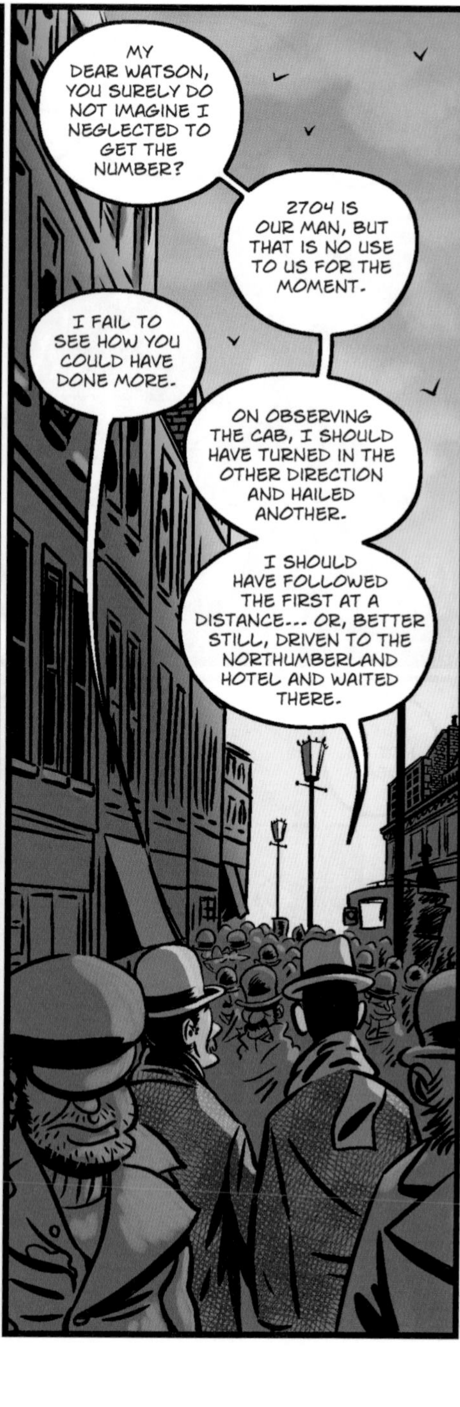
MY DEAR WATSON, YOU SURELY DO NOT IMAGINE I NEGLECTED TO GET THE NUMBER?
2704 IS OUR MAN, BUT THAT IS NO USE TO US FOR THE MOMENT.
I FAIL TO SEE HOW YOU COULD HAVE DONE MORE.
ON OBSERVING THE CAB, I SHOULD HAVE TURNED IN THE OTHER DIRECTION AND HAILED ANOTHER.
I SHOULD HAVE FOLLOWED THE FIRST AT A DISTANCE... OR, BETTER STILL, DRIVEN TO THE NORTHUMBERLAND HOTEL AND WAITED THERE.

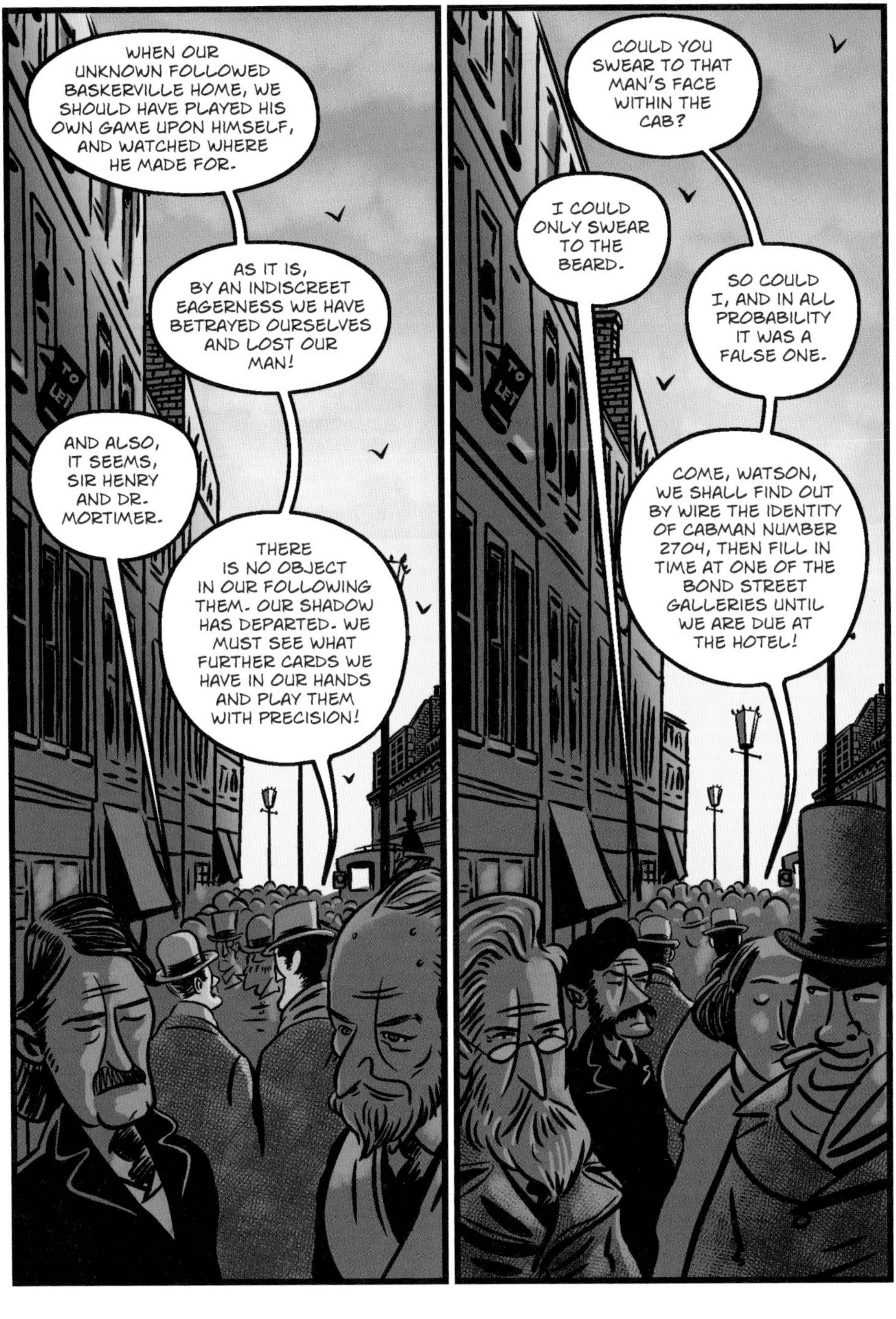
WHEN OUR UNKNOWN FOLLOWED BASKERVILLE HOME, WE SHOULD HAVE PLAYED HIS OWN GAME UPON HIMSELF, AND WATCHED WHERE HE MADE FOR.
AS IT IS, BY AN INDISCREET EAGERNESS WE HAVE BETRAYED OURSELVES AND LOST OUR MAN!
AND ALSO, IT SEEMS, SIR HENRY AND DR. MORTIMER.
THERE IS NO OBJECT IN OUR FOLLOWING THEM. OUR SHADOW HAS DEPARTED. WE MUST SEE WHAT FURTHER CARDS WE HAVE IN OUR HANDS AND PLAY THEM WITH PRECISION!
TO LET
COULD YOU SWEAR TO THAT MAN'S FACE WITHIN THE CAB?
I COULD ONLY SWEAR TO THE BEARD.
SO COULD I, AND IN ALL PROBABILITY IT WAS A FALSE ONE.
COME, WATSON, WE SHALL FIND OUT BY WIRE THE IDENTITY OF CABMAN NUMBER 2704, THEN FILL IN TIME AT ONE OF THE BOND STREET GALLERIES UNTIL WE ARE DUE AT THE HOTEL!
TO LET

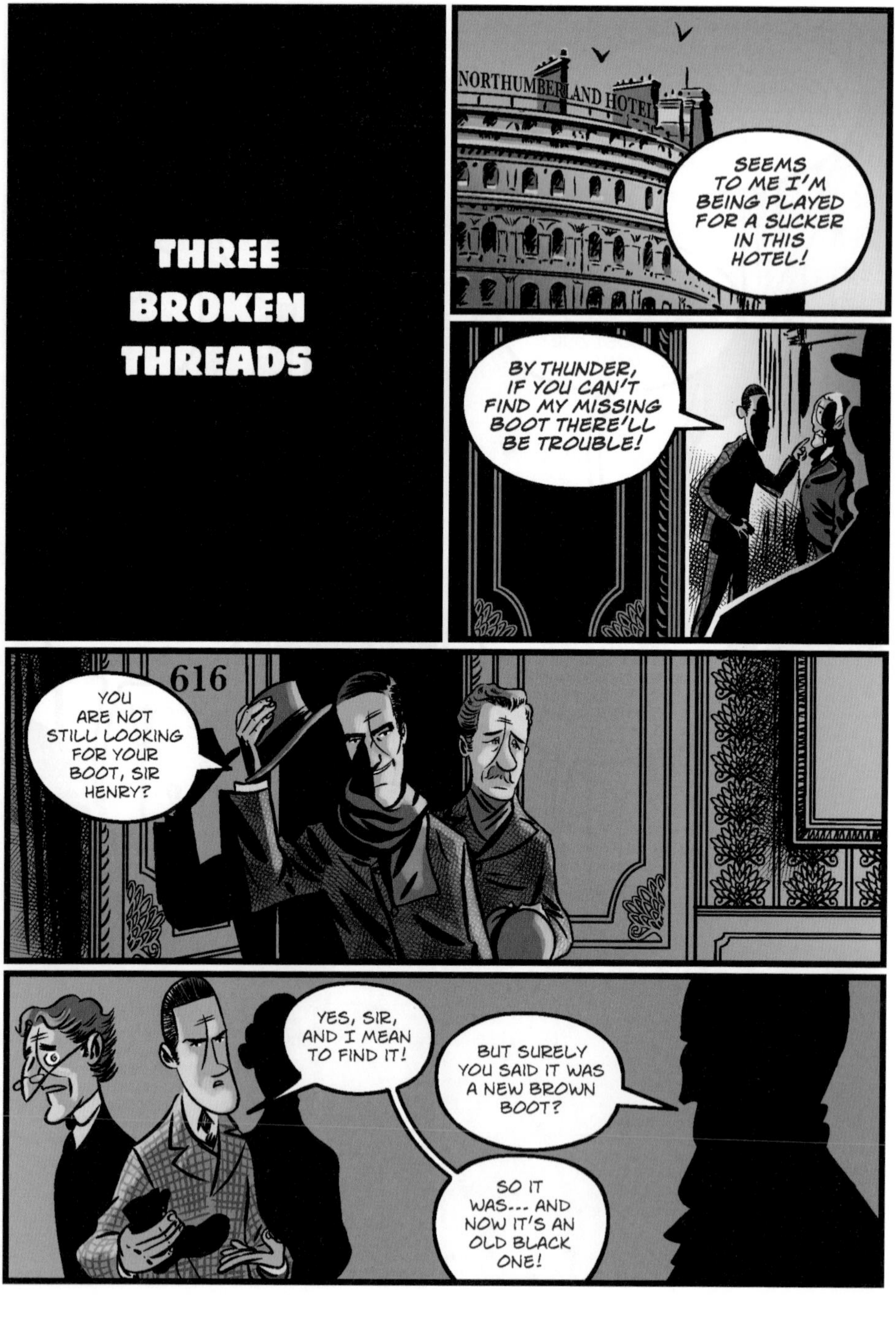
THREE BROKEN THREADS
NORTHUMBERLAND HOTEL
SEEMS TO ME I'M BEING PLAYED FOR A SUCKER IN THIS HOTEL!
BY THUNDER, IF YOU CAN'T FIND MY MISSING BOOT THERE'LL BE TROUBLE!
616
YOU ARE NOT STILL LOOKING FOR YOUR BOOT, SIR HENRY?
YES, SIR, AND I MEAN TO FIND IT!
BUT SURELY YOU SAID IT WAS A NEW BROWN BOOT?
SO IT WAS... AND NOW IT'S AN OLD BLACK ONE!

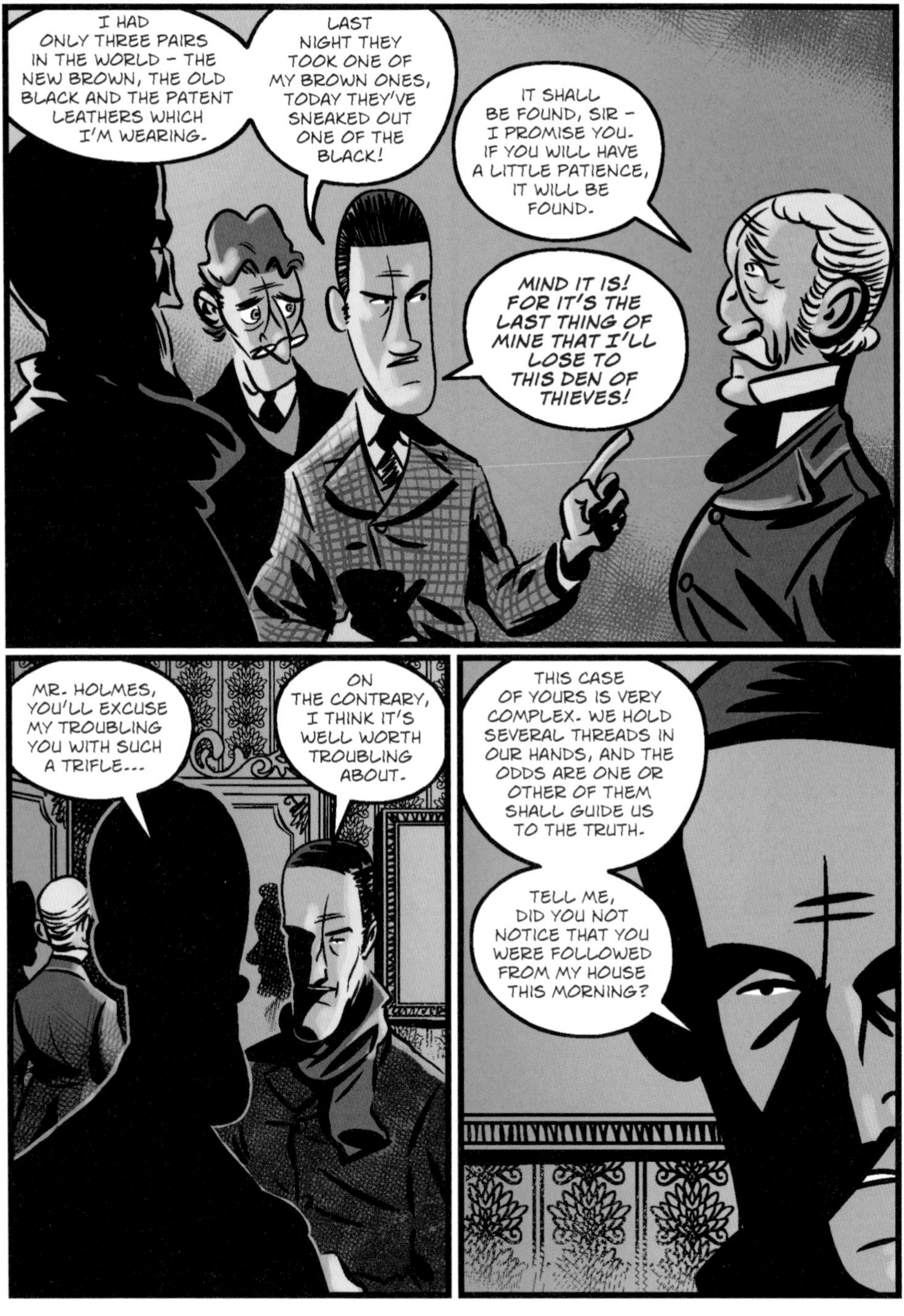
I HAD ONLY THREE PAIRS IN THE WORLD – THE NEW BROWN, THE OLD BLACK AND THE PATENT LEATHERS WHICH I'M WEARING.
LAST NIGHT THEY TOOK ONE OF MY BROWN ONES, TODAY THEY'VE SNEAKED OUT ONE OF THE BLACK!
IT SHALL BE FOUND, SIR – I PROMISE YOU. IF YOU WILL HAVE A LITTLE PATIENCE, IT WILL BE FOUND.
MIND IT IS! FOR IT'S THE LAST THING OF MINE THAT I'LL LOSE TO THIS DEN OF THIEVES!
MR. HOLMES, YOU'LL EXCUSE MY TROUBLING YOU WITH SUCH A TRIFLE...
ON THE CONTRARY, I THINK IT'S WELL WORTH TROUBLING ABOUT.
THIS CASE OF YOURS IS VERY COMPLEX. WE HOLD SEVERAL THREADS IN OUR HANDS, AND THE ODDS ARE ONE OR OTHER OF THEM SHALL GUIDE US TO THE TRUTH.
TELL ME, DID YOU NOT NOTICE THAT YOU WERE FOLLOWED FROM MY HOUSE THIS MORNING?

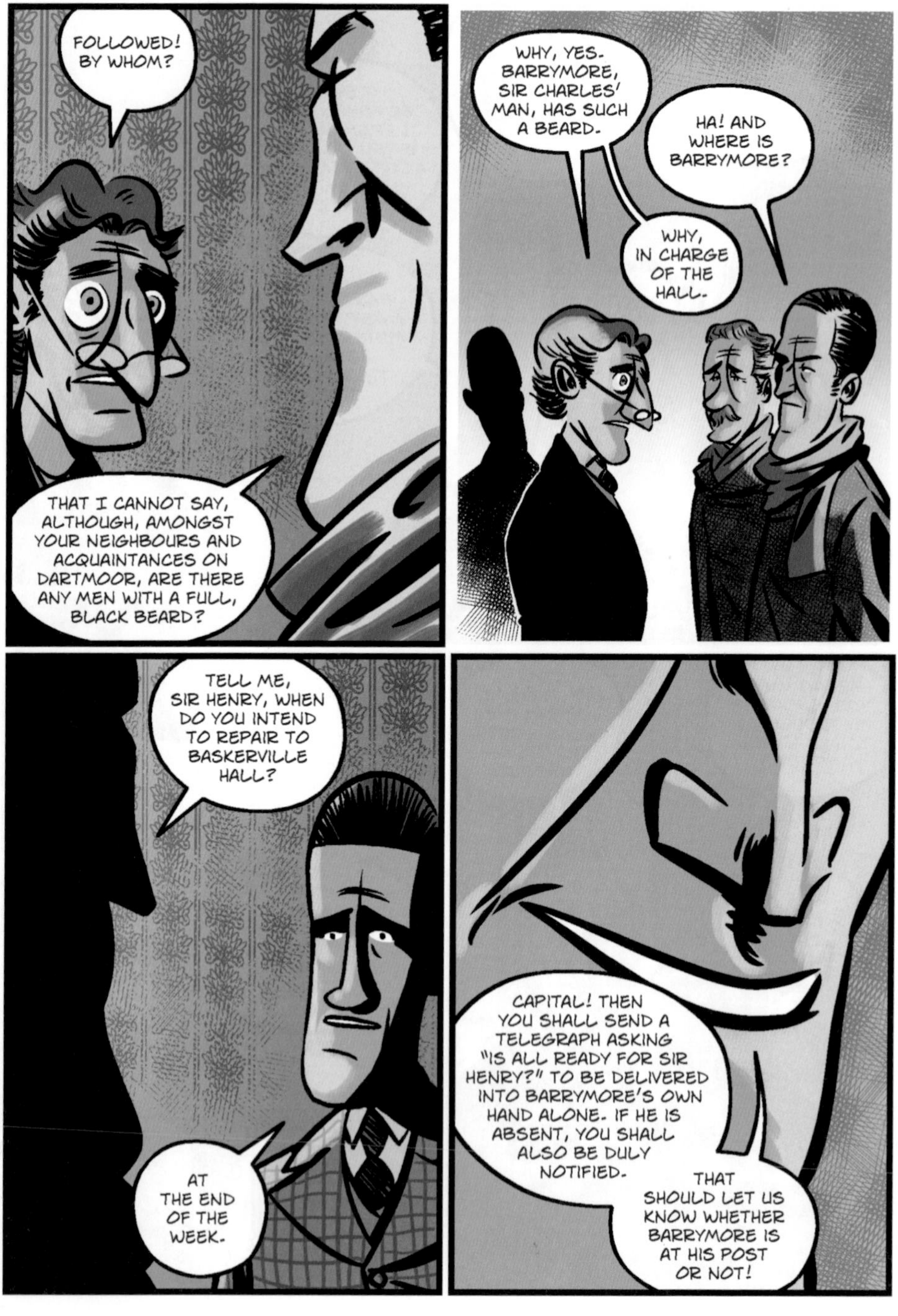
FOLLOWED! BY WHOM?
THAT I CANNOT SAY, ALTHOUGH, AMONGST YOUR NEIGHBOURS AND ACQUAINTANCES ON DARTMOOR, ARE THERE ANY MEN WITH A FULL, BLACK BEARD?
WHY, YES. BARRYMORE, SIR CHARLES' MAN, HAS SUCH A BEARD.
HA! AND WHERE IS BARRYMORE?
WHY, IN CHARGE OF THE HALL.
TELL ME, SIR HENRY, WHEN DO YOU INTEND TO REPAIR TO BASKERVILLE HALL?
AT THE END OF THE WEEK.
CAPITAL! THEN YOU SHALL SEND A TELEGRAPH ASKING "IS ALL READY FOR SIR HENRY?" TO BE DELIVERED INTO BARRYMORE'S OWN HAND ALONE. IF HE IS ABSENT, YOU SHALL ALSO BE DULY NOTIFIED.
THAT SHOULD LET US KNOW WHETHER BARRYMORE IS AT HIS POST OR NOT!

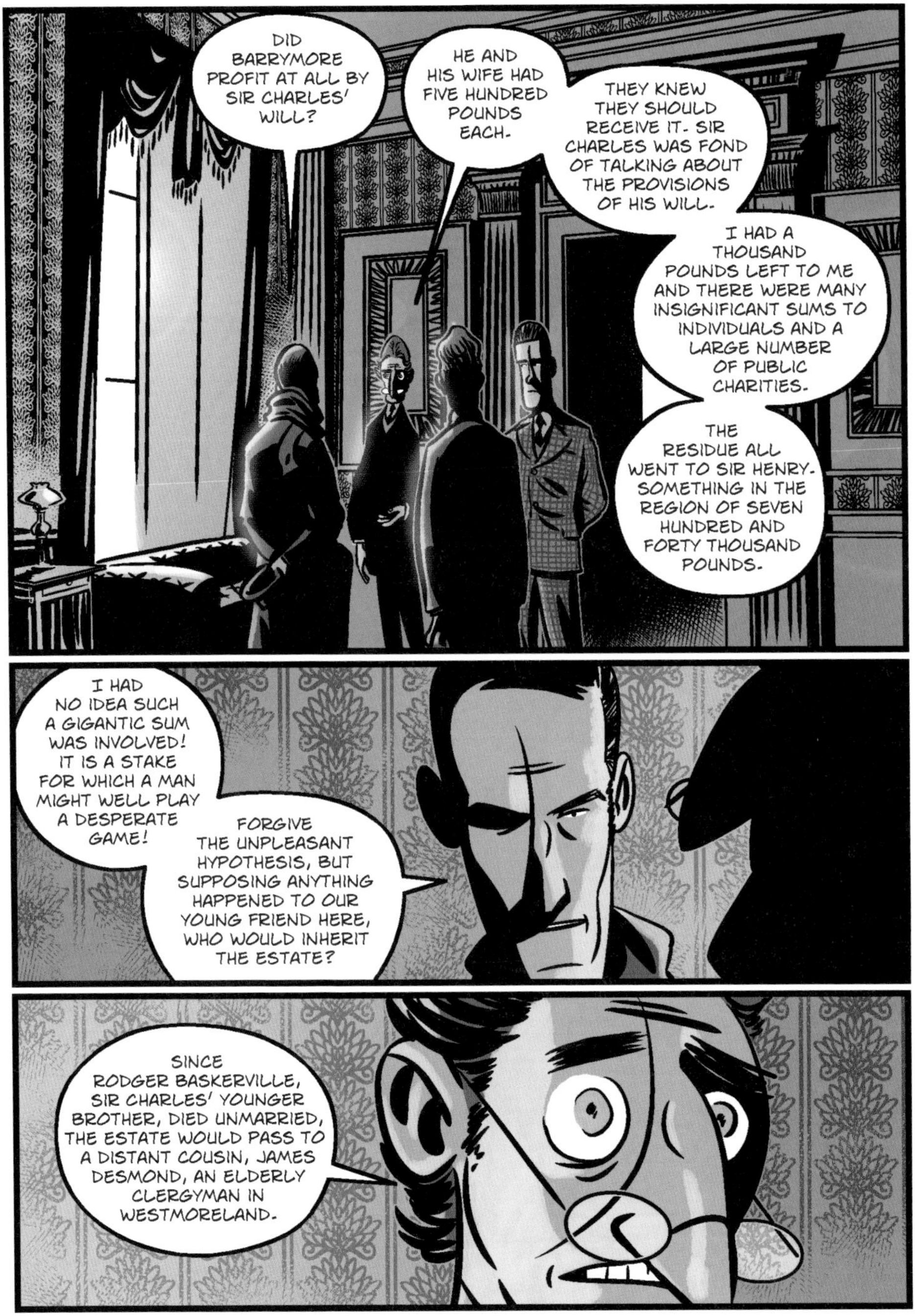
DID BARRYMORE PROFIT AT ALL BY SIR CHARLES' WILL?
HE AND HIS WIFE HAD FIVE HUNDRED POUNDS EACH.
THEY KNEW THEY SHOULD RECEIVE IT. SIR CHARLES WAS FOND OF TALKING ABOUT THE PROVISIONS OF HIS WILL.
I HAD A THOUSAND POUNDS LEFT TO ME AND THERE WERE MANY INSIGNIFICANT SUMS TO INDIVIDUALS AND A LARGE NUMBER OF PUBLIC CHARITIES.
THE RESIDUE ALL WENT TO SIR HENRY. SOMETHING IN THE REGION OF SEVEN HUNDRED AND FORTY THOUSAND POUNDS.
I HAD NO IDEA SUCH A GIGANTIC SUM WAS INVOLVED! IT IS A STAKE FOR WHICH A MAN MIGHT WELL PLAY A DESPERATE GAME!
FORGIVE THE UNPLEASANT HYPOTHESIS, BUT SUPPOSING ANYTHING HAPPENED TO OUR YOUNG FRIEND HERE, WHO WOULD INHERIT THE ESTATE?
SINCE RODGER BASKERVILLE, SIR CHARLES' YOUNGER BROTHER, DIED UNMARRIED, THE ESTATE WOULD PASS TO A DISTANT COUSIN, JAMES DESMOND, AN ELDERLY CLERGYMAN IN WESTMORELAND.

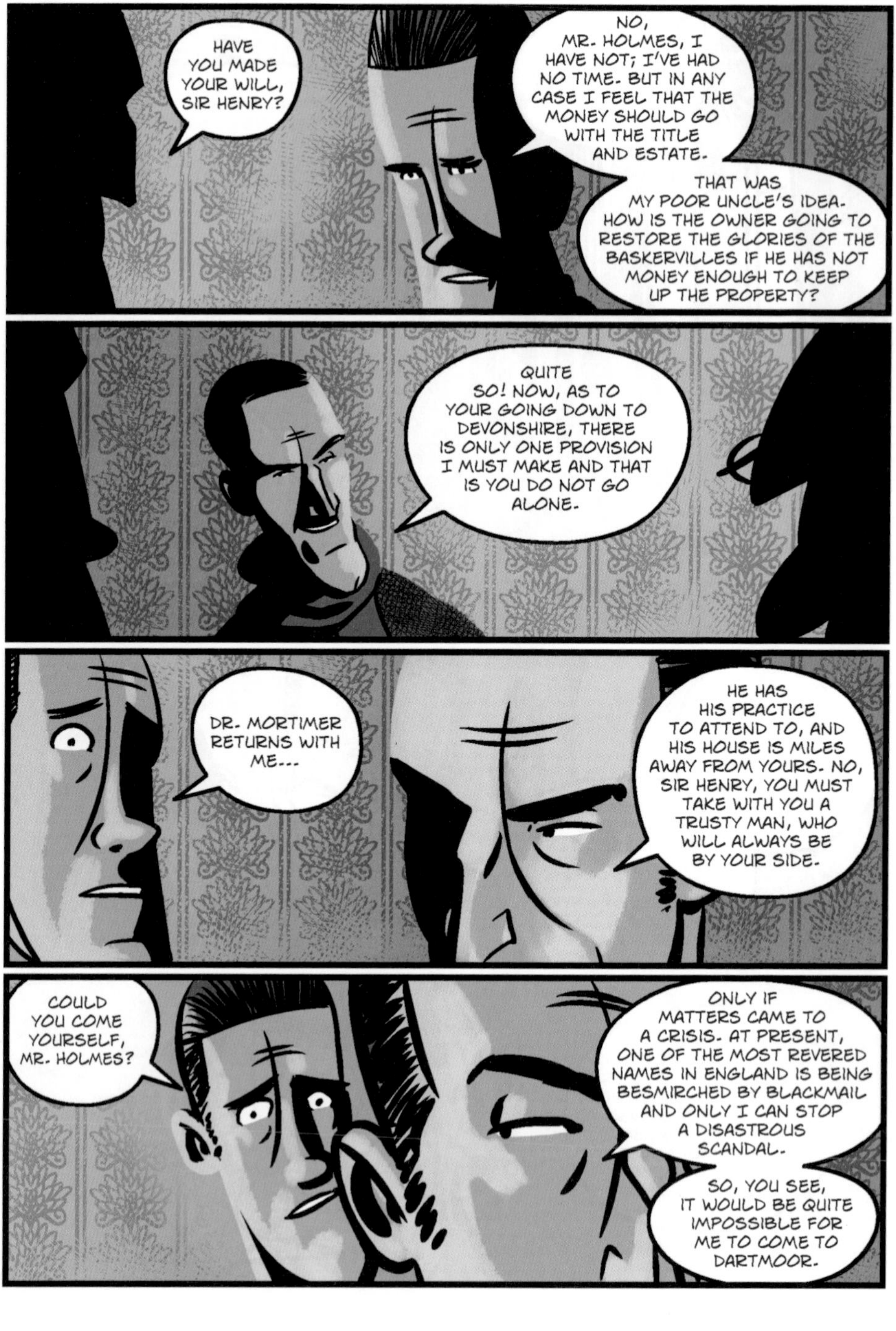
HAVE YOU MADE YOUR WILL, SIR HENRY?
NO, MR. HOLMES, I HAVE NOT; I'VE HAD NO TIME. BUT IN ANY CASE I FEEL THAT THE MONEY SHOULD GO WITH THE TITLE AND ESTATE.
THAT WAS MY POOR UNCLE'S IDEA. HOW IS THE OWNER GOING TO RESTORE THE GLORIES OF THE BASKERVILLES IF HE HAS NOT MONEY ENOUGH TO KEEP UP THE PROPERTY?
QUITE SO! NOW, AS TO YOUR GOING DOWN TO DEVONSHIRE, THERE IS ONLY ONE PROVISION I MUST MAKE AND THAT IS YOU DO NOT GO ALONE.
DR. MORTIMER RETURNS WITH ME...
HE HAS HIS PRACTICE TO ATTEND TO, AND HIS HOUSE IS MILES AWAY FROM YOURS. NO, SIR HENRY, YOU MUST TAKE WITH YOU A TRUSTY MAN, WHO WILL ALWAYS BE BY YOUR SIDE.
COULD YOU COME YOURSELF, MR. HOLMES?
ONLY IF MATTERS CAME TO A CRISIS. AT PRESENT, ONE OF THE MOST REVERED NAMES IN ENGLAND IS BEING BESMIRCHED BY BLACKMAIL AND ONLY I CAN STOP A DISASTROUS SCANDAL.
SO, YOU SEE, IT WOULD BE QUITE IMPOSSIBLE FOR ME TO COME TO DARTMOOR.

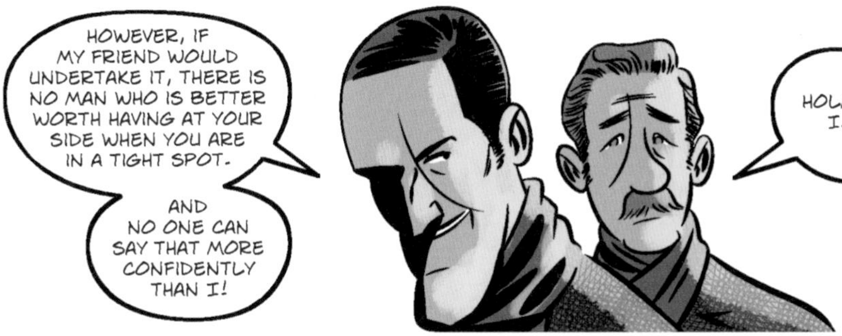
HOWEVER, IF MY FRIEND WOULD UNDERTAKE IT, THERE IS NO MAN WHO IS BETTER WORTH HAVING AT YOUR SIDE WHEN YOU ARE IN A TIGHT SPOT.
AND NO ONE CAN SAY THAT MORE CONFIDENTLY THAN I!
HOLMES, I...

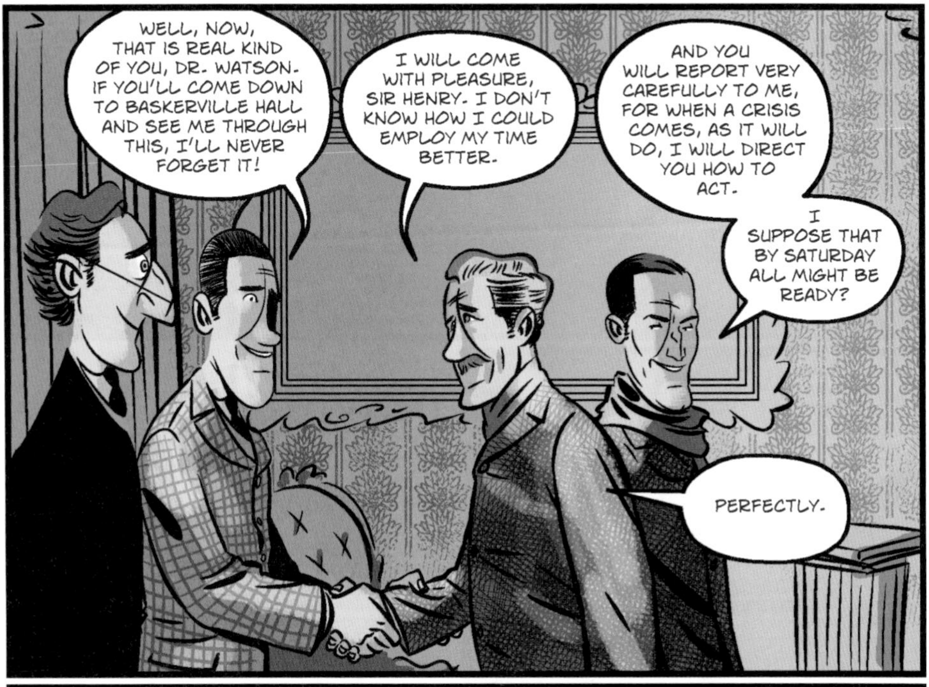
WELL, NOW, THAT IS REAL KIND OF YOU, DR. WATSON. IF YOU'LL COME DOWN TO BASKERVILLE HALL AND SEE ME THROUGH THIS, I'LL NEVER FORGET IT!
I WILL COME WITH PLEASURE, SIR HENRY. I DON'T KNOW HOW I COULD EMPLOY MY TIME BETTER.
AND YOU WILL REPORT VERY CAREFULLY TO ME, FOR WHEN A CRISIS COMES, AS IT WILL DO, I WILL DIRECT YOU HOW TO ACT.
I SUPPOSE THAT BY SATURDAY ALL MIGHT BE READY?
PERFECTLY.

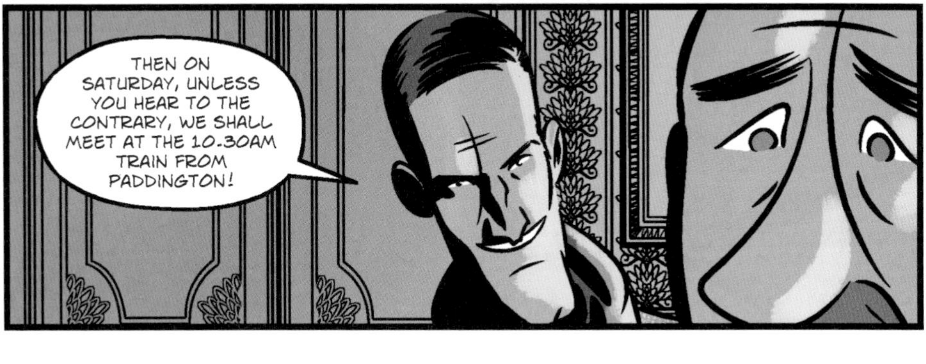
THEN ON SATURDAY, UNLESS YOU HEAR TO THE CONTRARY, WE SHALL MEET AT THE 10.30AM TRAIN FROM PADDINGTON!

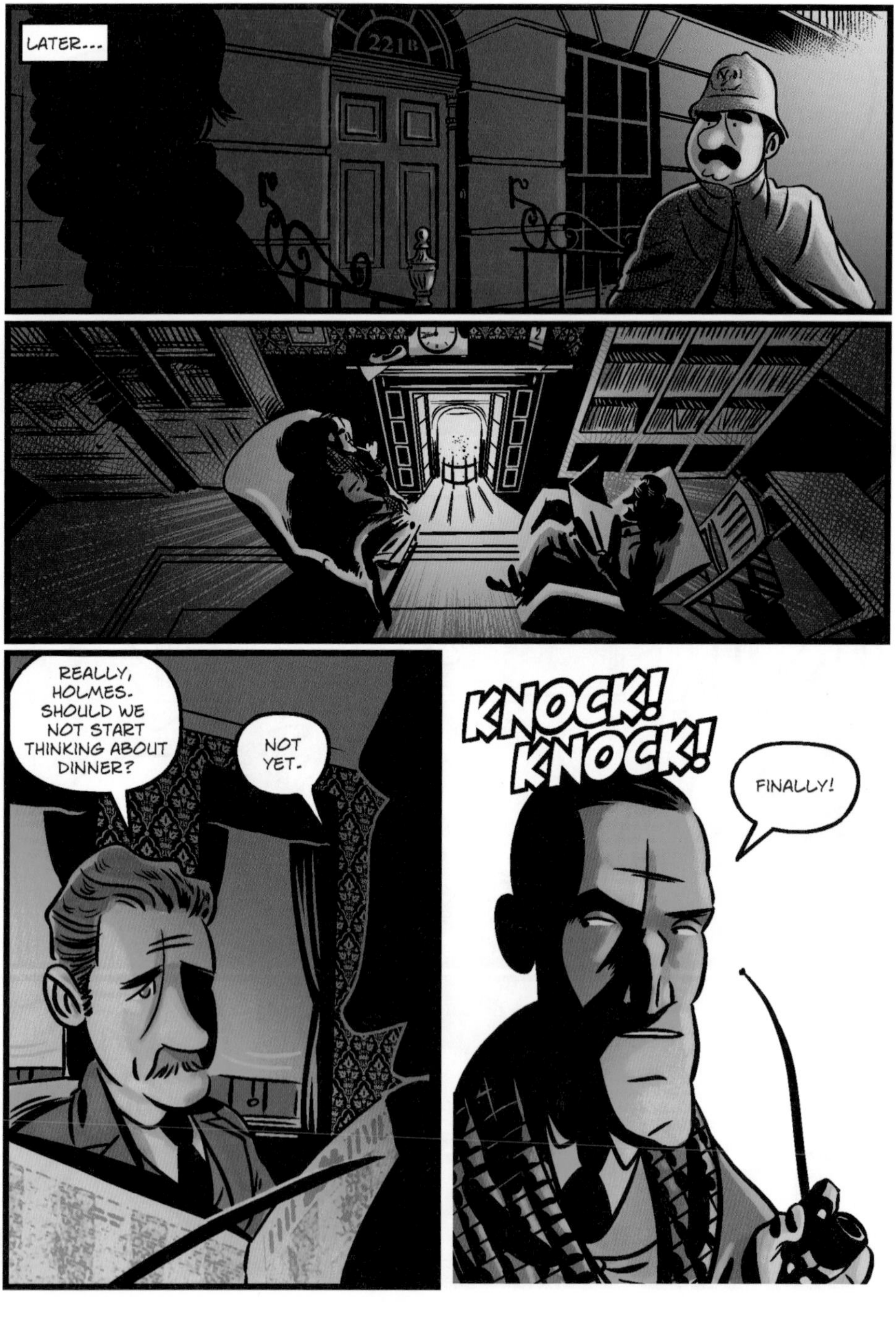
LATER...
221B
REALLY, HOLMES. SHOULD WE NOT START THINKING ABOUT DINNER?
NOT YET.
KNOCK! KNOCK!
FINALLY!

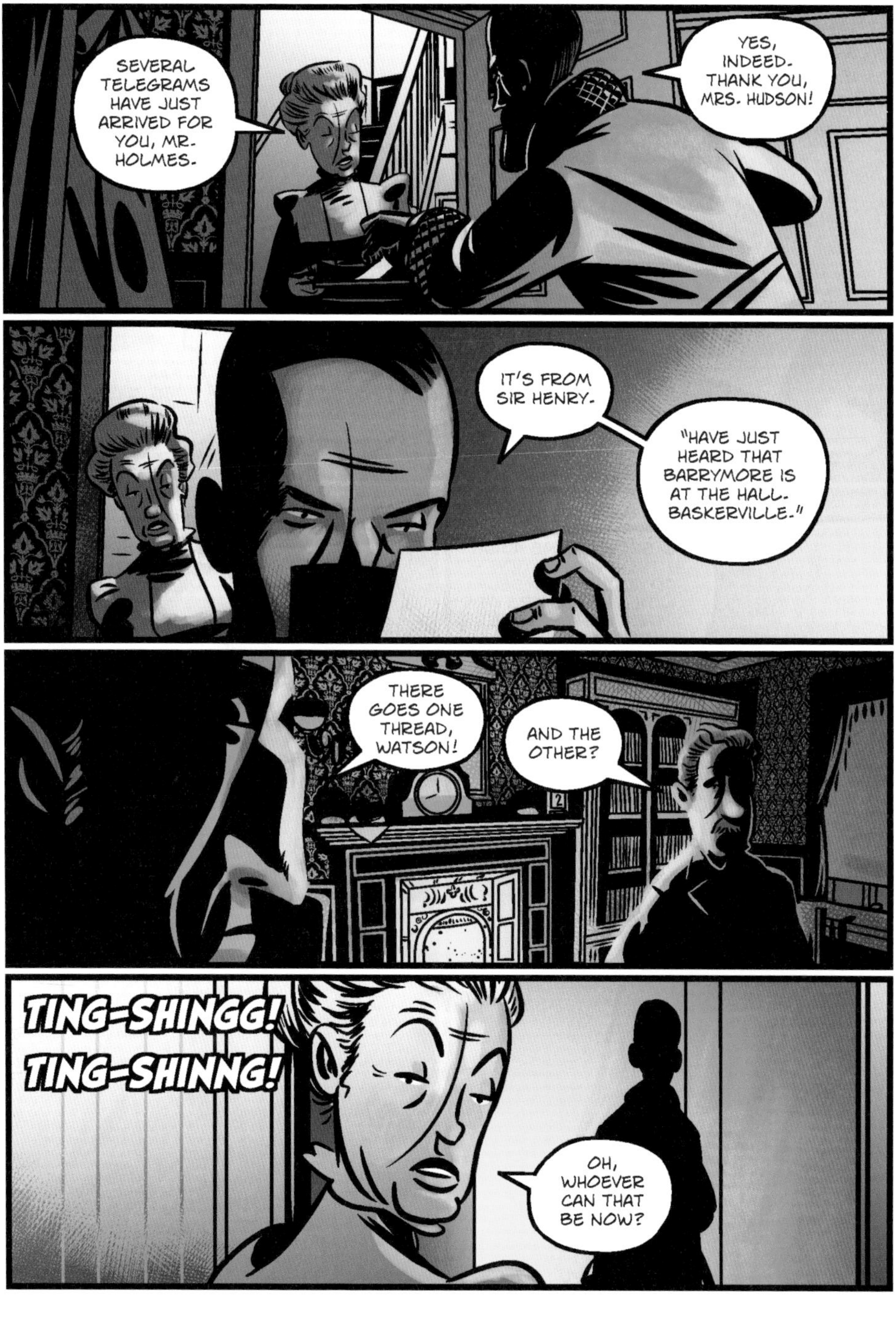
SEVERAL TELEGRAMS HAVE JUST ARRIVED FOR YOU, MR. HOLMES.
YES, INDEED. THANK YOU, MRS. HUDSON!
IT'S FROM SIR HENRY.
"HAVE JUST HEARD THAT BARRYMORE IS AT THE HALL. BASKERVILLE."
THERE GOES ONE THREAD, WATSON!
AND THE OTHER?
TING-SHINGG!
TING-SHINNG!
OH, WHOEVER CAN THAT BE NOW?

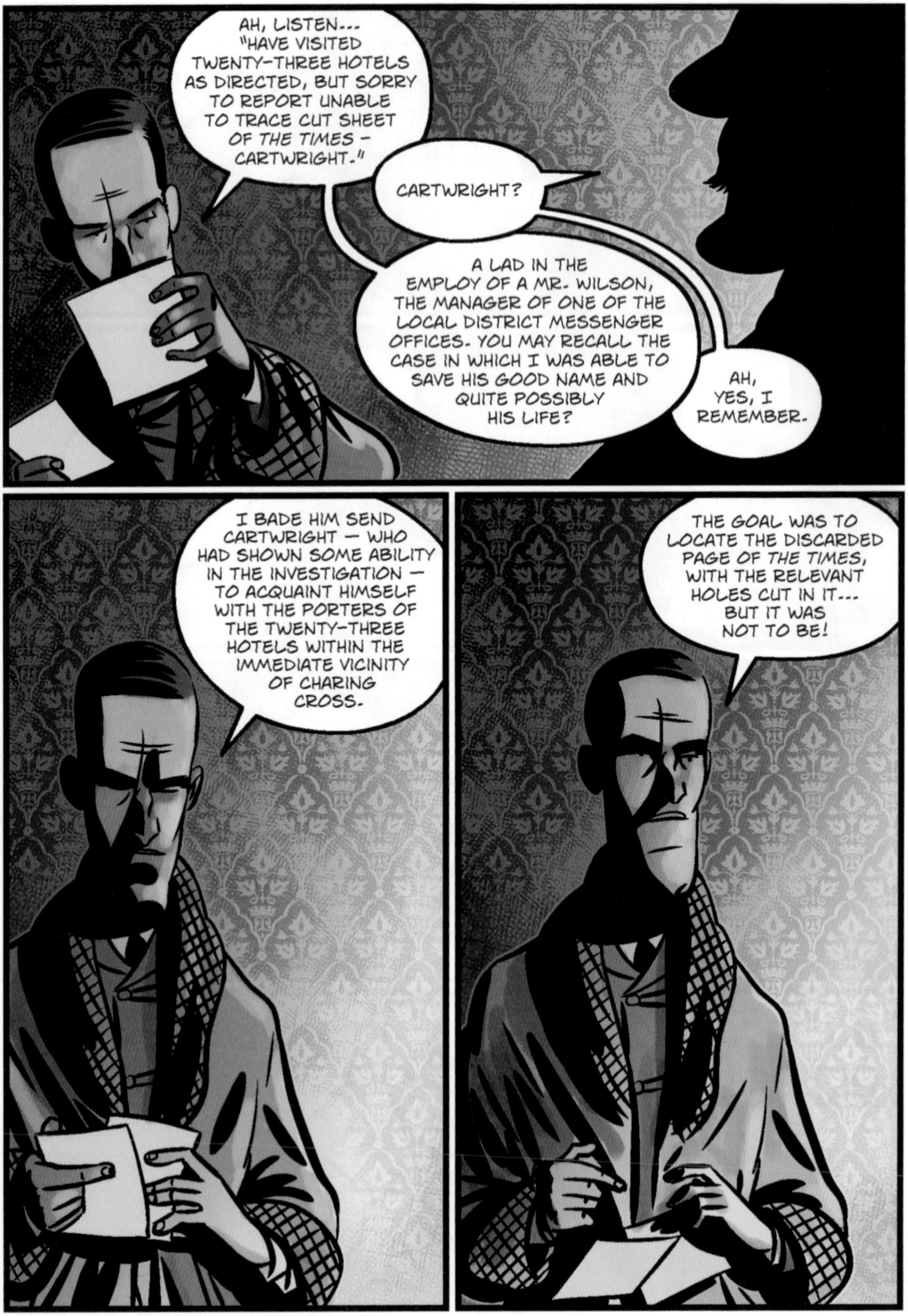
AH, LISTEN... "HAVE VISITED TWENTY-THREE HOTELS AS DIRECTED, BUT SORRY TO REPORT UNABLE TO TRACE CUT SHEET OF *THE TIMES* – CARTWRIGHT."
CARTWRIGHT?
A LAD IN THE EMPLOY OF A MR. WILSON, THE MANAGER OF ONE OF THE LOCAL DISTRICT MESSENGER OFFICES. YOU MAY RECALL THE CASE IN WHICH I WAS ABLE TO SAVE HIS GOOD NAME AND QUITE POSSIBLY HIS LIFE?
AH, YES, I REMEMBER.
I BADE HIM SEND CARTWRIGHT — WHO HAD SHOWN SOME ABILITY IN THE INVESTIGATION — TO ACQUAINT HIMSELF WITH THE PORTERS OF THE TWENTY-THREE HOTELS WITHIN THE IMMEDIATE VICINITY OF CHARING CROSS.
THE GOAL WAS TO LOCATE THE DISCARDED PAGE OF *THE TIMES*, WITH THE RELEVANT HOLES CUT IN IT... BUT IT WAS NOT TO BE!

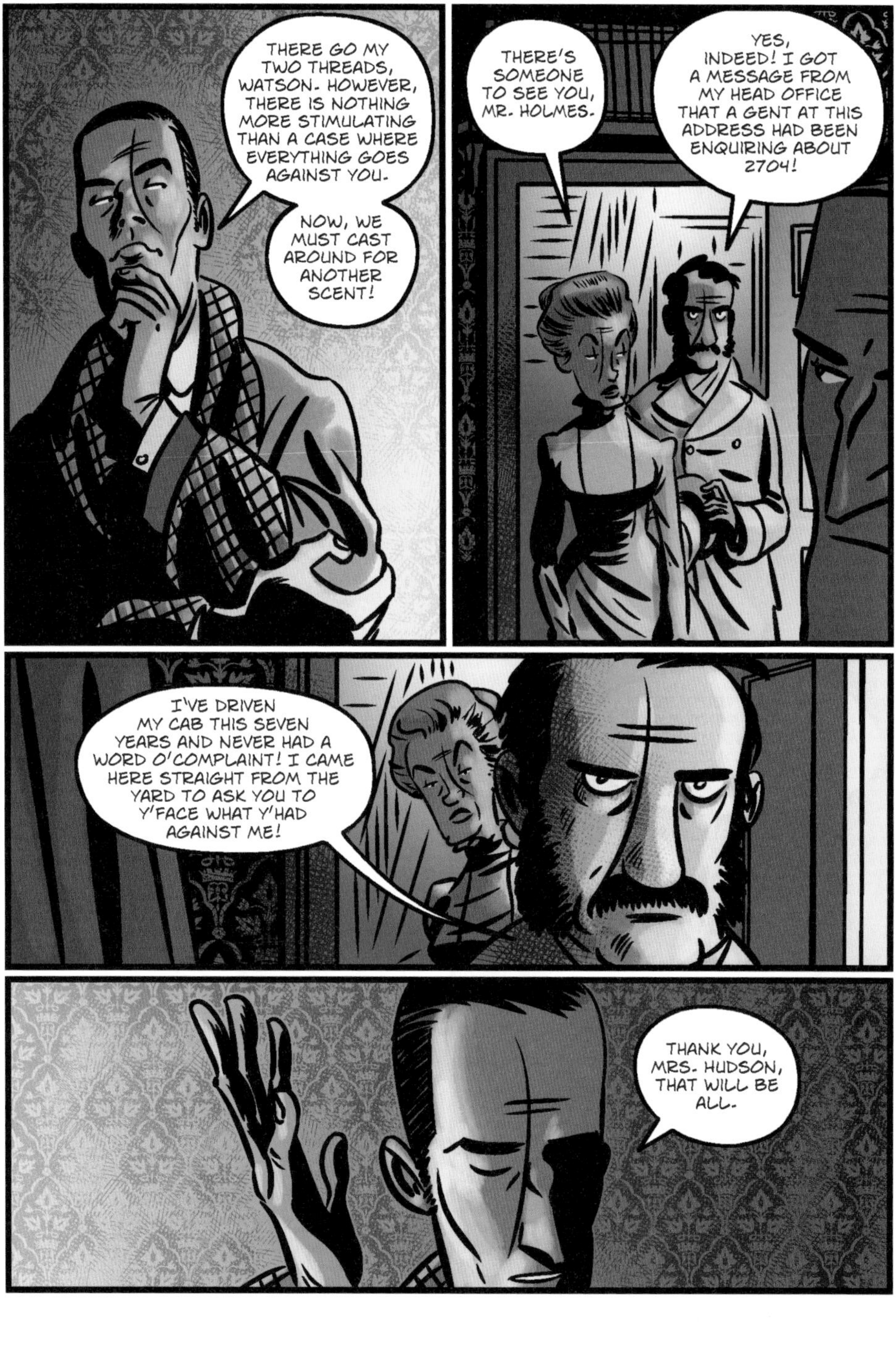
THERE GO MY TWO THREADS, WATSON. HOWEVER, THERE IS NOTHING MORE STIMULATING THAN A CASE WHERE EVERYTHING GOES AGAINST YOU.
NOW, WE MUST CAST AROUND FOR ANOTHER SCENT!
THERE'S SOMEONE TO SEE YOU, MR. HOLMES.
YES, INDEED! I GOT A MESSAGE FROM MY HEAD OFFICE THAT A GENT AT THIS ADDRESS HAD BEEN ENQUIRING ABOUT 2704!
I'VE DRIVEN MY CAB THIS SEVEN YEARS AND NEVER HAD A WORD O'COMPLAINT! I CAME HERE STRAIGHT FROM THE YARD TO ASK YOU TO Y'FACE WHAT Y'HAD AGAINST ME!
THANK YOU, MRS. HUDSON, THAT WILL BE ALL.

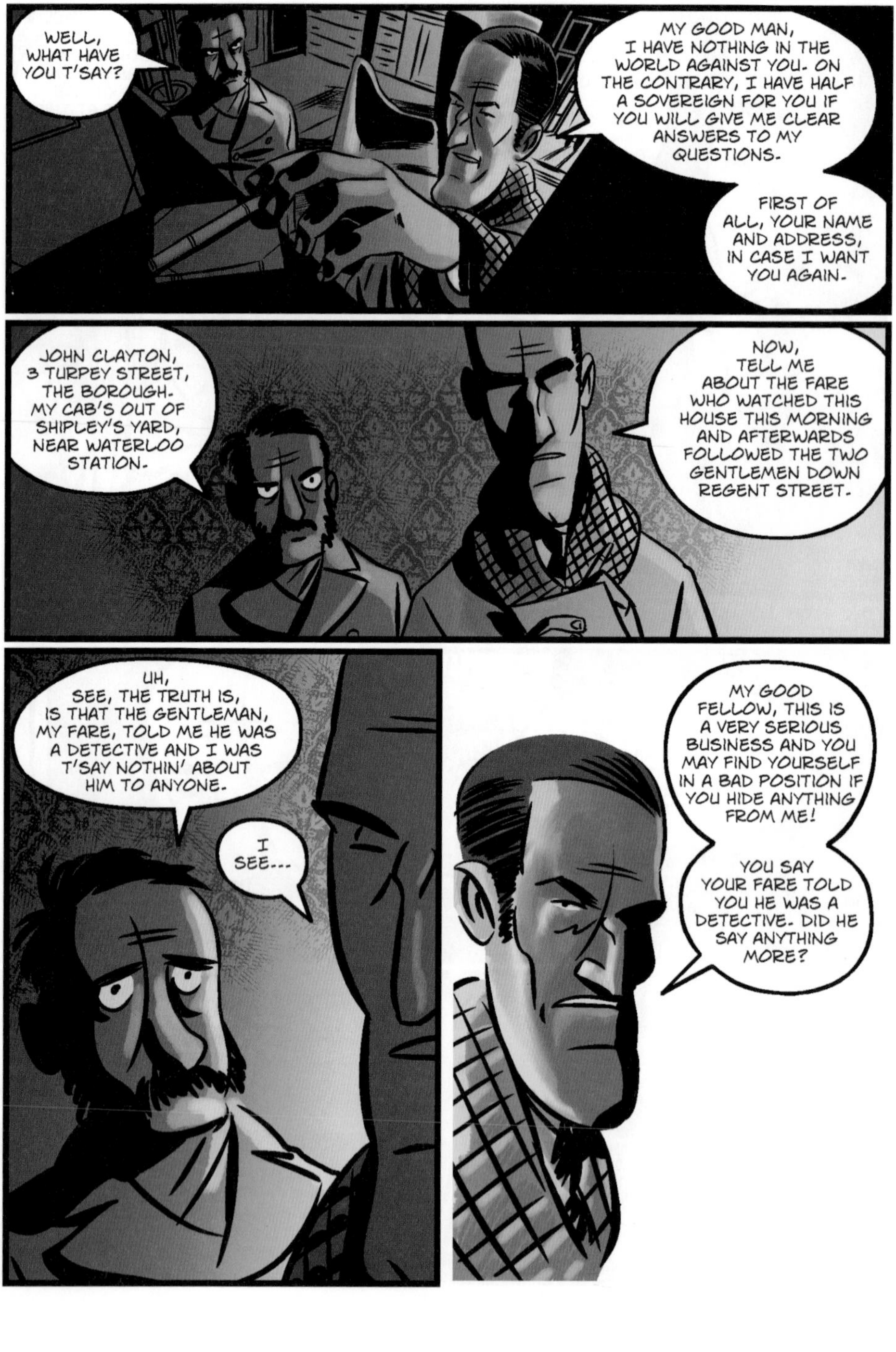
WELL, WHAT HAVE YOU T'SAY?
MY GOOD MAN, I HAVE NOTHING IN THE WORLD AGAINST YOU. ON THE CONTRARY, I HAVE HALF A SOVEREIGN FOR YOU IF YOU WILL GIVE ME CLEAR ANSWERS TO MY QUESTIONS.
FIRST OF ALL, YOUR NAME AND ADDRESS, IN CASE I WANT YOU AGAIN.
JOHN CLAYTON, 3 TURPEY STREET, THE BOROUGH. MY CAB'S OUT OF SHIPLEY'S YARD, NEAR WATERLOO STATION.
NOW, TELL ME ABOUT THE FARE WHO WATCHED THIS HOUSE THIS MORNING AND AFTERWARDS FOLLOWED THE TWO GENTLEMEN DOWN REGENT STREET.
UH, SEE, THE TRUTH IS, IS THAT THE GENTLEMAN, MY FARE, TOLD ME HE WAS A DETECTIVE AND I WAS T'SAY NOTHIN' ABOUT HIM TO ANYONE.
I SEE...
MY GOOD FELLOW, THIS IS A VERY SERIOUS BUSINESS AND YOU MAY FIND YOURSELF IN A BAD POSITION IF YOU HIDE ANYTHING FROM ME!
YOU SAY YOUR FARE TOLD YOU HE WAS A DETECTIVE. DID HE SAY ANYTHING MORE?

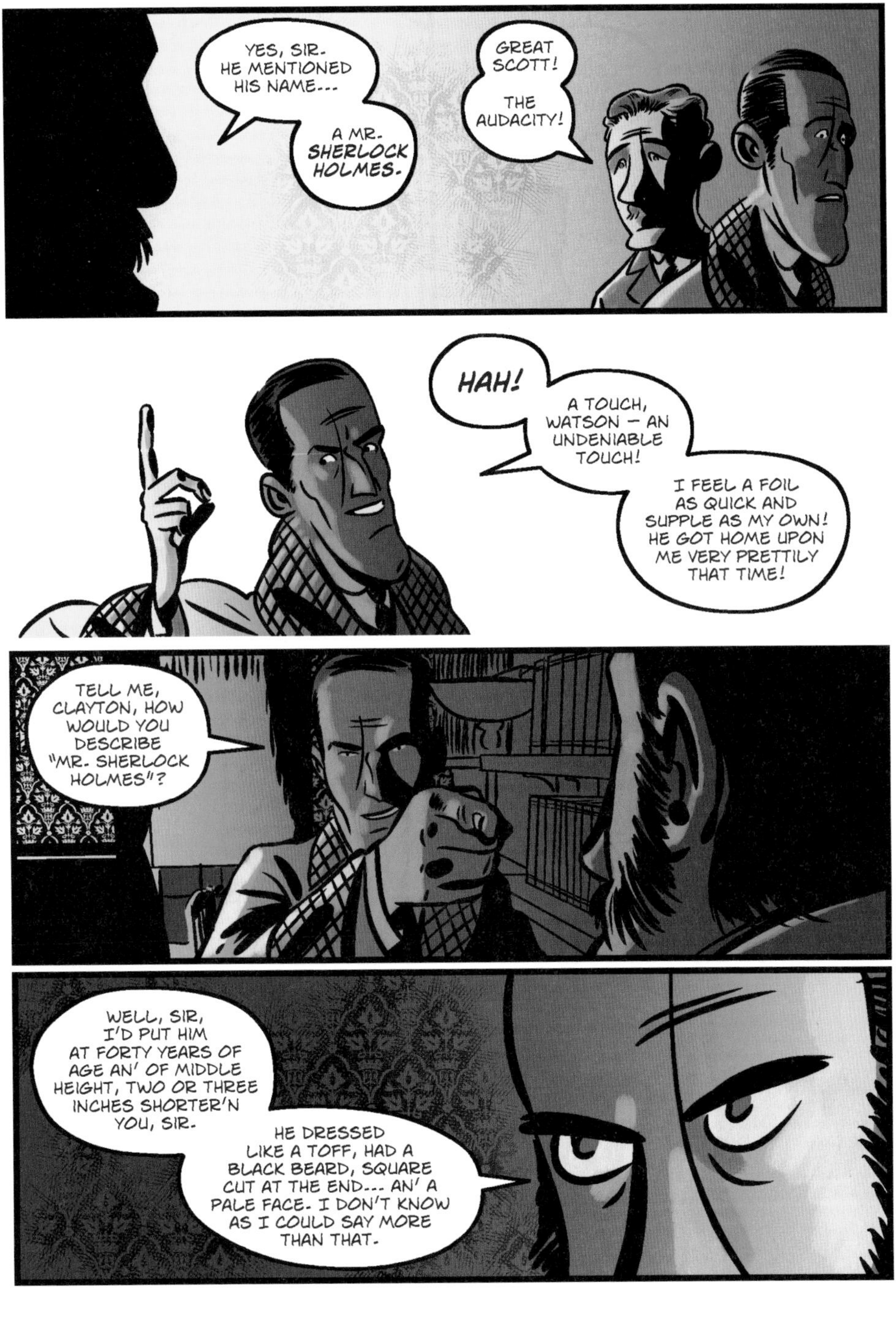
YES, SIR. HE MENTIONED HIS NAME...
A MR. SHERLOCK HOLMES.
GREAT SCOTT!
THE AUDACITY!
HAH!
A TOUCH, WATSON — AN UNDENIABLE TOUCH!
I FEEL A FOIL AS QUICK AND SUPPLE AS MY OWN! HE GOT HOME UPON ME VERY PRETTILY THAT TIME!
TELL ME, CLAYTON, HOW WOULD YOU DESCRIBE "MR. SHERLOCK HOLMES"?
WELL, SIR, I'D PUT HIM AT FORTY YEARS OF AGE AN' OF MIDDLE HEIGHT, TWO OR THREE INCHES SHORTER'N YOU, SIR.
HE DRESSED LIKE A TOFF, HAD A BLACK BEARD, SQUARE CUT AT THE END... AN' A PALE FACE. I DON'T KNOW AS I COULD SAY MORE THAN THAT.

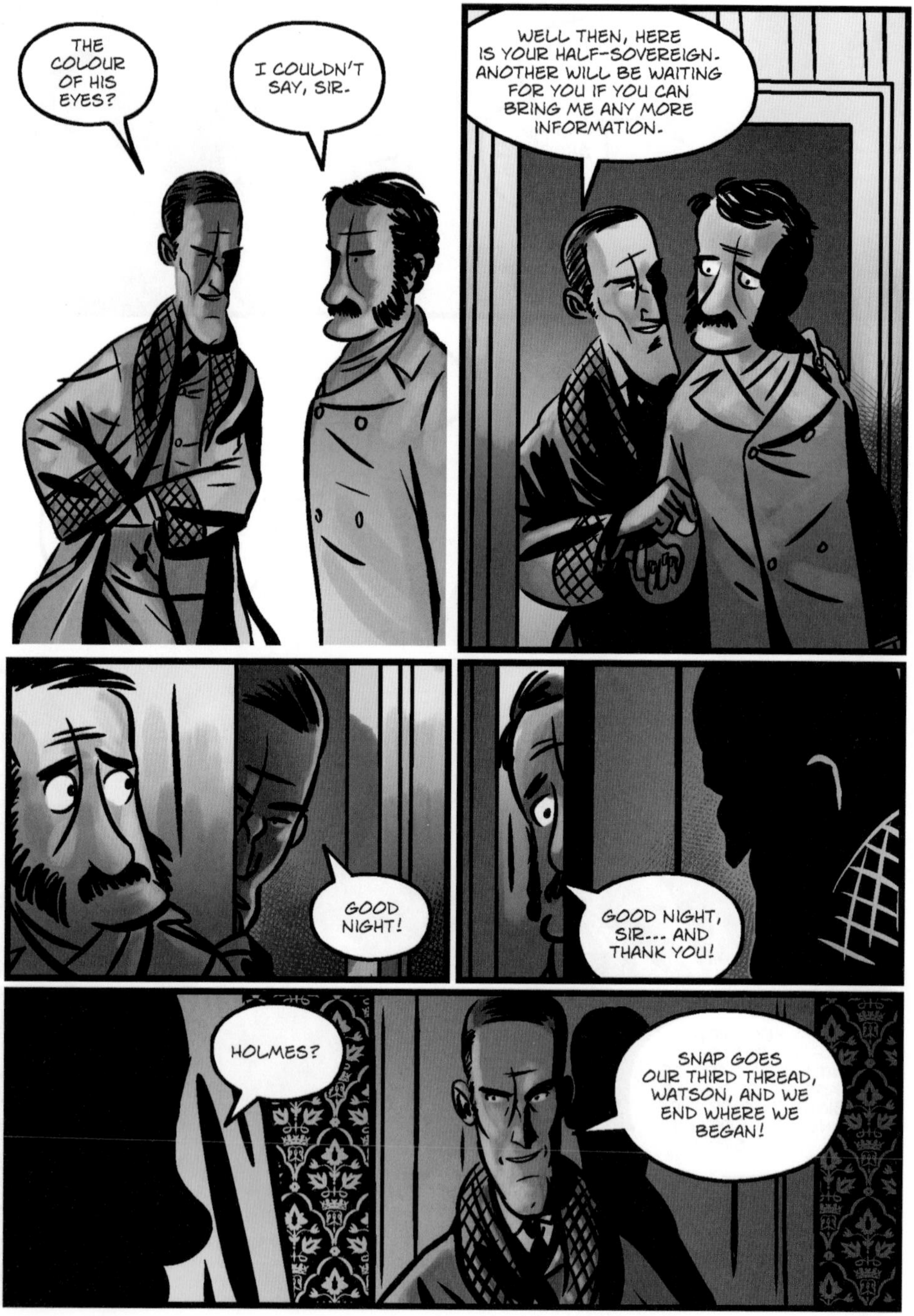
THE COLOUR OF HIS EYES?
I COULDN'T SAY, SIR.
WELL THEN, HERE IS YOUR HALF-SOVEREIGN. ANOTHER WILL BE WAITING FOR YOU IF YOU CAN BRING ME ANY MORE INFORMATION.
GOOD NIGHT!
GOOD NIGHT, SIR... AND THANK YOU!
HOLMES?
SNAP GOES OUR THIRD THREAD, WATSON, AND WE END WHERE WE BEGAN!

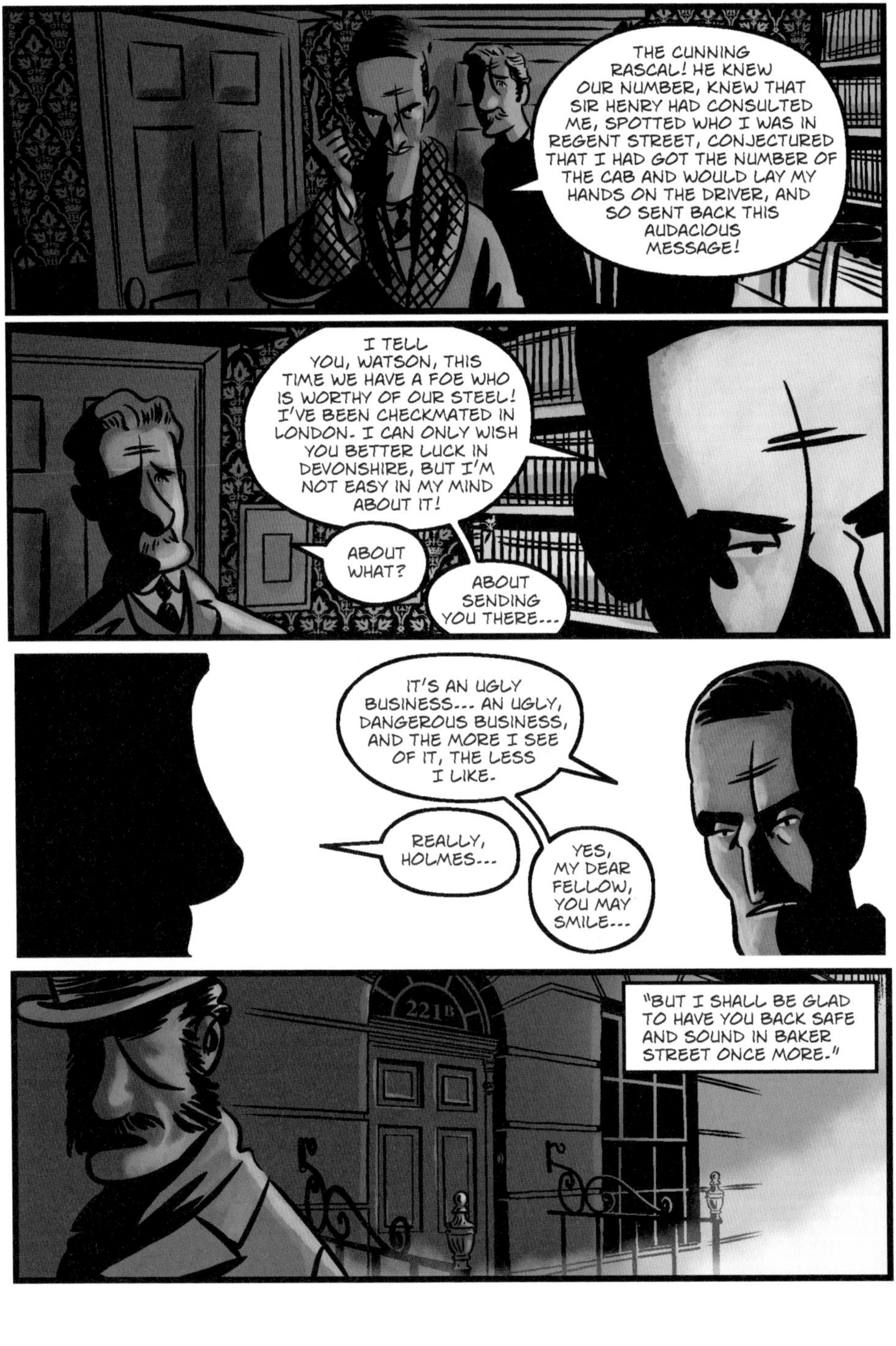
THE CUNNING RASCAL! HE KNEW OUR NUMBER, KNEW THAT SIR HENRY HAD CONSULTED ME, SPOTTED WHO I WAS IN REGENT STREET, CONJECTURED THAT I HAD GOT THE NUMBER OF THE CAB AND WOULD LAY MY HANDS ON THE DRIVER, AND SO SENT BACK THIS AUDACIOUS MESSAGE!
I TELL YOU, WATSON, THIS TIME WE HAVE A FOE WHO IS WORTHY OF OUR STEEL! I'VE BEEN CHECKMATED IN LONDON. I CAN ONLY WISH YOU BETTER LUCK IN DEVONSHIRE, BUT I'M NOT EASY IN MY MIND ABOUT IT!
ABOUT WHAT?
ABOUT SENDING YOU THERE...
IT'S AN UGLY BUSINESS... AN UGLY, DANGEROUS BUSINESS, AND THE MORE I SEE OF IT, THE LESS I LIKE.
REALLY, HOLMES...
YES, MY DEAR FELLOW, YOU MAY SMILE...
221B
"BUT I SHALL BE GLAD TO HAVE YOU BACK SAFE AND SOUND IN BAKER STREET ONCE MORE."

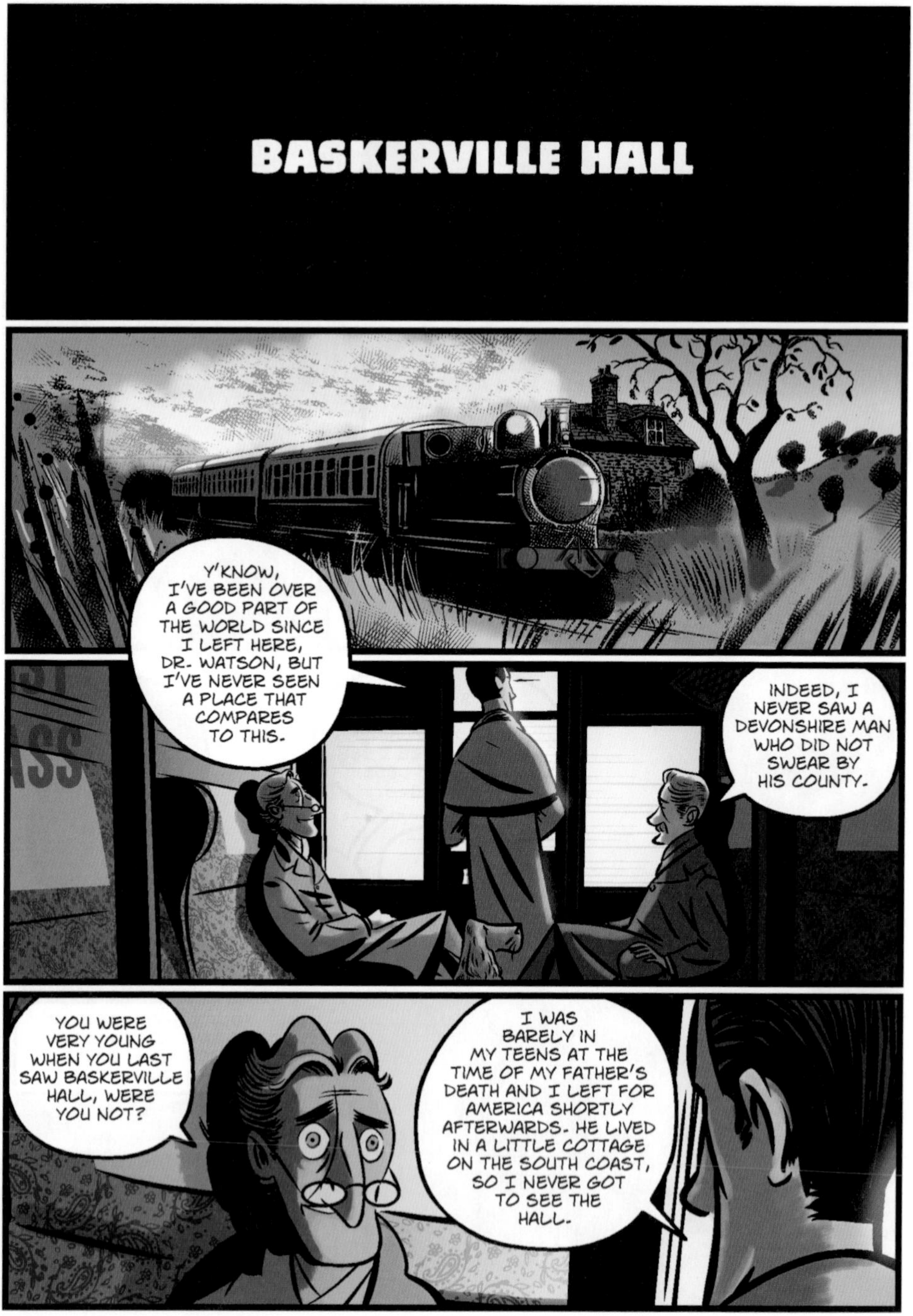
BASKERVILLE HALL
Y'KNOW, I'VE BEEN OVER A GOOD PART OF THE WORLD SINCE I LEFT HERE, DR. WATSON, BUT I'VE NEVER SEEN A PLACE THAT COMPARES TO THIS.
INDEED, I NEVER SAW A DEVONSHIRE MAN WHO DID NOT SWEAR BY HIS COUNTY.
YOU WERE VERY YOUNG WHEN YOU LAST SAW BASKERVILLE HALL, WERE YOU NOT?
I WAS BARELY IN MY TEENS AT THE TIME OF MY FATHER'S DEATH AND I LEFT FOR AMERICA SHORTLY AFTERWARDS. HE LIVED IN A LITTLE COTTAGE ON THE SOUTH COAST, SO I NEVER GOT TO SEE THE HALL.

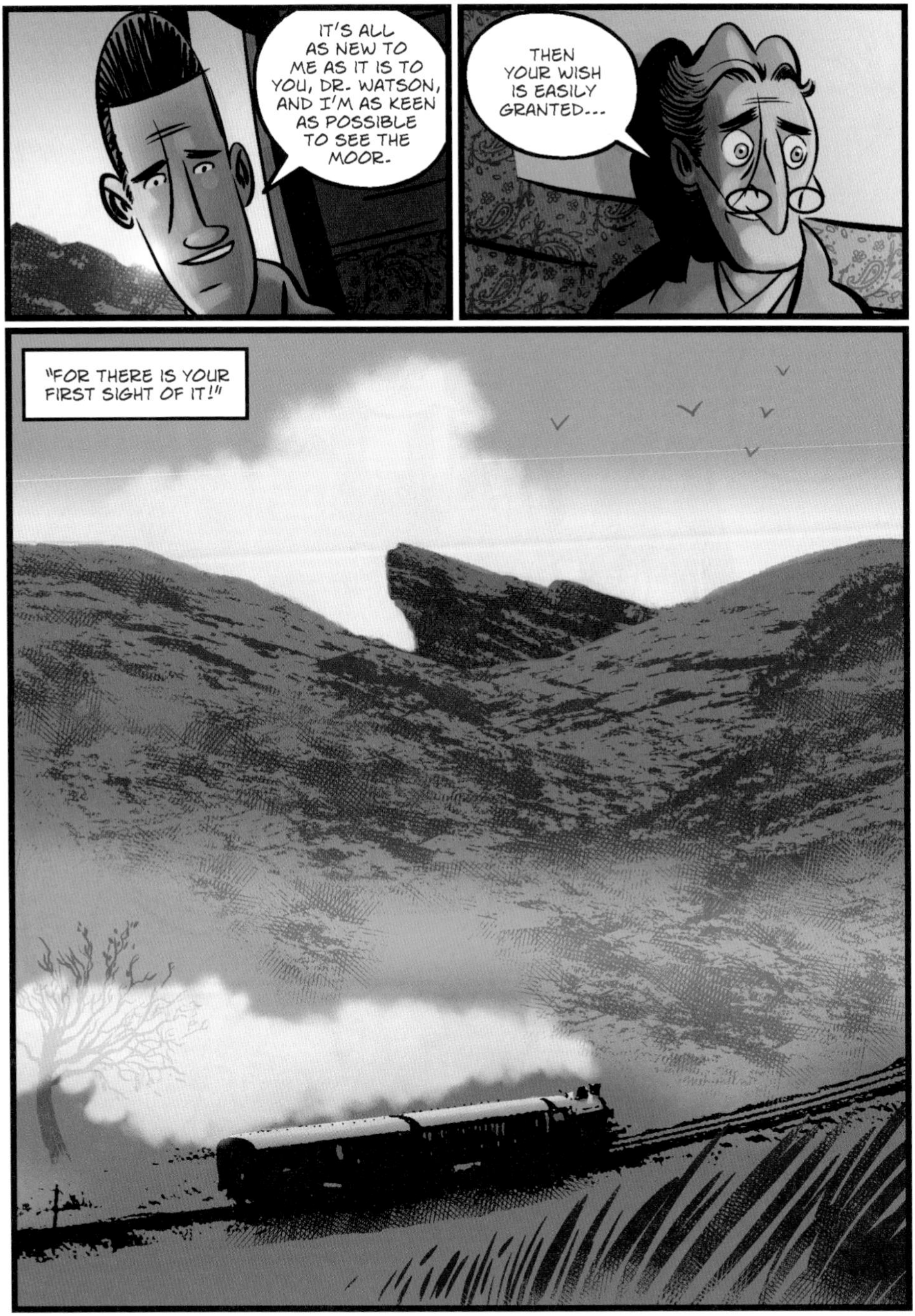
IT'S ALL AS NEW TO ME AS IT IS TO YOU, DR. WATSON, AND I'M AS KEEN AS POSSIBLE TO SEE THE MOOR.
THEN YOUR WISH IS EASILY GRANTED...
"FOR THERE IS YOUR FIRST SIGHT OF IT!"

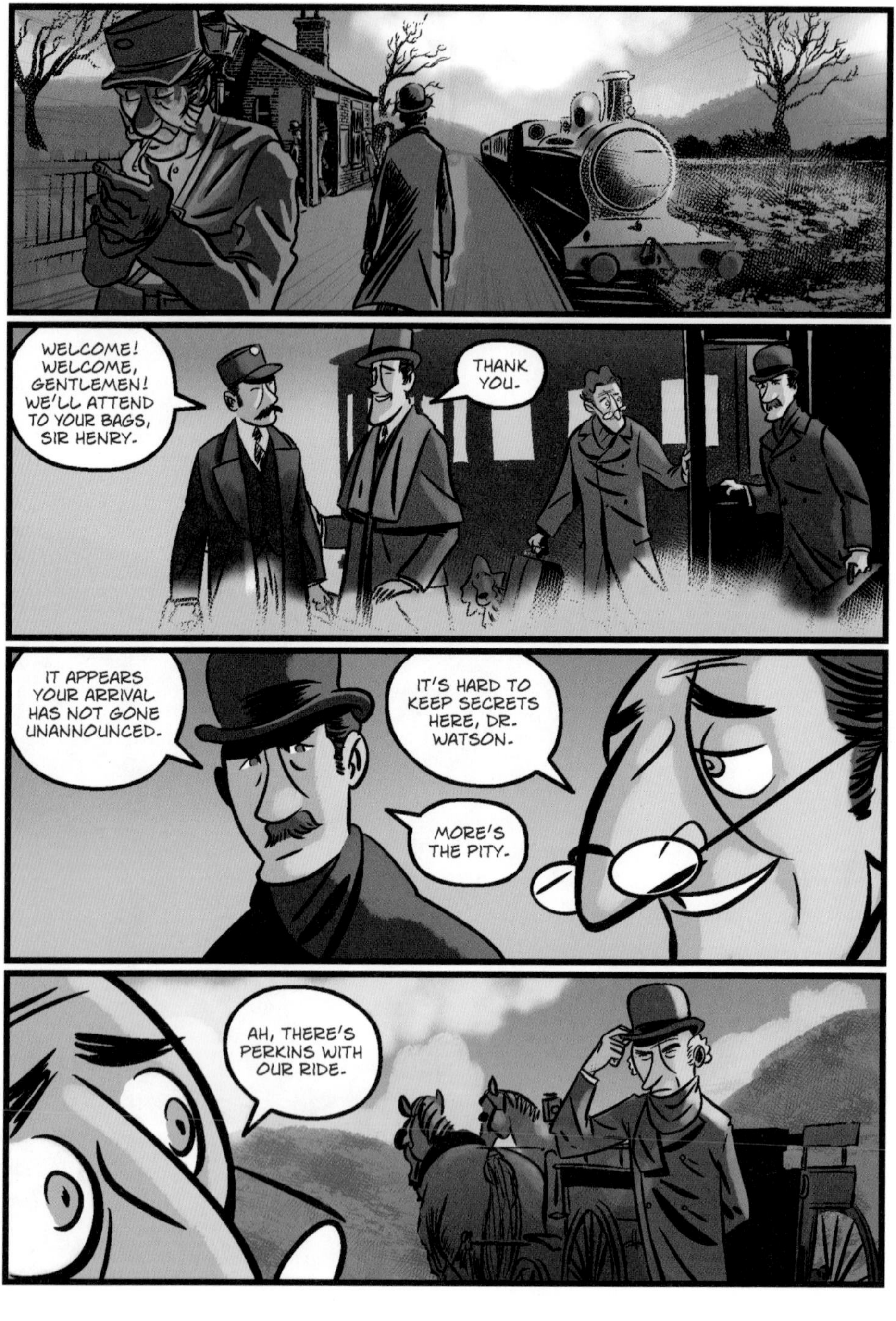
WELCOME! WELCOME, GENTLEMEN! WE'LL ATTEND TO YOUR BAGS, SIR HENRY.
THANK YOU.
IT APPEARS YOUR ARRIVAL HAS NOT GONE UNANNOUNCED.
IT'S HARD TO KEEP SECRETS HERE, DR. WATSON.
MORE'S THE PITY.
AH, THERE'S PERKINS WITH OUR RIDE.

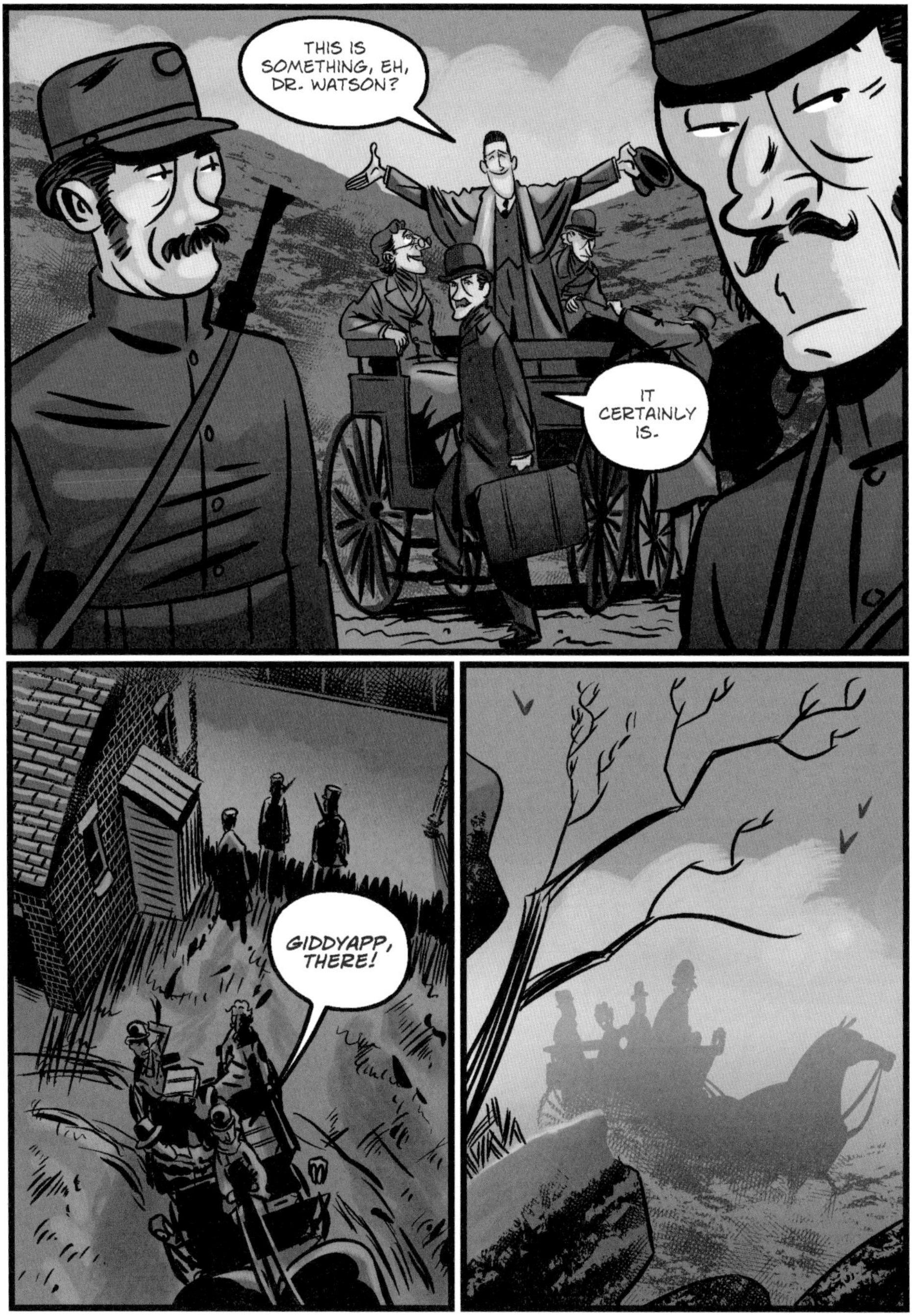
THIS IS SOMETHING, EH, DR. WATSON?
IT CERTAINLY IS.
GIDDYAPP, THERE!

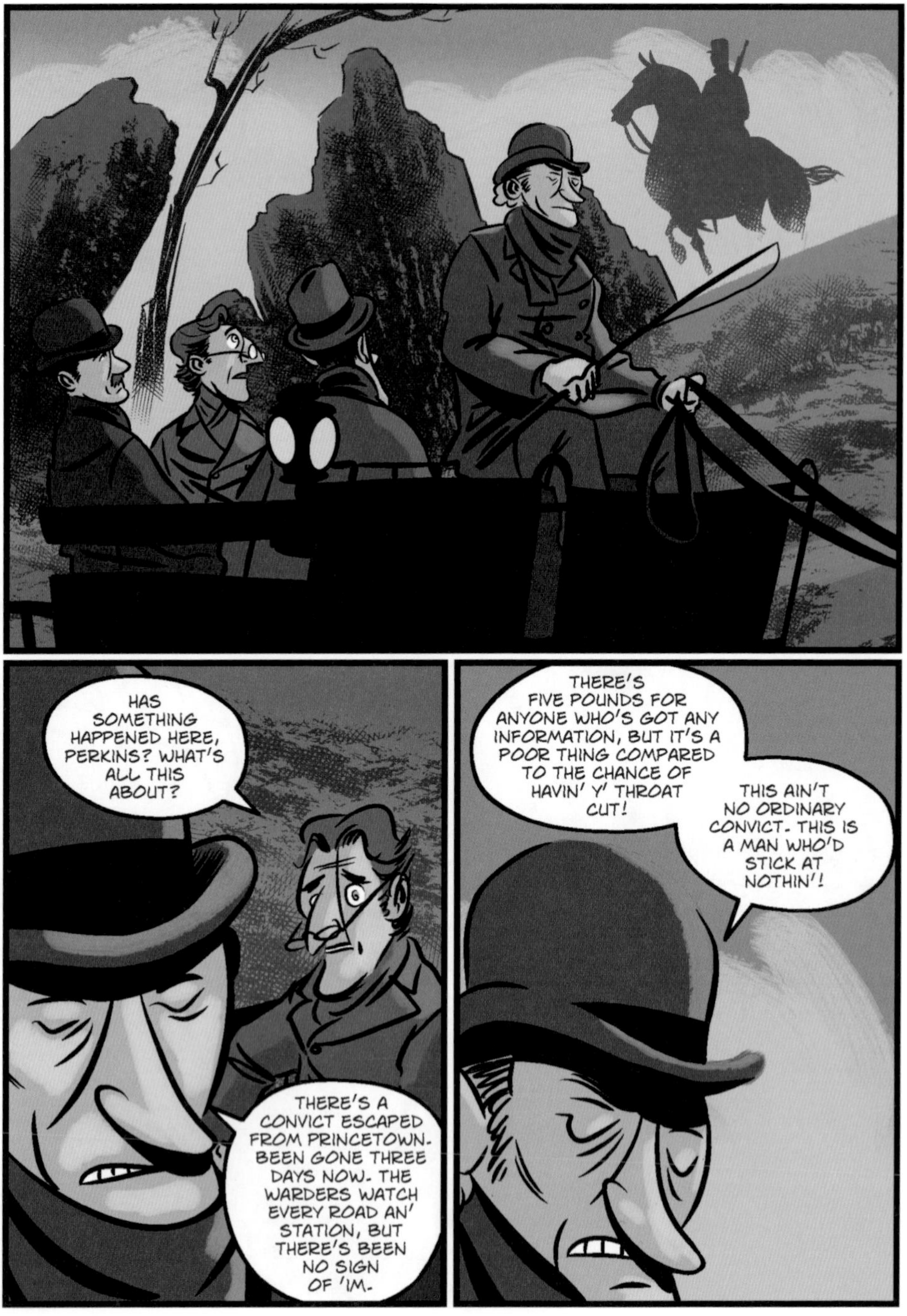
HAS SOMETHING HAPPENED HERE, PERKINS? WHAT'S ALL THIS ABOUT?
THERE'S A CONVICT ESCAPED FROM PRINCETOWN. BEEN GONE THREE DAYS NOW. THE WARDERS WATCH EVERY ROAD AN' STATION, BUT THERE'S BEEN NO SIGN OF 'IM.
THERE'S FIVE POUNDS FOR ANYONE WHO'S GOT ANY INFORMATION, BUT IT'S A POOR THING COMPARED TO THE CHANCE OF HAVIN' Y' THROAT CUT!
THIS AIN'T NO ORDINARY CONVICT. THIS IS A MAN WHO'D STICK AT NOTHIN'!

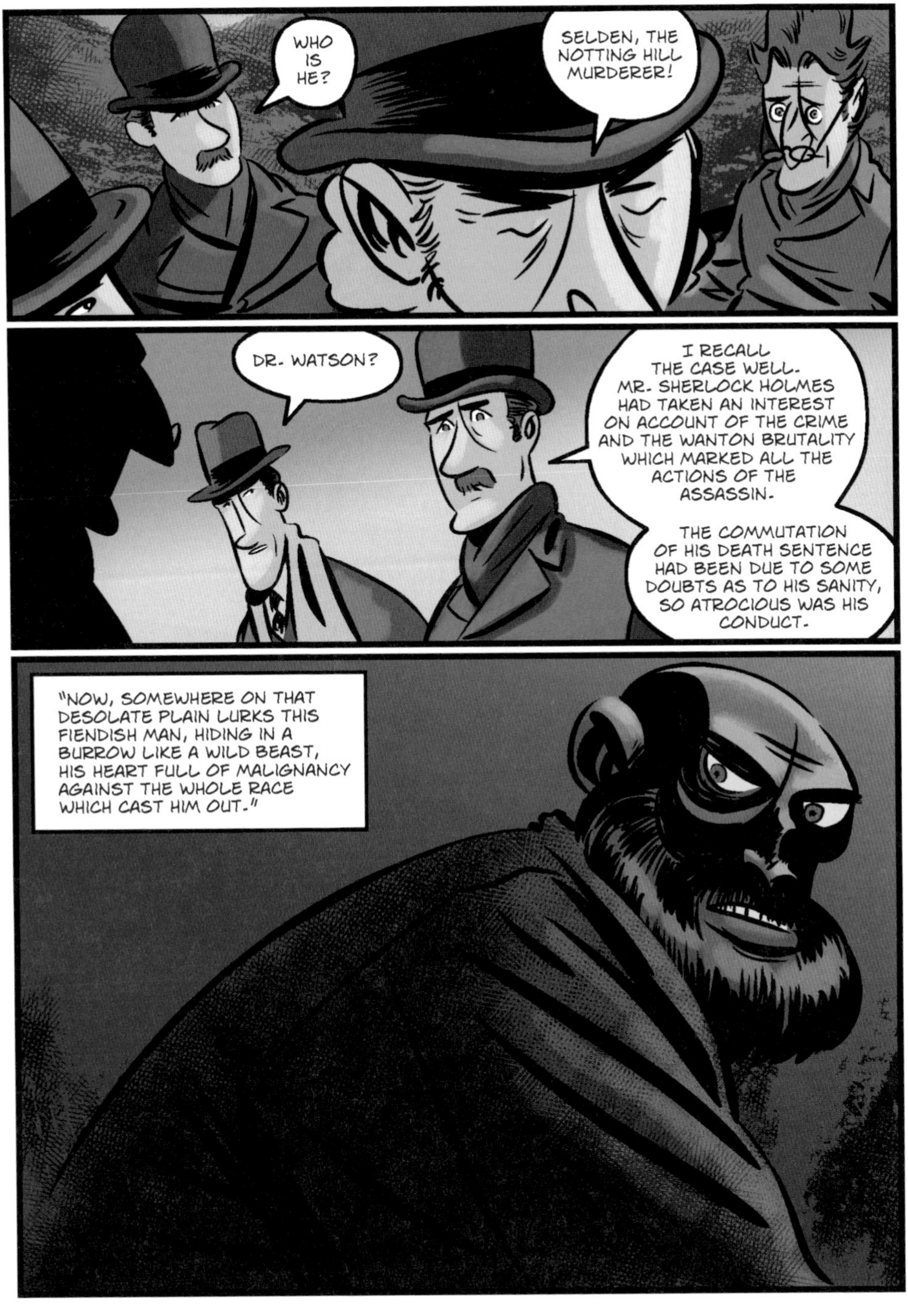
WHO IS HE?
SELDEN, THE NOTTING HILL MURDERER!
DR. WATSON?
I RECALL THE CASE WELL. MR. SHERLOCK HOLMES HAD TAKEN AN INTEREST ON ACCOUNT OF THE CRIME AND THE WANTON BRUTALITY WHICH MARKED ALL THE ACTIONS OF THE ASSASSIN.
THE COMMUTATION OF HIS DEATH SENTENCE HAD BEEN DUE TO SOME DOUBTS AS TO HIS SANITY, SO ATROCIOUS WAS HIS CONDUCT.
"NOW, SOMEWHERE ON THAT DESOLATE PLAIN LURKS THIS FIENDISH MAN, HIDING IN A BURROW LIKE A WILD BEAST, HIS HEART FULL OF MALIGNANCY AGAINST THE WHOLE RACE WHICH CAST HIM OUT."

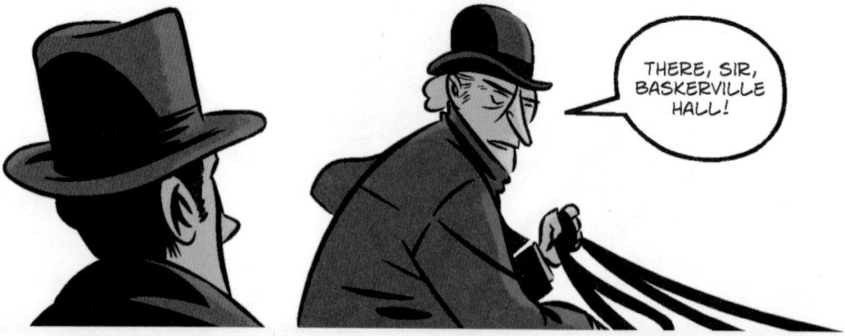
THERE, SIR, BASKERVILLE HALL!

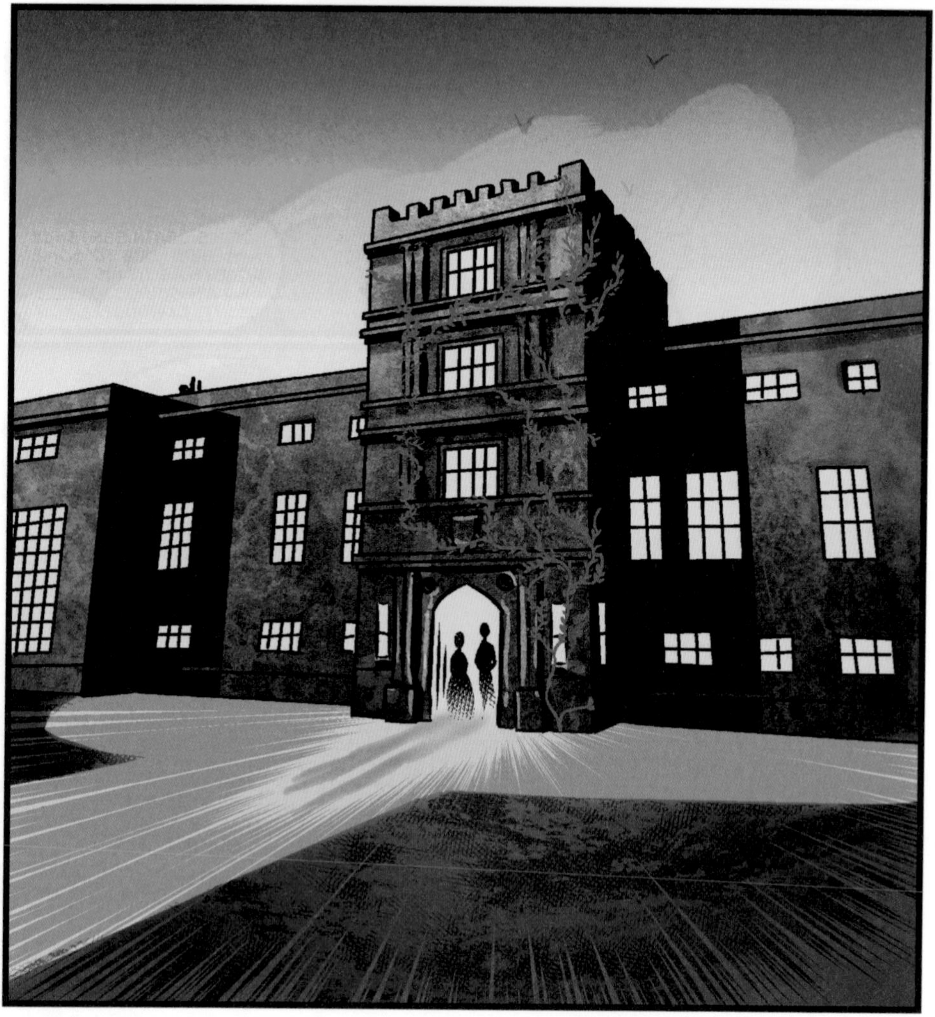

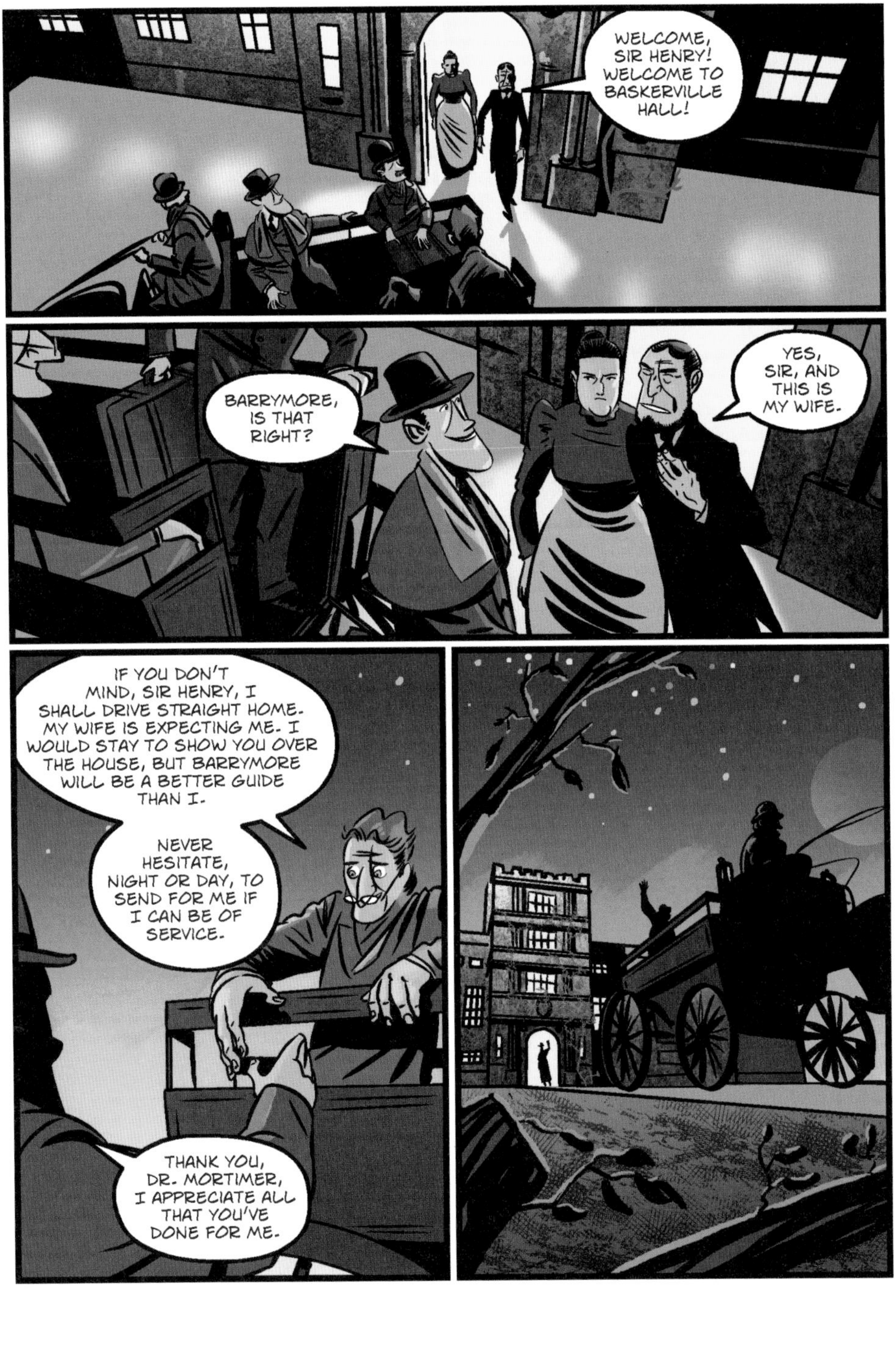
WELCOME, SIR HENRY! WELCOME TO BASKERVILLE HALL!
BARRYMORE, IS THAT RIGHT?
YES, SIR, AND THIS IS MY WIFE.
IF YOU DON'T MIND, SIR HENRY, I SHALL DRIVE STRAIGHT HOME. MY WIFE IS EXPECTING ME. I WOULD STAY TO SHOW YOU OVER THE HOUSE, BUT BARRYMORE WILL BE A BETTER GUIDE THAN I.
NEVER HESITATE, NIGHT OR DAY, TO SEND FOR ME IF I CAN BE OF SERVICE.
THANK YOU, DR. MORTIMER, I APPRECIATE ALL THAT YOU'VE DONE FOR ME.

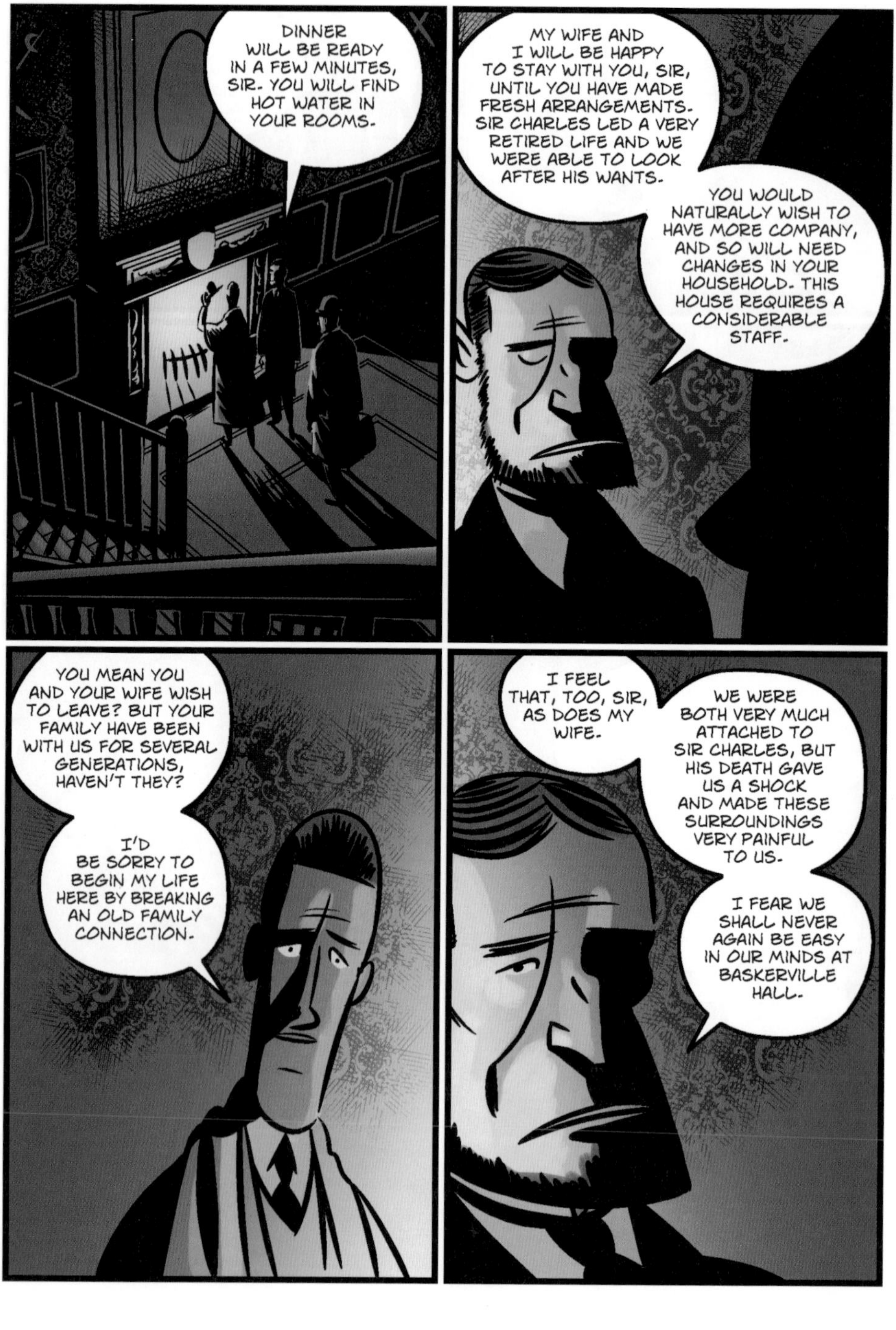
DINNER WILL BE READY IN A FEW MINUTES, SIR. YOU WILL FIND HOT WATER IN YOUR ROOMS.
MY WIFE AND I WILL BE HAPPY TO STAY WITH YOU, SIR, UNTIL YOU HAVE MADE FRESH ARRANGEMENTS. SIR CHARLES LED A VERY RETIRED LIFE AND WE WERE ABLE TO LOOK AFTER HIS WANTS.
YOU WOULD NATURALLY WISH TO HAVE MORE COMPANY, AND SO WILL NEED CHANGES IN YOUR HOUSEHOLD. THIS HOUSE REQUIRES A CONSIDERABLE STAFF.
YOU MEAN YOU AND YOUR WIFE WISH TO LEAVE? BUT YOUR FAMILY HAVE BEEN WITH US FOR SEVERAL GENERATIONS, HAVEN'T THEY?
I'D BE SORRY TO BEGIN MY LIFE HERE BY BREAKING AN OLD FAMILY CONNECTION.
I FEEL THAT, TOO, SIR, AS DOES MY WIFE.
WE WERE BOTH VERY MUCH ATTACHED TO SIR CHARLES, BUT HIS DEATH GAVE US A SHOCK AND MADE THESE SURROUNDINGS VERY PAINFUL TO US.
I FEAR WE SHALL NEVER AGAIN BE EASY IN OUR MINDS AT BASKERVILLE HALL.

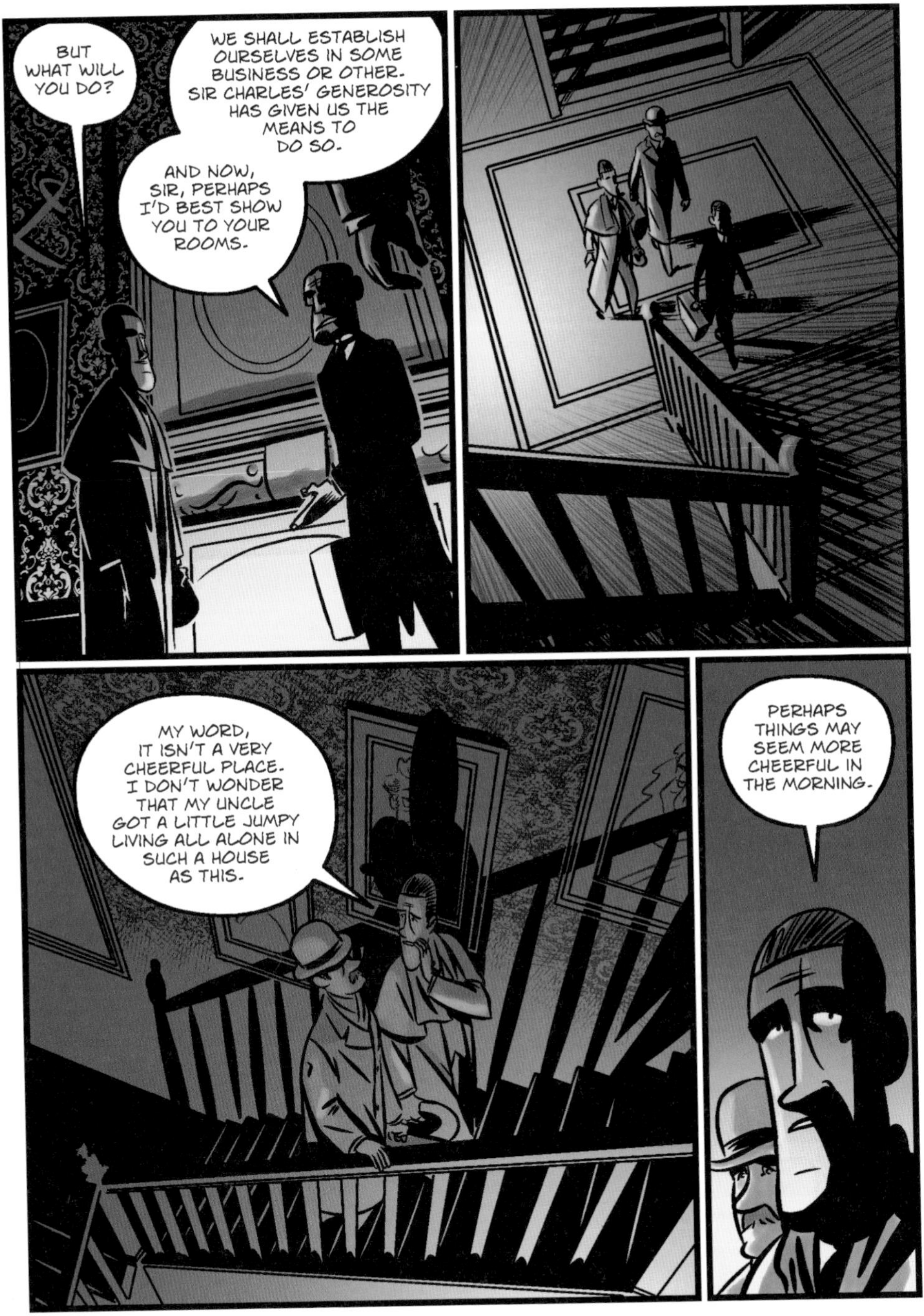
BUT WHAT WILL YOU DO?
WE SHALL ESTABLISH OURSELVES IN SOME BUSINESS OR OTHER. SIR CHARLES' GENEROSITY HAS GIVEN US THE MEANS TO DO SO.
AND NOW, SIR, PERHAPS I'D BEST SHOW YOU TO YOUR ROOMS.
MY WORD, IT ISN'T A VERY CHEERFUL PLACE. I DON'T WONDER THAT MY UNCLE GOT A LITTLE JUMPY LIVING ALL ALONE IN SUCH A HOUSE AS THIS.
PERHAPS THINGS MAY SEEM MORE CHEERFUL IN THE MORNING.

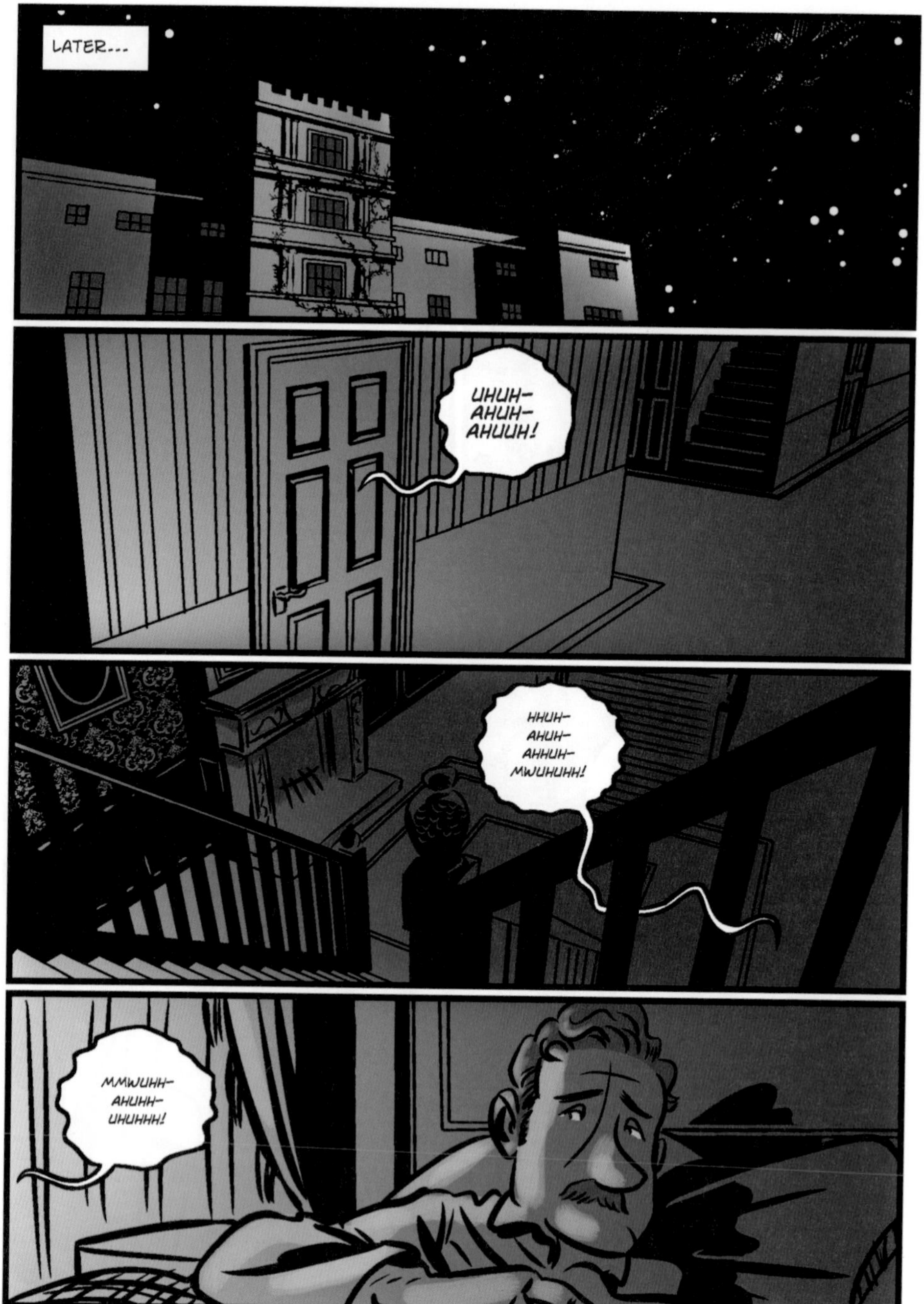
LATER...
UHUH-
AHUH-
AHUUH!
HHUH-
AHUH-
AHHUH-
MWUHUHH!
MMWUHH-
AHUHH-
UHUHHH!

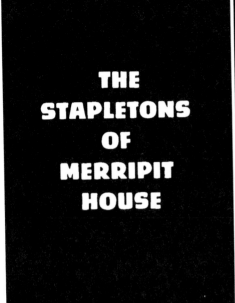

THE STAPLETONS OF MERRIPIT HOUSE

WELL, THIS IS CERTAINLY A WELCOME CHANGE. IT ALL SEEMS QUITE DIFFERENT IN THE DAYLIGHT.

I GUESS IT'S OURSELVES AND NOT THE HOUSE WE HAVE TO BLAME! WE WERE TIRED FROM OUR JOURNEY AND CHILLED FROM THE DRIVE, SO WE TOOK A GREY VIEW OF THE PLACE.

AND YET... DID YOU HAPPEN TO HEAR SOMEONE... A WOMAN, I THINK, SOBBING IN THE NIGHT?

THAT IS CURIOUS. I DID FANCY THAT I HEARD SOMETHING OF THE SORT. I ASKED BARRYMORE ABOUT IT EARLIER. HE SAID THERE ARE ONLY TWO WOMEN IN THE HOUSE: A SCULLERY MAID WHO SLEEPS WAY OFF IN THE OTHER WING, AND MRS. BARRYMORE — AND HE SAYS IT WASN'T HER.

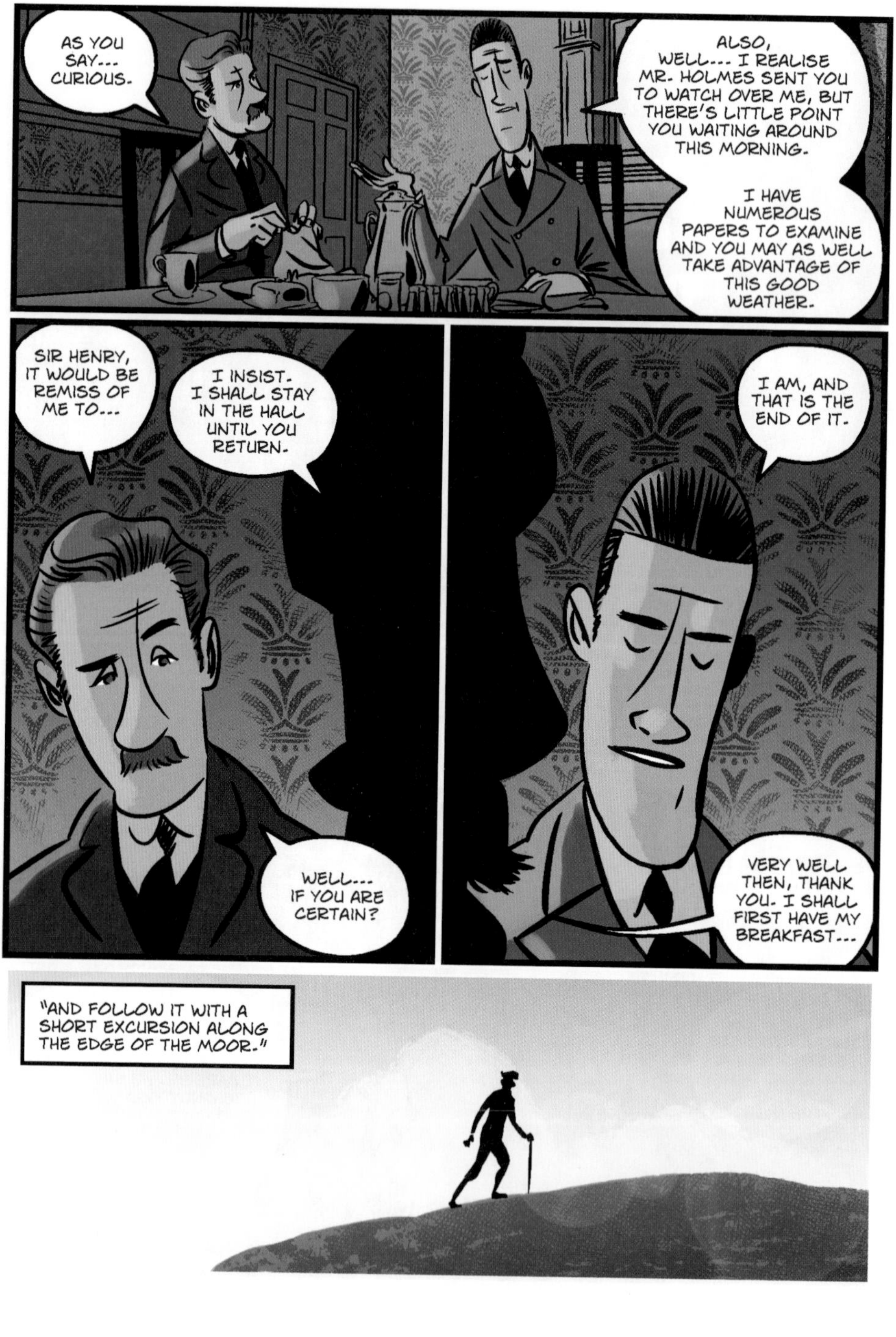
AS YOU SAY... CURIOUS.
ALSO, WELL... I REALISE MR. HOLMES SENT YOU TO WATCH OVER ME, BUT THERE'S LITTLE POINT YOU WAITING AROUND THIS MORNING.
I HAVE NUMEROUS PAPERS TO EXAMINE AND YOU MAY AS WELL TAKE ADVANTAGE OF THIS GOOD WEATHER.
SIR HENRY, IT WOULD BE REMISS OF ME TO...
I INSIST. I SHALL STAY IN THE HALL UNTIL YOU RETURN.
WELL... IF YOU ARE CERTAIN?
I AM, AND THAT IS THE END OF IT.
VERY WELL THEN, THANK YOU. I SHALL FIRST HAVE MY BREAKFAST...
"AND FOLLOW IT WITH A SHORT EXCURSION ALONG THE EDGE OF THE MOOR."

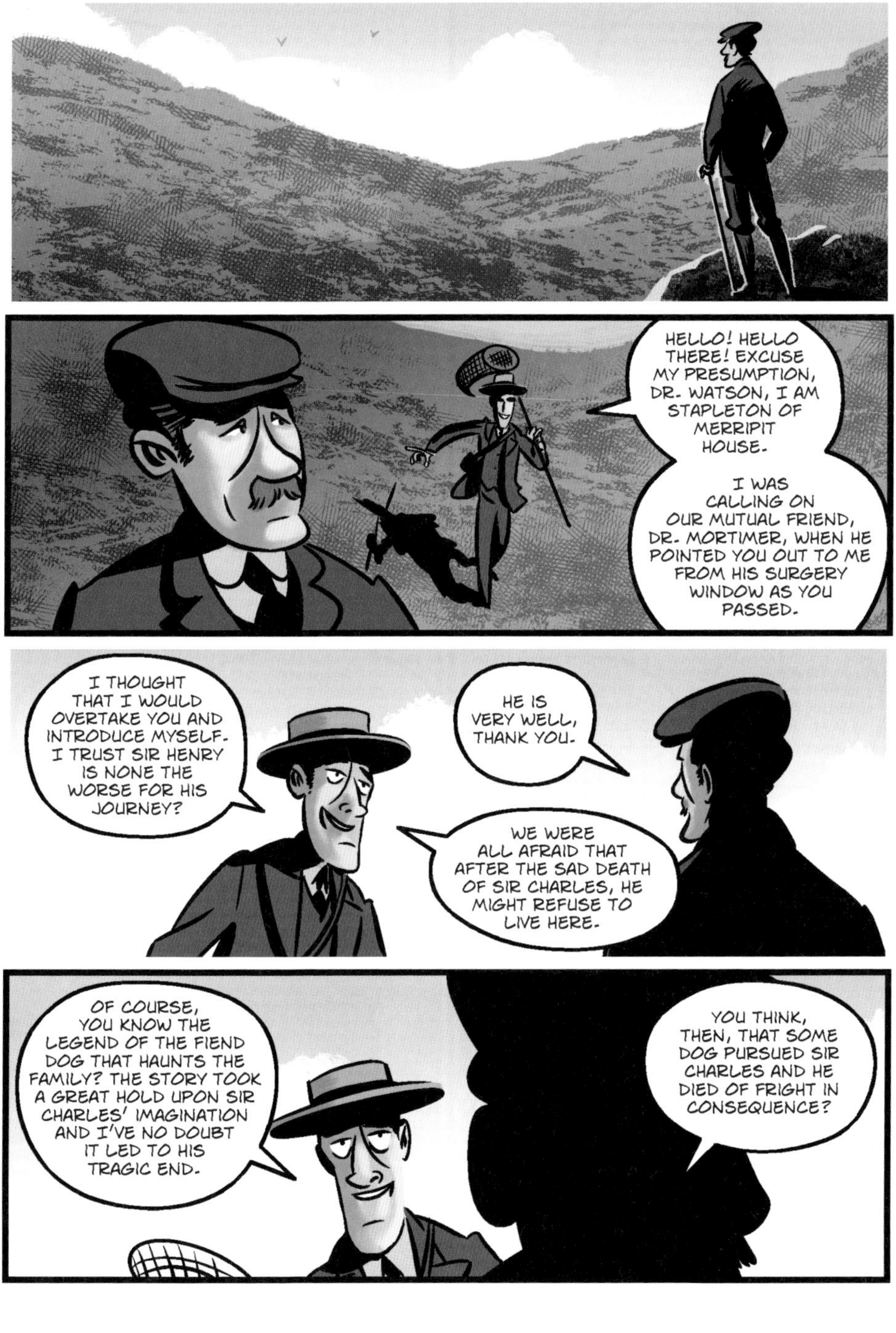
HELLO! HELLO THERE! EXCUSE MY PRESUMPTION, DR. WATSON, I AM STAPLETON OF MERRIPIT HOUSE.
I WAS CALLING ON OUR MUTUAL FRIEND, DR. MORTIMER, WHEN HE POINTED YOU OUT TO ME FROM HIS SURGERY WINDOW AS YOU PASSED.
I THOUGHT THAT I WOULD OVERTAKE YOU AND INTRODUCE MYSELF. I TRUST SIR HENRY IS NONE THE WORSE FOR HIS JOURNEY?
HE IS VERY WELL, THANK YOU.
WE WERE ALL AFRAID THAT AFTER THE SAD DEATH OF SIR CHARLES, HE MIGHT REFUSE TO LIVE HERE.
OF COURSE, YOU KNOW THE LEGEND OF THE FIEND DOG THAT HAUNTS THE FAMILY? THE STORY TOOK A GREAT HOLD UPON SIR CHARLES' IMAGINATION AND I'VE NO DOUBT IT LED TO HIS TRAGIC END.
YOU THINK, THEN, THAT SOME DOG PURSUED SIR CHARLES AND HE DIED OF FRIGHT IN CONSEQUENCE?

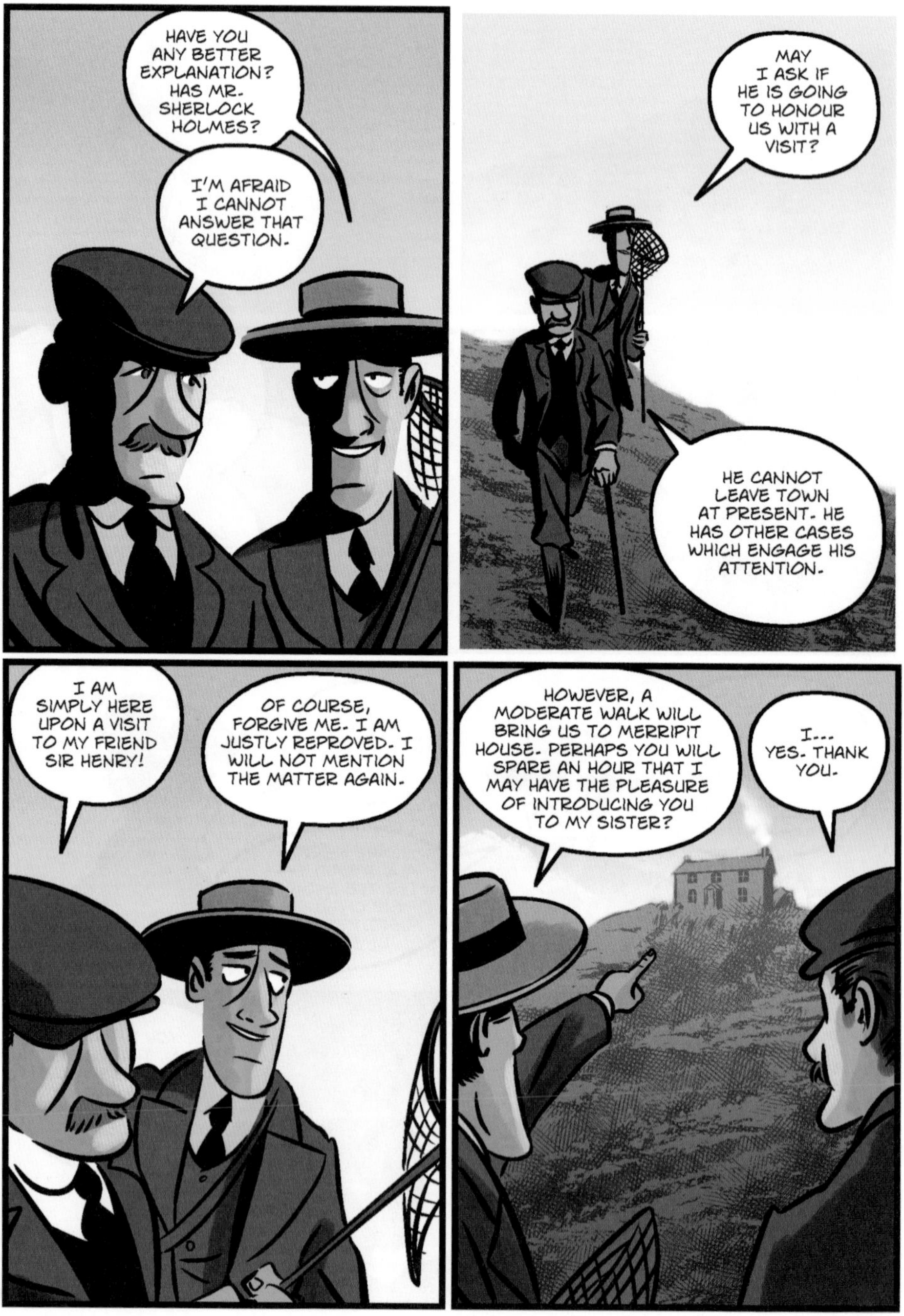
HAVE YOU ANY BETTER EXPLANATION? HAS MR. SHERLOCK HOLMES?
I'M AFRAID I CANNOT ANSWER THAT QUESTION.
MAY I ASK IF HE IS GOING TO HONOUR US WITH A VISIT?
HE CANNOT LEAVE TOWN AT PRESENT. HE HAS OTHER CASES WHICH ENGAGE HIS ATTENTION.
I AM SIMPLY HERE UPON A VISIT TO MY FRIEND SIR HENRY!
OF COURSE, FORGIVE ME. I AM JUSTLY REPROVED. I WILL NOT MENTION THE MATTER AGAIN.
HOWEVER, A MODERATE WALK WILL BRING US TO MERRIPIT HOUSE. PERHAPS YOU WILL SPARE AN HOUR THAT I MAY HAVE THE PLEASURE OF INTRODUCING YOU TO MY SISTER?
I... YES. THANK YOU.

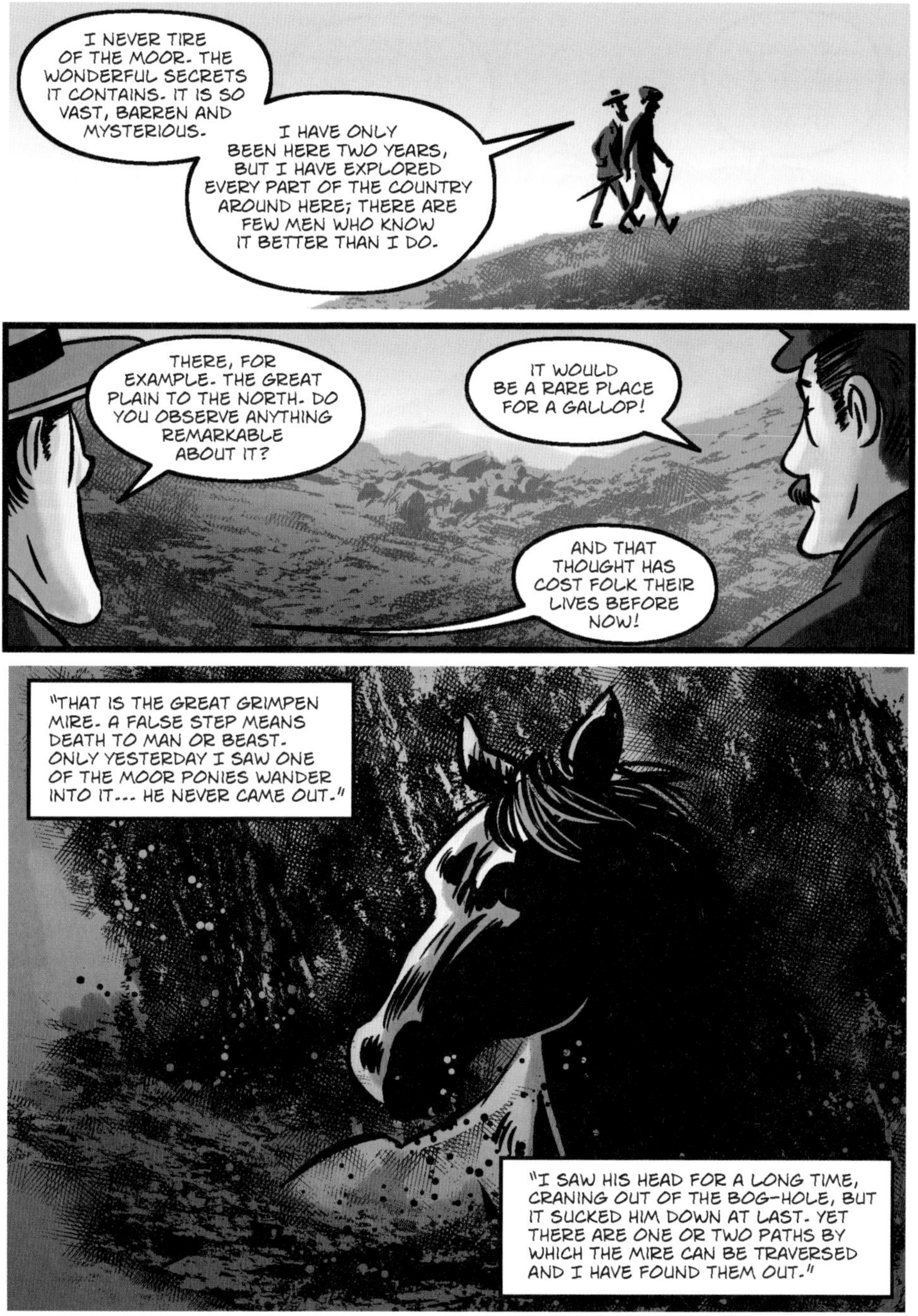
I NEVER TIRE OF THE MOOR. THE WONDERFUL SECRETS IT CONTAINS. IT IS SO VAST, BARREN AND MYSTERIOUS.
I HAVE ONLY BEEN HERE TWO YEARS, BUT I HAVE EXPLORED EVERY PART OF THE COUNTRY AROUND HERE; THERE ARE FEW MEN WHO KNOW IT BETTER THAN I DO.
THERE, FOR EXAMPLE. THE GREAT PLAIN TO THE NORTH. DO YOU OBSERVE ANYTHING REMARKABLE ABOUT IT?
IT WOULD BE A RARE PLACE FOR A GALLOP!
AND THAT THOUGHT HAS COST FOLK THEIR LIVES BEFORE NOW!
"THAT IS THE GREAT GRIMPEN MIRE. A FALSE STEP MEANS DEATH TO MAN OR BEAST. ONLY YESTERDAY I SAW ONE OF THE MOOR PONIES WANDER INTO IT... HE NEVER CAME OUT."
"I SAW HIS HEAD FOR A LONG TIME, CRANING OUT OF THE BOG-HOLE, BUT IT SUCKED HIM DOWN AT LAST. YET THERE ARE ONE OR TWO PATHS BY WHICH THE MIRE CAN BE TRAVERSED AND I HAVE FOUND THEM OUT."

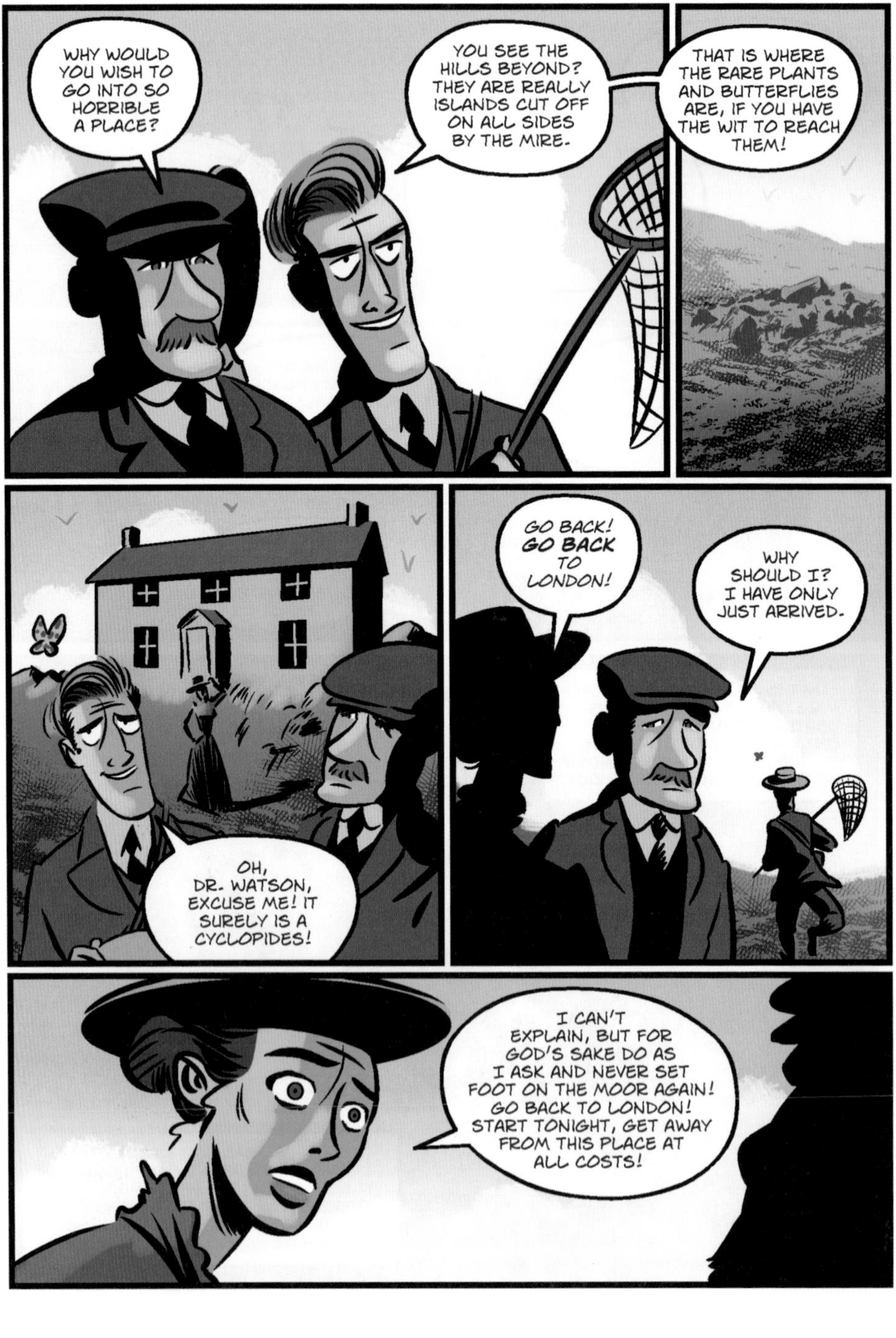
WHY WOULD YOU WISH TO GO INTO SO HORRIBLE A PLACE?
YOU SEE THE HILLS BEYOND? THEY ARE REALLY ISLANDS CUT OFF ON ALL SIDES BY THE MIRE.
THAT IS WHERE THE RARE PLANTS AND BUTTERFLIES ARE, IF YOU HAVE THE WIT TO REACH THEM!
OH, DR. WATSON, EXCUSE ME! IT SURELY IS A CYCLOPIDES!
GO BACK! GO BACK TO LONDON!
WHY SHOULD I? I HAVE ONLY JUST ARRIVED.
I CAN'T EXPLAIN, BUT FOR GOD'S SAKE DO AS I ASK AND NEVER SET FOOT ON THE MOOR AGAIN! GO BACK TO LONDON! START TONIGHT, GET AWAY FROM THIS PLACE AT ALL COSTS!

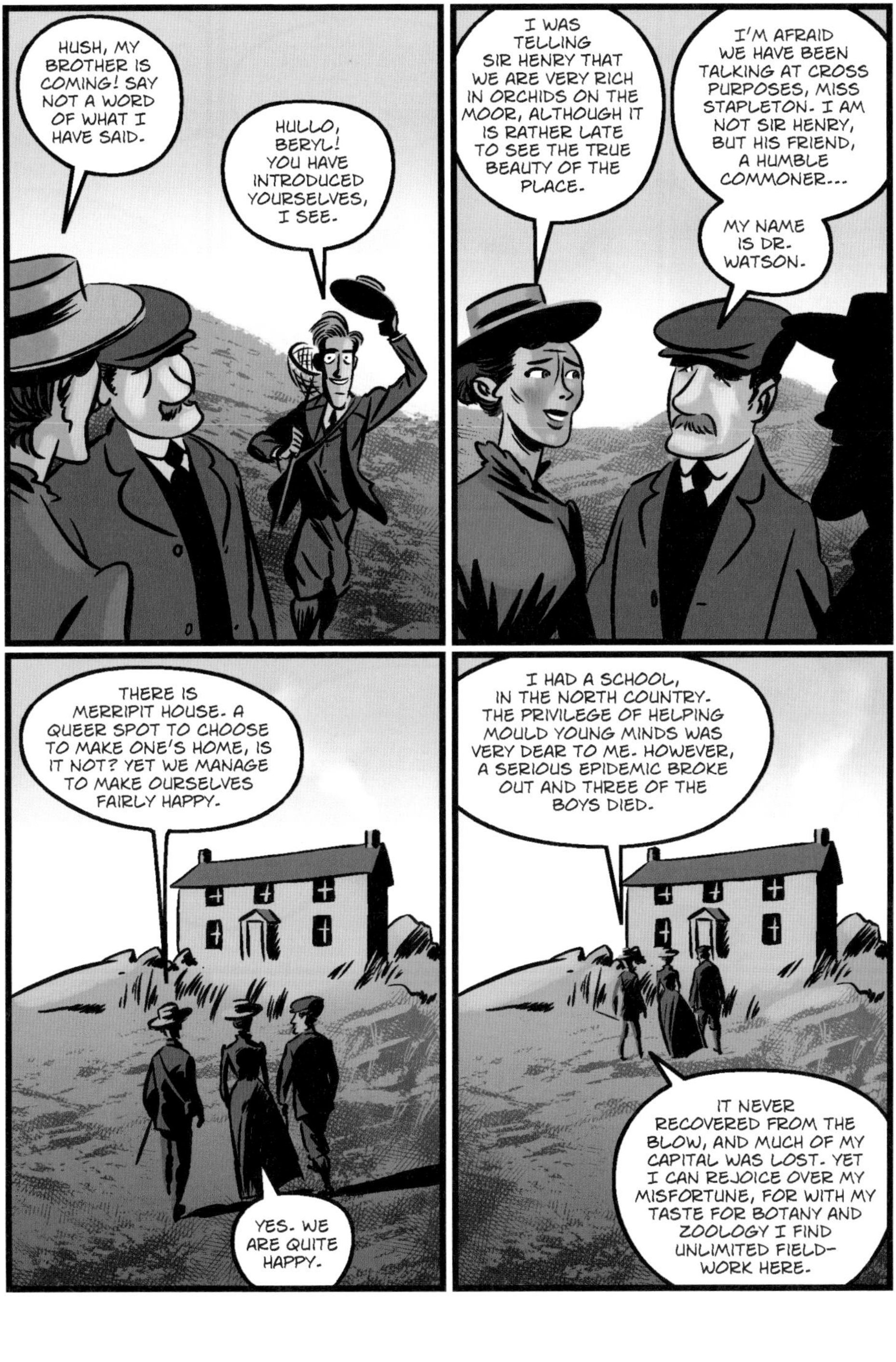
HUSH, MY BROTHER IS COMING! SAY NOT A WORD OF WHAT I HAVE SAID.
HULLO, BERYL! YOU HAVE INTRODUCED YOURSELVES, I SEE.
I WAS TELLING SIR HENRY THAT WE ARE VERY RICH IN ORCHIDS ON THE MOOR, ALTHOUGH IT IS RATHER LATE TO SEE THE TRUE BEAUTY OF THE PLACE.
I'M AFRAID WE HAVE BEEN TALKING AT CROSS PURPOSES, MISS STAPLETON. I AM NOT SIR HENRY, BUT HIS FRIEND, A HUMBLE COMMONER...
MY NAME IS DR. WATSON.
THERE IS MERRIPIT HOUSE. A QUEER SPOT TO CHOOSE TO MAKE ONE'S HOME, IS IT NOT? YET WE MANAGE TO MAKE OURSELVES FAIRLY HAPPY.
YES. WE ARE QUITE HAPPY.
I HAD A SCHOOL, IN THE NORTH COUNTRY. THE PRIVILEGE OF HELPING MOULD YOUNG MINDS WAS VERY DEAR TO ME. HOWEVER, A SERIOUS EPIDEMIC BROKE OUT AND THREE OF THE BOYS DIED.
IT NEVER RECOVERED FROM THE BLOW, AND MUCH OF MY CAPITAL WAS LOST. YET I CAN REJOICE OVER MY MISFORTUNE, FOR WITH MY TASTE FOR BOTANY AND ZOOLOGY I FIND UNLIMITED FIELD-WORK HERE.

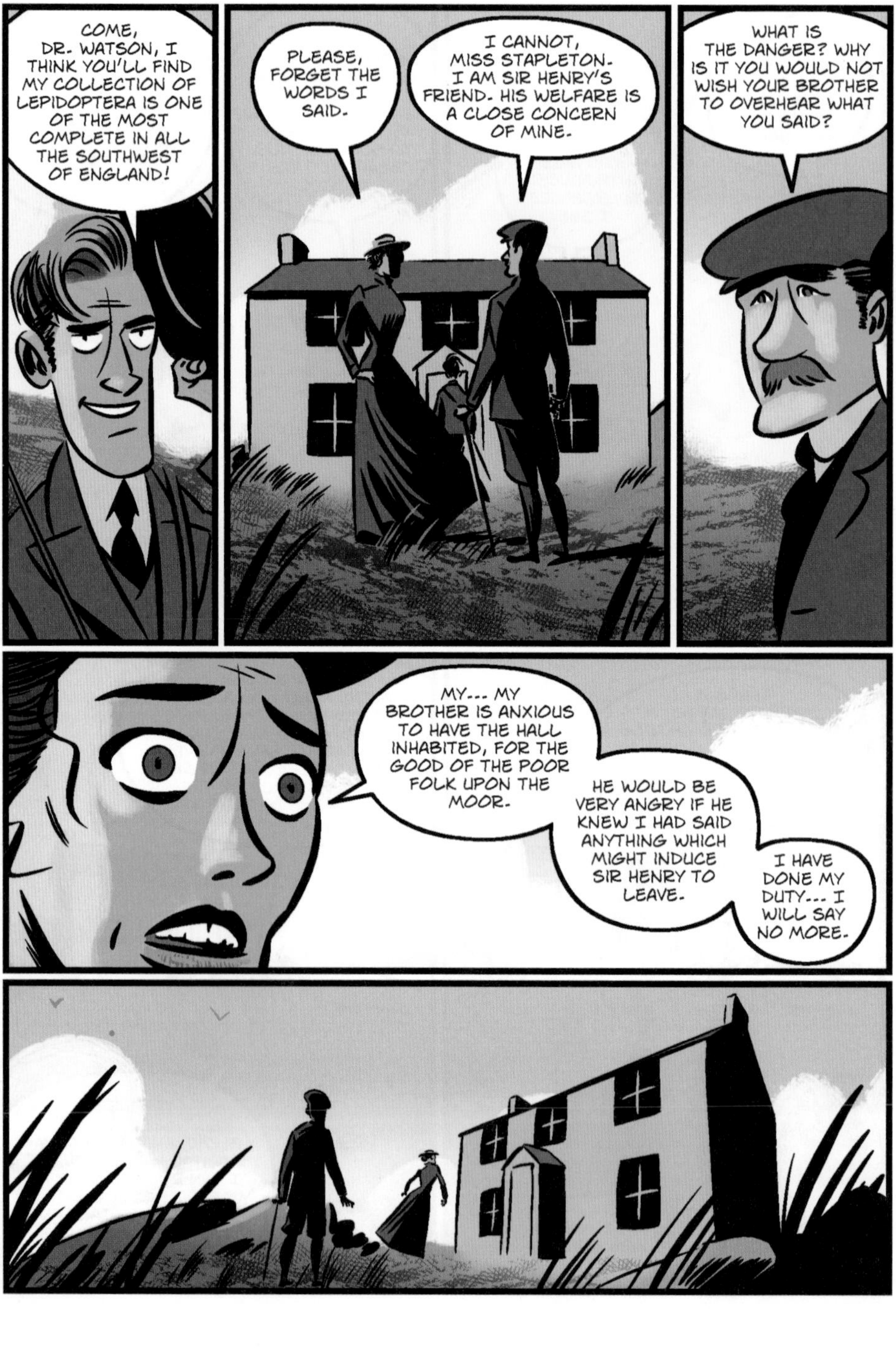
COME, DR. WATSON, I THINK YOU'LL FIND MY COLLECTION OF LEPIDOPTERA IS ONE OF THE MOST COMPLETE IN ALL THE SOUTHWEST OF ENGLAND!
PLEASE, FORGET THE WORDS I SAID.
I CANNOT, MISS STAPLETON. I AM SIR HENRY'S FRIEND. HIS WELFARE IS A CLOSE CONCERN OF MINE.
WHAT IS THE DANGER? WHY IS IT YOU WOULD NOT WISH YOUR BROTHER TO OVERHEAR WHAT YOU SAID?
MY... MY BROTHER IS ANXIOUS TO HAVE THE HALL INHABITED, FOR THE GOOD OF THE POOR FOLK UPON THE MOOR.
HE WOULD BE VERY ANGRY IF HE KNEW I HAD SAID ANYTHING WHICH MIGHT INDUCE SIR HENRY TO LEAVE.
I HAVE DONE MY DUTY... I WILL SAY NO MORE.

FIRST REPORT OF DR. WATSON

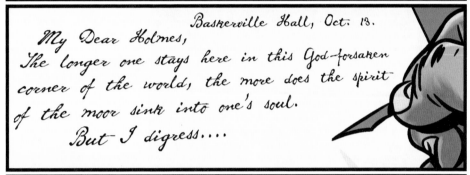

Baskerville Hall, Oct. 13.

My Dear Holmes,
The longer one stays here in this God-forsaken corner of the world, the more does the spirit of the moor sink into one's soul.
But I digress....

SEVERAL INCIDENTS HAVE OCCURRED OF LATE, NOT LEAST OF WHICH IS THE BELIEF THAT THE MURDERER, SELDEN, HAS GOT AWAY.

A FORTNIGHT HAS PASSED SINCE HIS FLIGHT, DURING WHICH HE HAS NOT BEEN SEEN NOR HEARD OF.

IT IS INCONCEIVABLE THAT HE HELD OUT UPON THE MOOR ALL THAT TIME. WE THINK THEREFORE THAT HE HAS GONE.

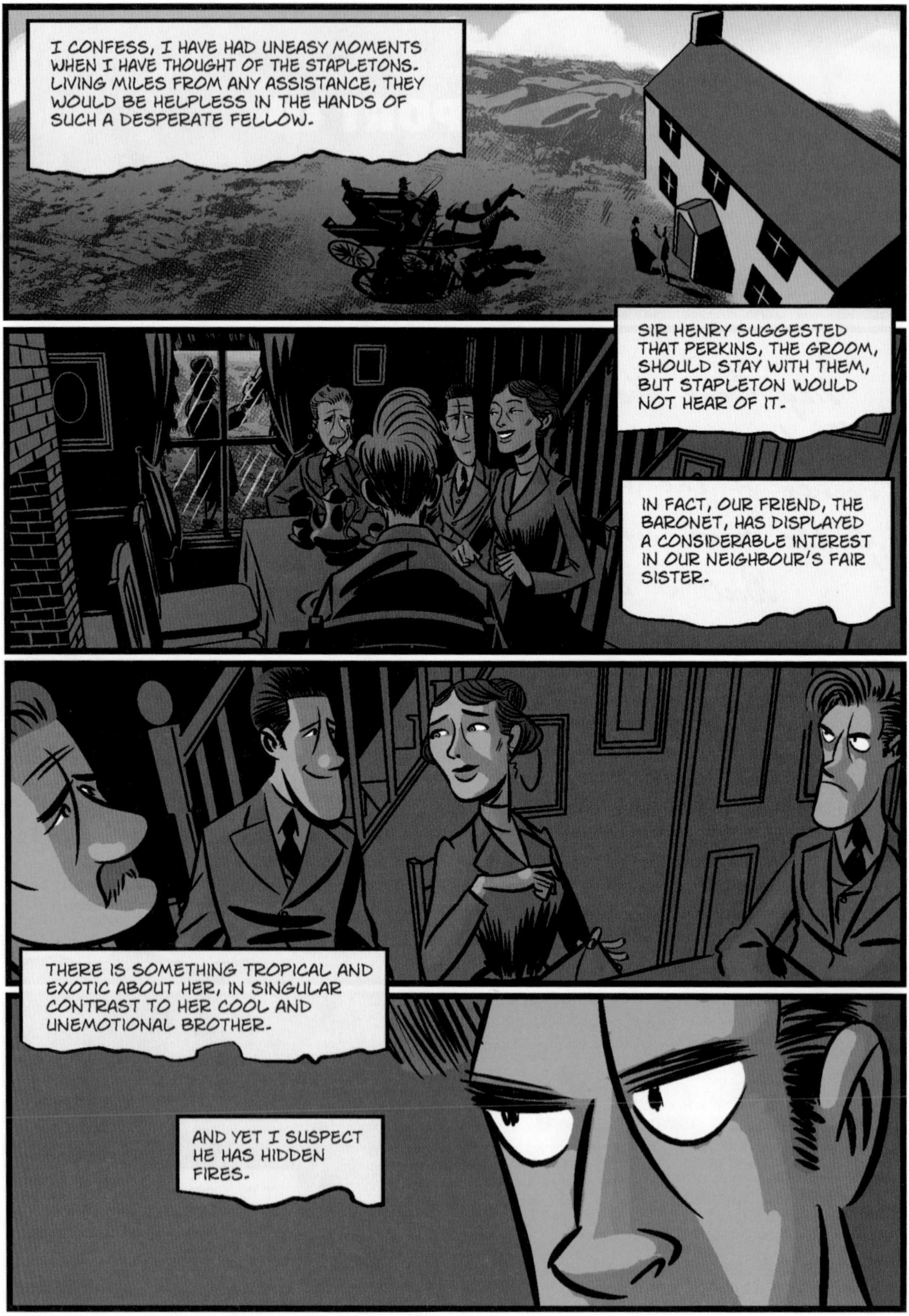
I CONFESS, I HAVE HAD UNEASY MOMENTS WHEN I HAVE THOUGHT OF THE STAPLETONS. LIVING MILES FROM ANY ASSISTANCE, THEY WOULD BE HELPLESS IN THE HANDS OF SUCH A DESPERATE FELLOW.
SIR HENRY SUGGESTED THAT PERKINS, THE GROOM, SHOULD STAY WITH THEM, BUT STAPLETON WOULD NOT HEAR OF IT.
IN FACT, OUR FRIEND, THE BARONET, HAS DISPLAYED A CONSIDERABLE INTEREST IN OUR NEIGHBOUR'S FAIR SISTER.
THERE IS SOMETHING TROPICAL AND EXOTIC ABOUT HER, IN SINGULAR CONTRAST TO HER COOL AND UNEMOTIONAL BROTHER.
AND YET I SUSPECT HE HAS HIDDEN FIRES.

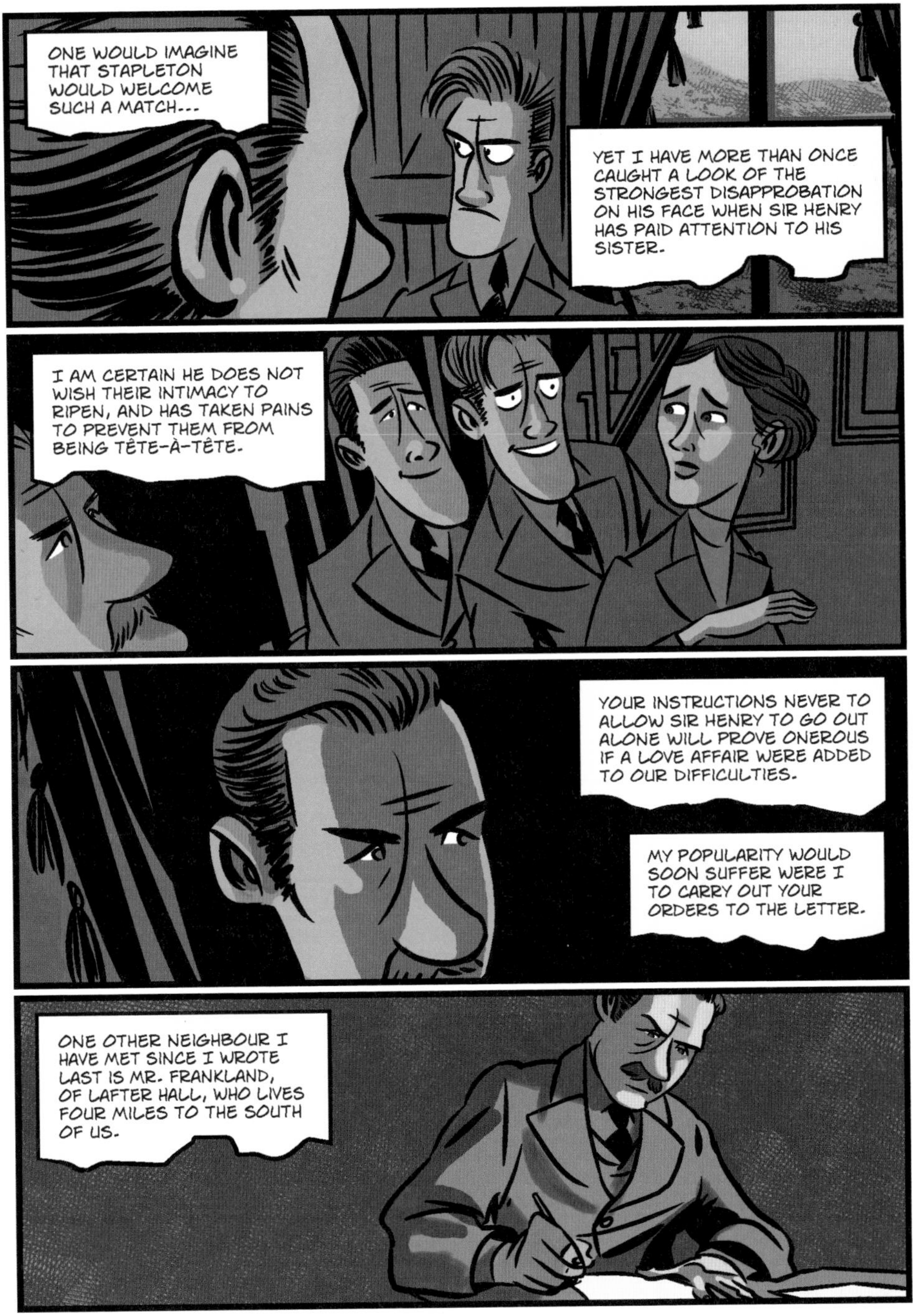
ONE WOULD IMAGINE THAT STAPLETON WOULD WELCOME SUCH A MATCH...
YET I HAVE MORE THAN ONCE CAUGHT A LOOK OF THE STRONGEST DISAPPROBATION ON HIS FACE WHEN SIR HENRY HAS PAID ATTENTION TO HIS SISTER.
I AM CERTAIN HE DOES NOT WISH THEIR INTIMACY TO RIPEN, AND HAS TAKEN PAINS TO PREVENT THEM FROM BEING TÊTE-À-TÊTE.
YOUR INSTRUCTIONS NEVER TO ALLOW SIR HENRY TO GO OUT ALONE WILL PROVE ONEROUS IF A LOVE AFFAIR WERE ADDED TO OUR DIFFICULTIES.
MY POPULARITY WOULD SOON SUFFER WERE I TO CARRY OUT YOUR ORDERS TO THE LETTER.
ONE OTHER NEIGHBOUR I HAVE MET SINCE I WROTE LAST IS MR. FRANKLAND, OF LAFTER HALL, WHO LIVES FOUR MILES TO THE SOUTH OF US.

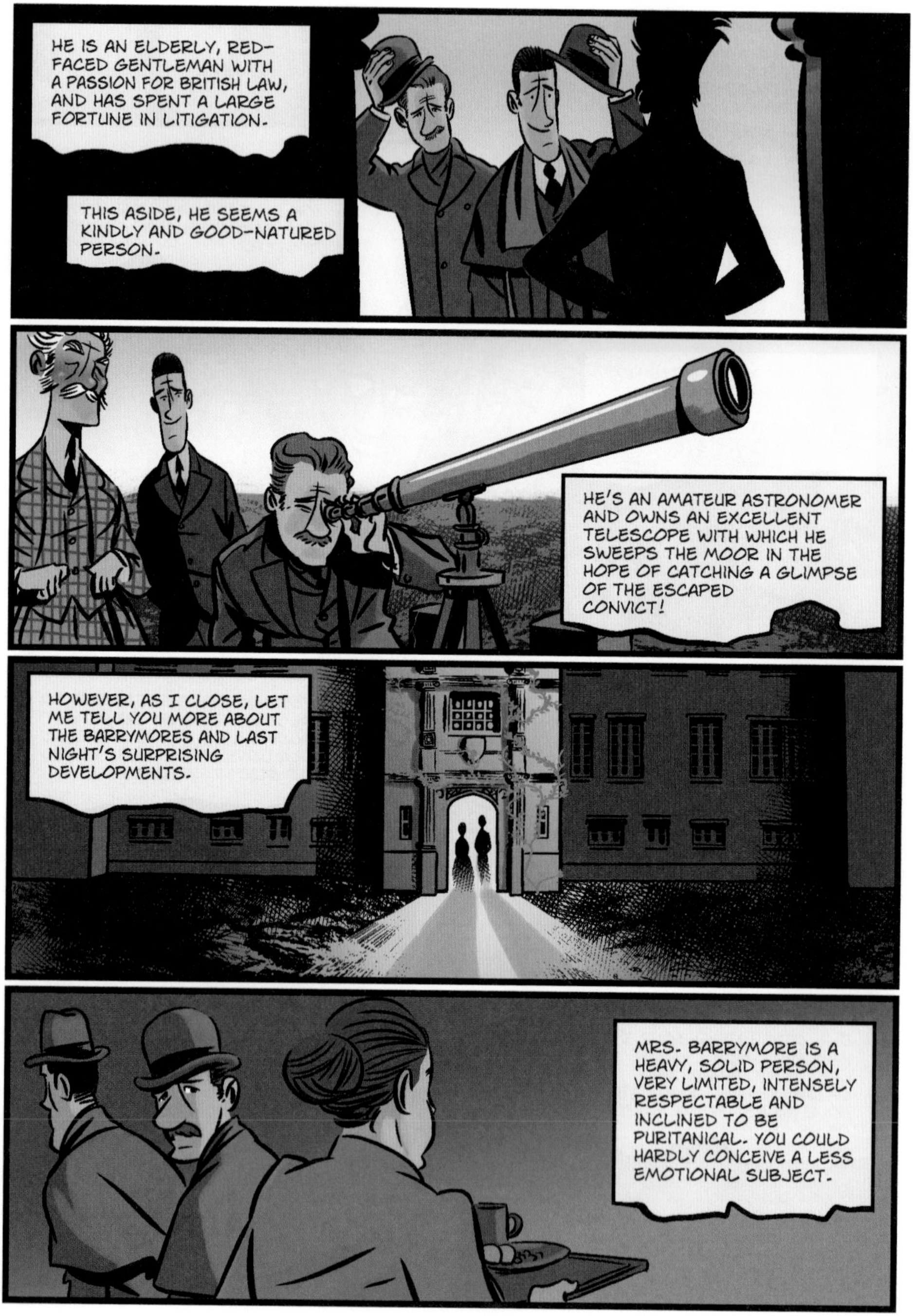
HE IS AN ELDERLY, RED-FACED GENTLEMAN WITH A PASSION FOR BRITISH LAW, AND HAS SPENT A LARGE FORTUNE IN LITIGATION.
THIS ASIDE, HE SEEMS A KINDLY AND GOOD-NATURED PERSON.
HE'S AN AMATEUR ASTRONOMER AND OWNS AN EXCELLENT TELESCOPE WITH WHICH HE SWEEPS THE MOOR IN THE HOPE OF CATCHING A GLIMPSE OF THE ESCAPED CONVICT!
HOWEVER, AS I CLOSE, LET ME TELL YOU MORE ABOUT THE BARRYMORES AND LAST NIGHT'S SURPRISING DEVELOPMENTS.
MRS. BARRYMORE IS A HEAVY, SOLID PERSON, VERY LIMITED, INTENSELY RESPECTABLE AND INCLINED TO BE PURITANICAL. YOU COULD HARDLY CONCEIVE A LESS EMOTIONAL SUBJECT.

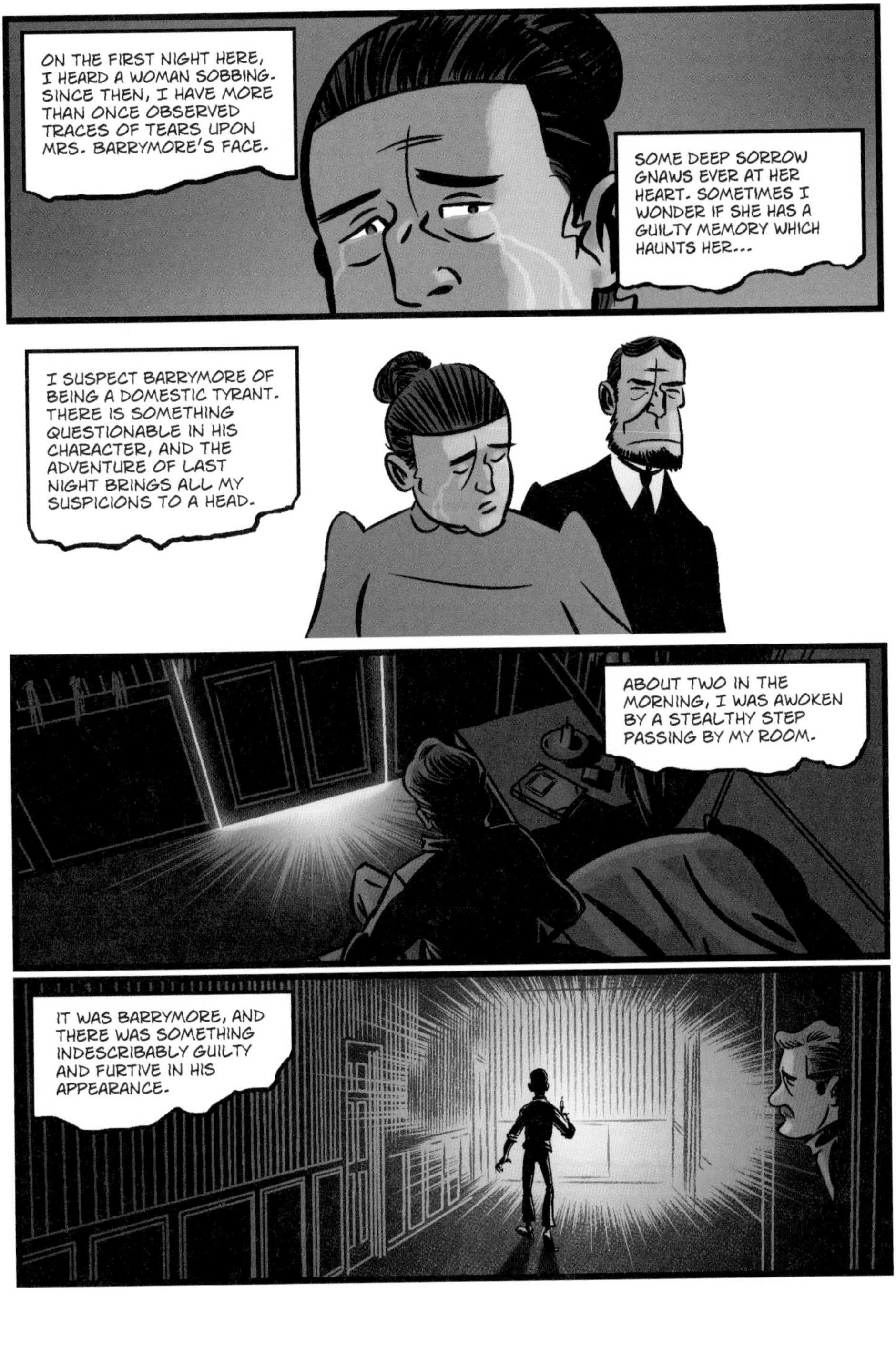
ON THE FIRST NIGHT HERE, I HEARD A WOMAN SOBBING. SINCE THEN, I HAVE MORE THAN ONCE OBSERVED TRACES OF TEARS UPON MRS. BARRYMORE'S FACE.
SOME DEEP SORROW GNAWS EVER AT HER HEART. SOMETIMES I WONDER IF SHE HAS A GUILTY MEMORY WHICH HAUNTS HER...
I SUSPECT BARRYMORE OF BEING A DOMESTIC TYRANT. THERE IS SOMETHING QUESTIONABLE IN HIS CHARACTER, AND THE ADVENTURE OF LAST NIGHT BRINGS ALL MY SUSPICIONS TO A HEAD.
ABOUT TWO IN THE MORNING, I WAS AWOKEN BY A STEALTHY STEP PASSING BY MY ROOM.
IT WAS BARRYMORE, AND THERE WAS SOMETHING INDESCRIBABLY GUILTY AND FURTIVE IN HIS APPEARANCE.

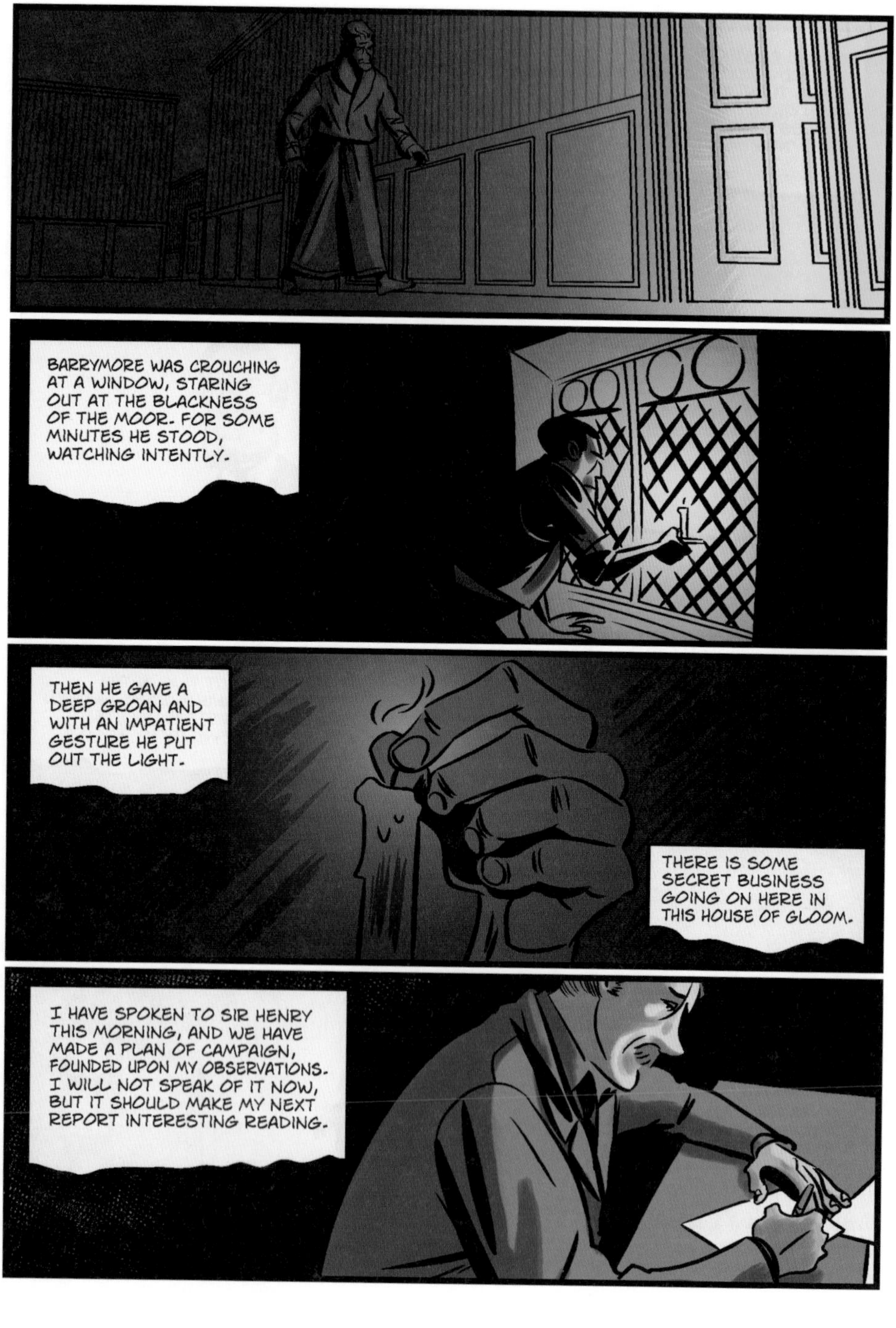
BARRYMORE WAS CROUCHING AT A WINDOW, STARING OUT AT THE BLACKNESS OF THE MOOR. FOR SOME MINUTES HE STOOD, WATCHING INTENTLY.
THEN HE GAVE A DEEP GROAN AND WITH AN IMPATIENT GESTURE HE PUT OUT THE LIGHT.
THERE IS SOME SECRET BUSINESS GOING ON HERE IN THIS HOUSE OF GLOOM.
I HAVE SPOKEN TO SIR HENRY THIS MORNING, AND WE HAVE MADE A PLAN OF CAMPAIGN, FOUNDED UPON MY OBSERVATIONS. I WILL NOT SPEAK OF IT NOW, BUT IT SHOULD MAKE MY NEXT REPORT INTERESTING READING.

THE LIGHT UPON THE MOOR
(SECOND REPORT OF DR. WATSON)

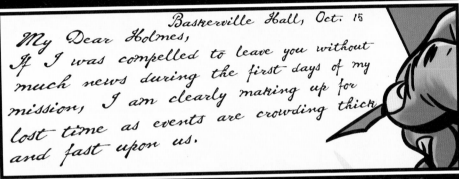

Baskerville Hall, Oct. 15

My Dear Holmes,
If I was compelled to leave you without much news during the first days of my mission, I am clearly making up for lost time as events are crowding thick and fast upon us.

SIR HENRY MEANS TO SPARE NO EXPENSE IN RESTORING THE GRANDEUR OF HIS FAMILY.

THERE HAVE BEEN DECORATORS AND FURNISHERS UP FROM PLYMOUTH AND A CONTRACTOR FROM LONDON.

WITH THE HOUSE REFURBISHED, ALL HE WILL NEED IS A WIFE TO MAKE IT COMPLETE – AND, BETWEEN OURSELVES, THERE ARE SIGNS THIS WILL NOT BE WANTING IF THE LADY IS WILLING.

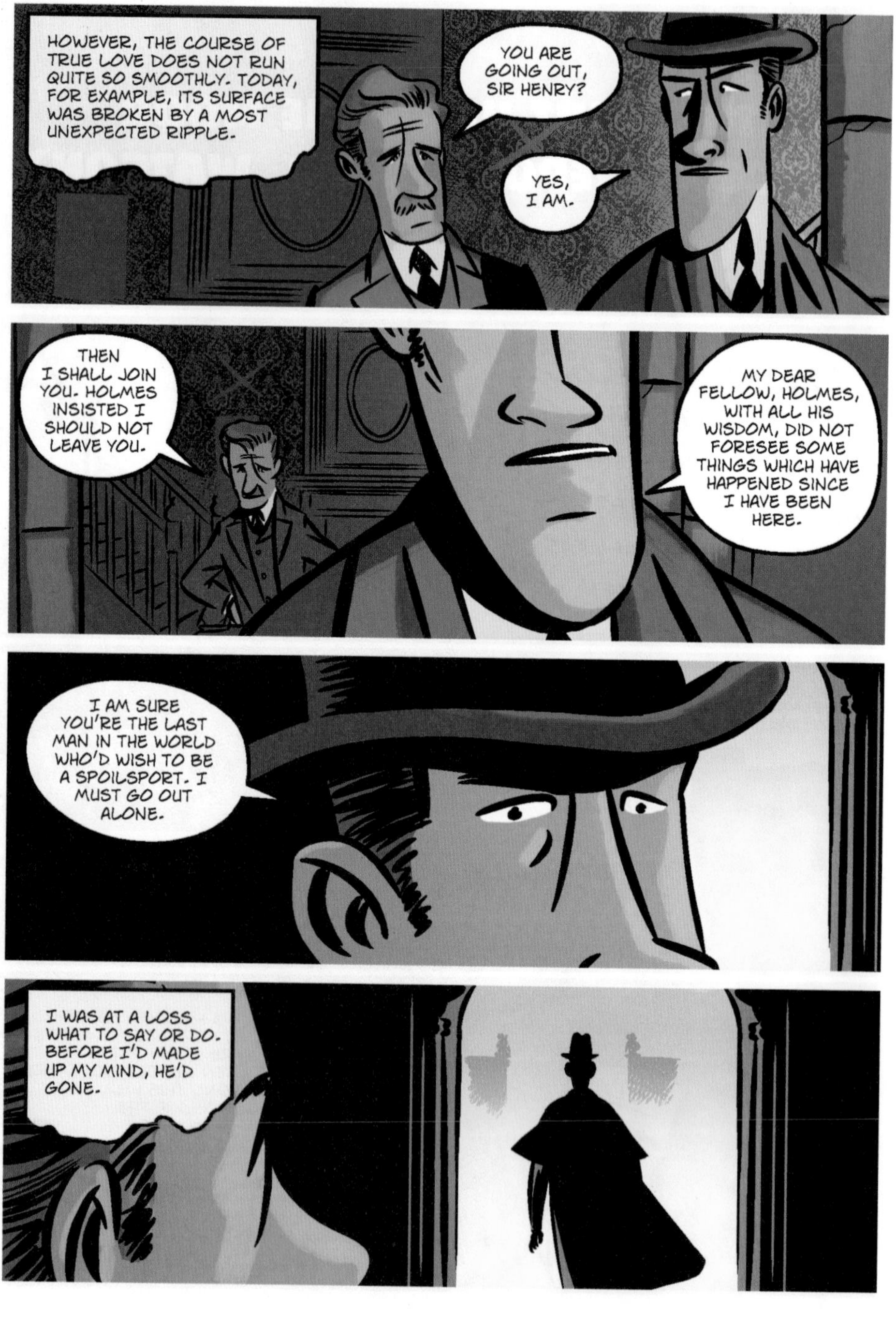
HOWEVER, THE COURSE OF TRUE LOVE DOES NOT RUN QUITE SO SMOOTHLY. TODAY, FOR EXAMPLE, ITS SURFACE WAS BROKEN BY A MOST UNEXPECTED RIPPLE.
YOU ARE GOING OUT, SIR HENRY?
YES, I AM.
THEN I SHALL JOIN YOU. HOLMES INSISTED I SHOULD NOT LEAVE YOU.
MY DEAR FELLOW, HOLMES, WITH ALL HIS WISDOM, DID NOT FORESEE SOME THINGS WHICH HAVE HAPPENED SINCE I HAVE BEEN HERE.
I AM SURE YOU'RE THE LAST MAN IN THE WORLD WHO'D WISH TO BE A SPOILSPORT. I MUST GO OUT ALONE.
I WAS AT A LOSS WHAT TO SAY OR DO. BEFORE I'D MADE UP MY MIND, HE'D GONE.

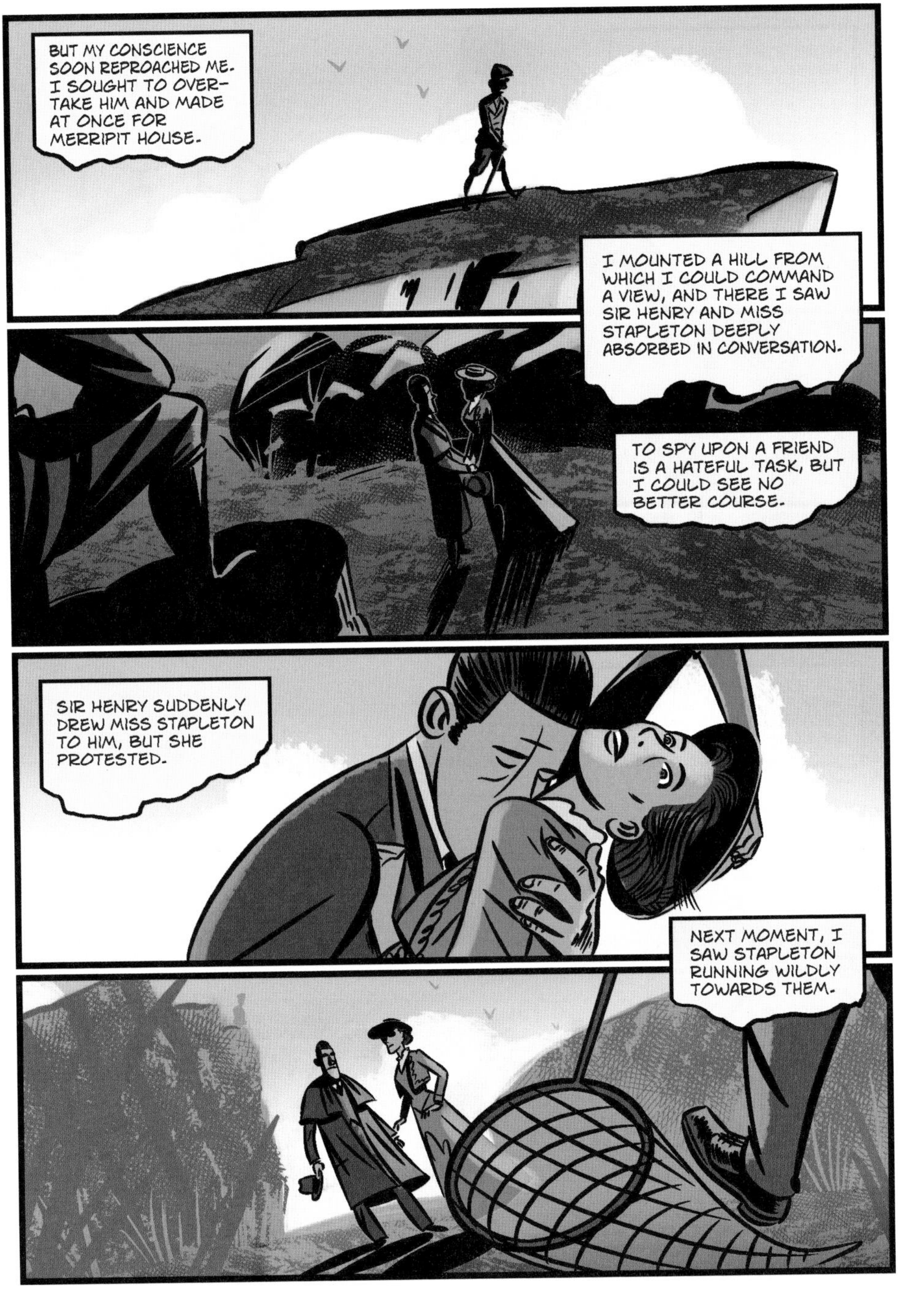
BUT MY CONSCIENCE SOON REPROACHED ME. I SOUGHT TO OVER-TAKE HIM AND MADE AT ONCE FOR MERRIPIT HOUSE.
I MOUNTED A HILL FROM WHICH I COULD COMMAND A VIEW, AND THERE I SAW SIR HENRY AND MISS STAPLETON DEEPLY ABSORBED IN CONVERSATION.
TO SPY UPON A FRIEND IS A HATEFUL TASK, BUT I COULD SEE NO BETTER COURSE.
SIR HENRY SUDDENLY DREW MISS STAPLETON TO HIM, BUT SHE PROTESTED.
NEXT MOMENT, I SAW STAPLETON RUNNING WILDLY TOWARDS THEM.

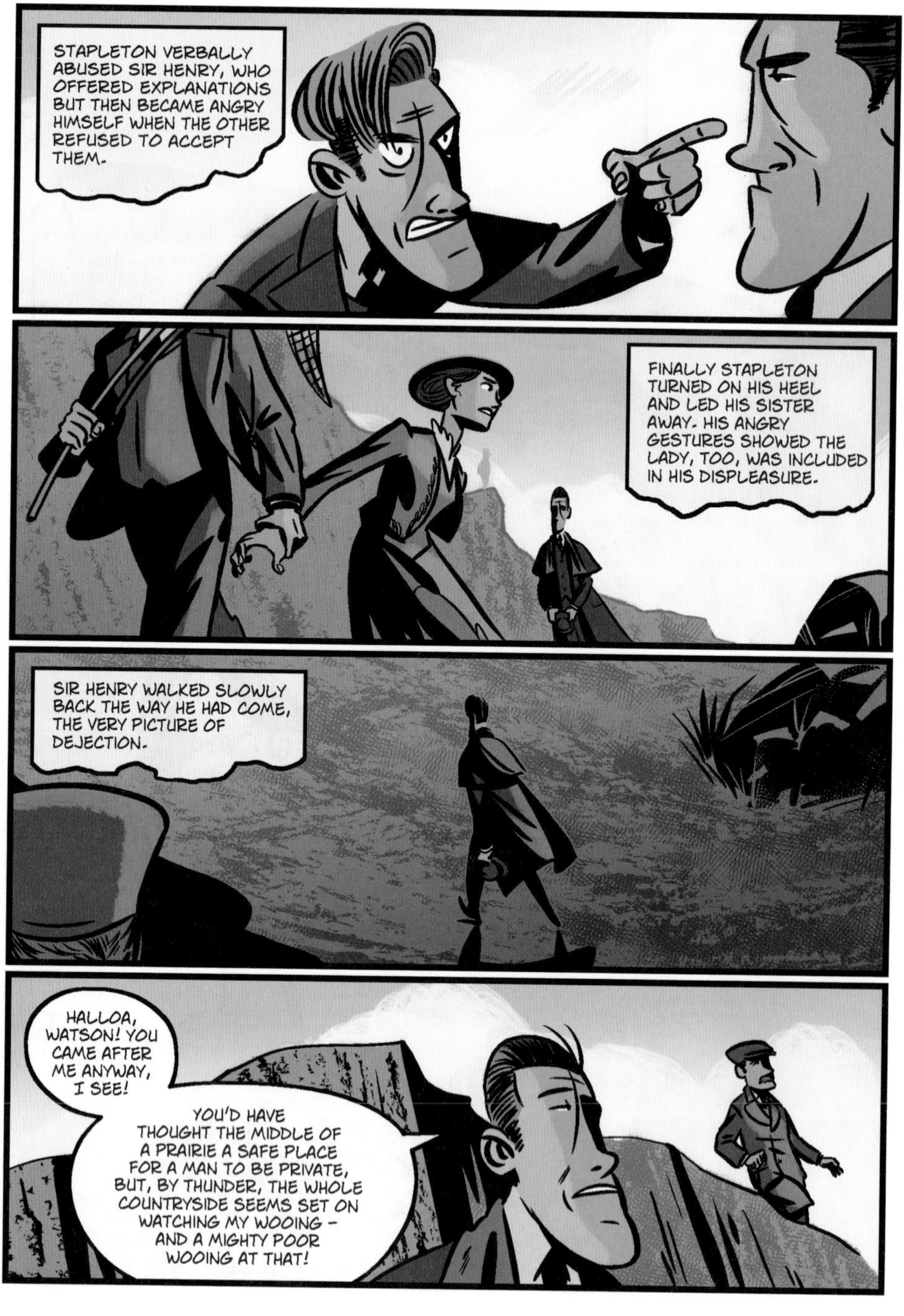
STAPLETON VERBALLY ABUSED SIR HENRY, WHO OFFERED EXPLANATIONS BUT THEN BECAME ANGRY HIMSELF WHEN THE OTHER REFUSED TO ACCEPT THEM.
FINALLY STAPLETON TURNED ON HIS HEEL AND LED HIS SISTER AWAY. HIS ANGRY GESTURES SHOWED THE LADY, TOO, WAS INCLUDED IN HIS DISPLEASURE.
SIR HENRY WALKED SLOWLY BACK THE WAY HE HAD COME, THE VERY PICTURE OF DEJECTION.
HALLOA, WATSON! YOU CAME AFTER ME ANYWAY, I SEE!
YOU'D HAVE THOUGHT THE MIDDLE OF A PRAIRIE A SAFE PLACE FOR A MAN TO BE PRIVATE, BUT, BY THUNDER, THE WHOLE COUNTRYSIDE SEEMS SET ON WATCHING MY WOOING – AND A MIGHTY POOR WOOING AT THAT!

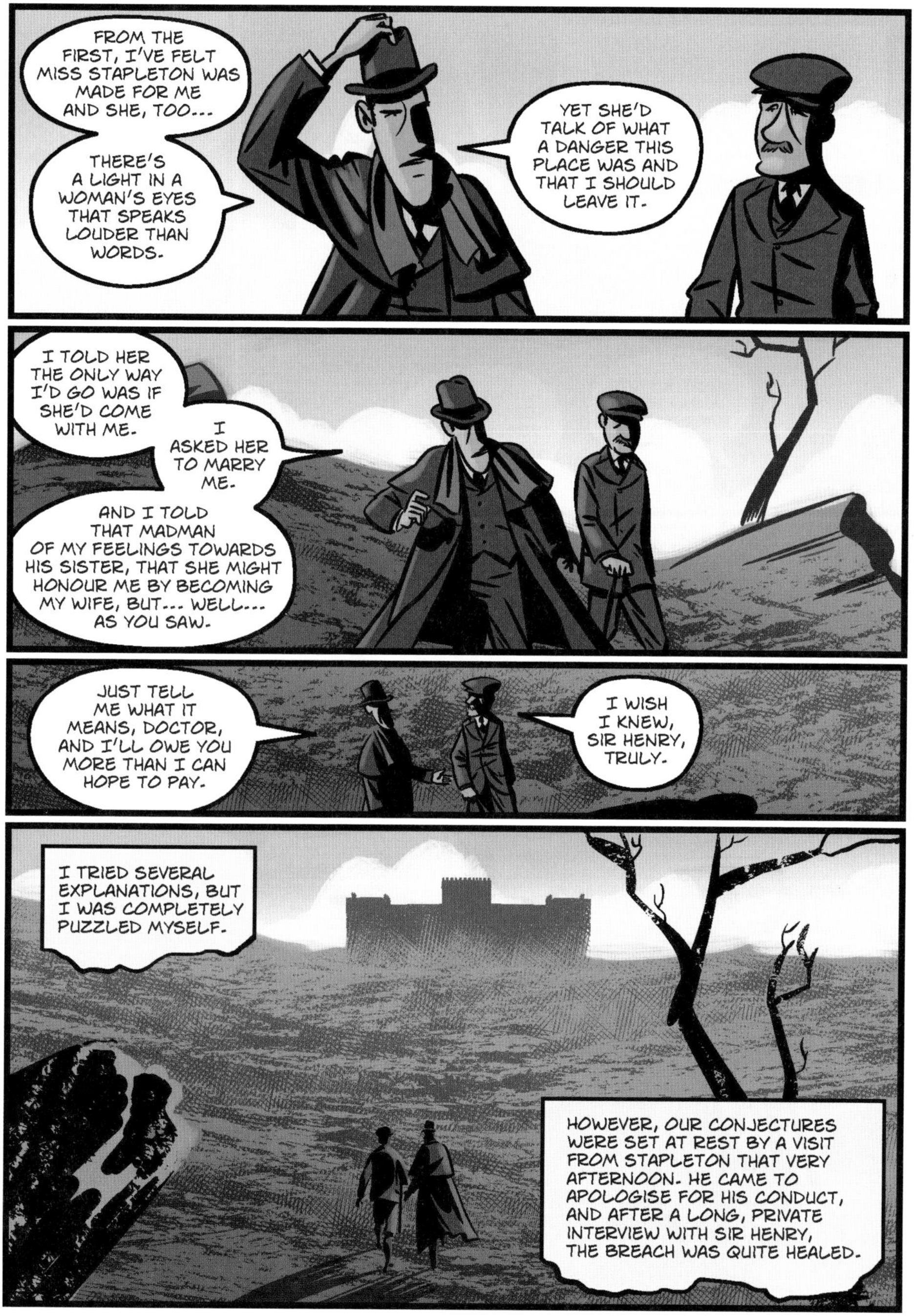
FROM THE FIRST, I'VE FELT MISS STAPLETON WAS MADE FOR ME AND SHE, TOO...
THERE'S A LIGHT IN A WOMAN'S EYES THAT SPEAKS LOUDER THAN WORDS.
YET SHE'D TALK OF WHAT A DANGER THIS PLACE WAS AND THAT I SHOULD LEAVE IT.
I TOLD HER THE ONLY WAY I'D GO WAS IF SHE'D COME WITH ME.
I ASKED HER TO MARRY ME.
AND I TOLD THAT MADMAN OF MY FEELINGS TOWARDS HIS SISTER, THAT SHE MIGHT HONOUR ME BY BECOMING MY WIFE, BUT... WELL... AS YOU SAW.
JUST TELL ME WHAT IT MEANS, DOCTOR, AND I'LL OWE YOU MORE THAN I CAN HOPE TO PAY.
I WISH I KNEW, SIR HENRY, TRULY.
I TRIED SEVERAL EXPLANATIONS, BUT I WAS COMPLETELY PUZZLED MYSELF.
HOWEVER, OUR CONJECTURES WERE SET AT REST BY A VISIT FROM STAPLETON THAT VERY AFTERNOON. HE CAME TO APOLOGISE FOR HIS CONDUCT, AND AFTER A LONG, PRIVATE INTERVIEW WITH SIR HENRY, THE BREACH WAS QUITE HEALED.

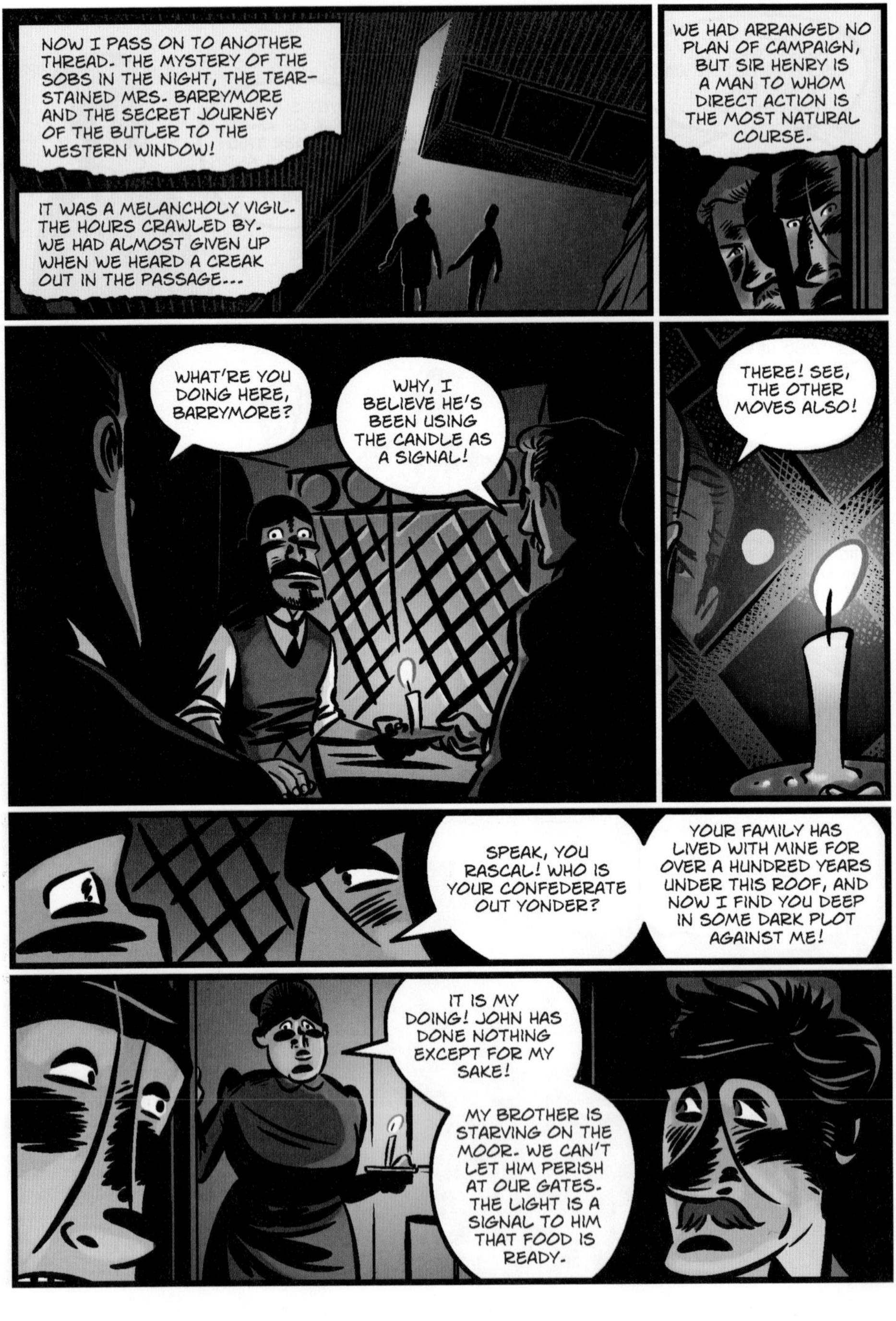
NOW I PASS ON TO ANOTHER THREAD. THE MYSTERY OF THE SOBS IN THE NIGHT, THE TEAR-STAINED MRS. BARRYMORE AND THE SECRET JOURNEY OF THE BUTLER TO THE WESTERN WINDOW!
IT WAS A MELANCHOLY VIGIL. THE HOURS CRAWLED BY. WE HAD ALMOST GIVEN UP WHEN WE HEARD A CREAK OUT IN THE PASSAGE...
WE HAD ARRANGED NO PLAN OF CAMPAIGN, BUT SIR HENRY IS A MAN TO WHOM DIRECT ACTION IS THE MOST NATURAL COURSE.
WHAT'RE YOU DOING HERE, BARRYMORE?
WHY, I BELIEVE HE'S BEEN USING THE CANDLE AS A SIGNAL!
THERE! SEE, THE OTHER MOVES ALSO!
SPEAK, YOU RASCAL! WHO IS YOUR CONFEDERATE OUT YONDER?
YOUR FAMILY HAS LIVED WITH MINE FOR OVER A HUNDRED YEARS UNDER THIS ROOF, AND NOW I FIND YOU DEEP IN SOME DARK PLOT AGAINST ME!
IT IS MY DOING! JOHN HAS DONE NOTHING EXCEPT FOR MY SAKE!
MY BROTHER IS STARVING ON THE MOOR. WE CAN'T LET HIM PERISH AT OUR GATES. THE LIGHT IS A SIGNAL TO HIM THAT FOOD IS READY.

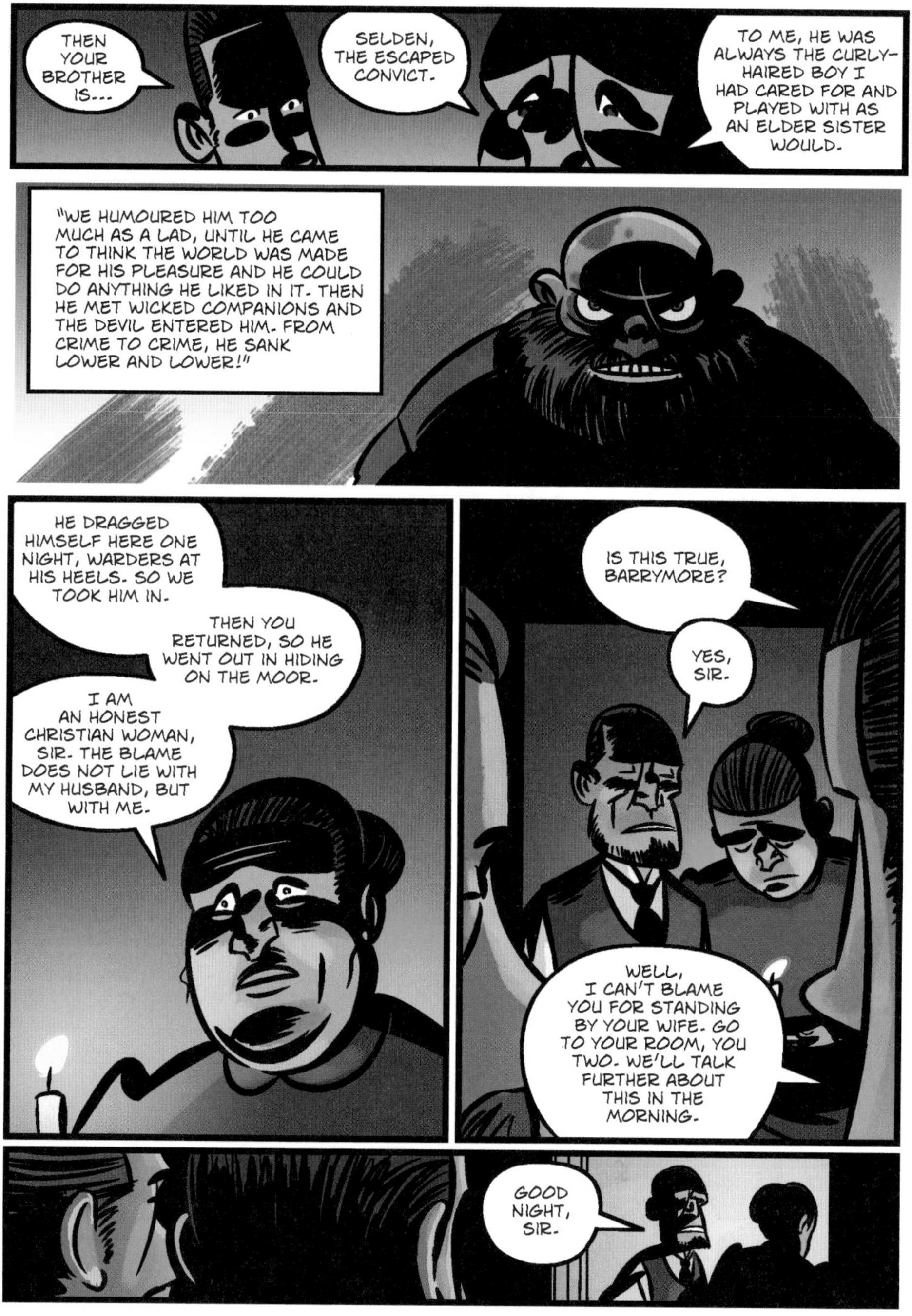
THEN YOUR BROTHER IS...
SELDEN, THE ESCAPED CONVICT.
TO ME, HE WAS ALWAYS THE CURLY-HAIRED BOY I HAD CARED FOR AND PLAYED WITH AS AN ELDER SISTER WOULD.
"WE HUMOURED HIM TOO MUCH AS A LAD, UNTIL HE CAME TO THINK THE WORLD WAS MADE FOR HIS PLEASURE AND HE COULD DO ANYTHING HE LIKED IN IT. THEN HE MET WICKED COMPANIONS AND THE DEVIL ENTERED HIM. FROM CRIME TO CRIME, HE SANK LOWER AND LOWER!"
HE DRAGGED HIMSELF HERE ONE NIGHT, WARDERS AT HIS HEELS. SO WE TOOK HIM IN.
THEN YOU RETURNED, SO HE WENT OUT IN HIDING ON THE MOOR.
I AM AN HONEST CHRISTIAN WOMAN, SIR. THE BLAME DOES NOT LIE WITH MY HUSBAND, BUT WITH ME.
IS THIS TRUE, BARRYMORE?
YES, SIR.
WELL, I CAN'T BLAME YOU FOR STANDING BY YOUR WIFE. GO TO YOUR ROOM, YOU TWO. WE'LL TALK FURTHER ABOUT THIS IN THE MORNING.
GOOD NIGHT, SIR.

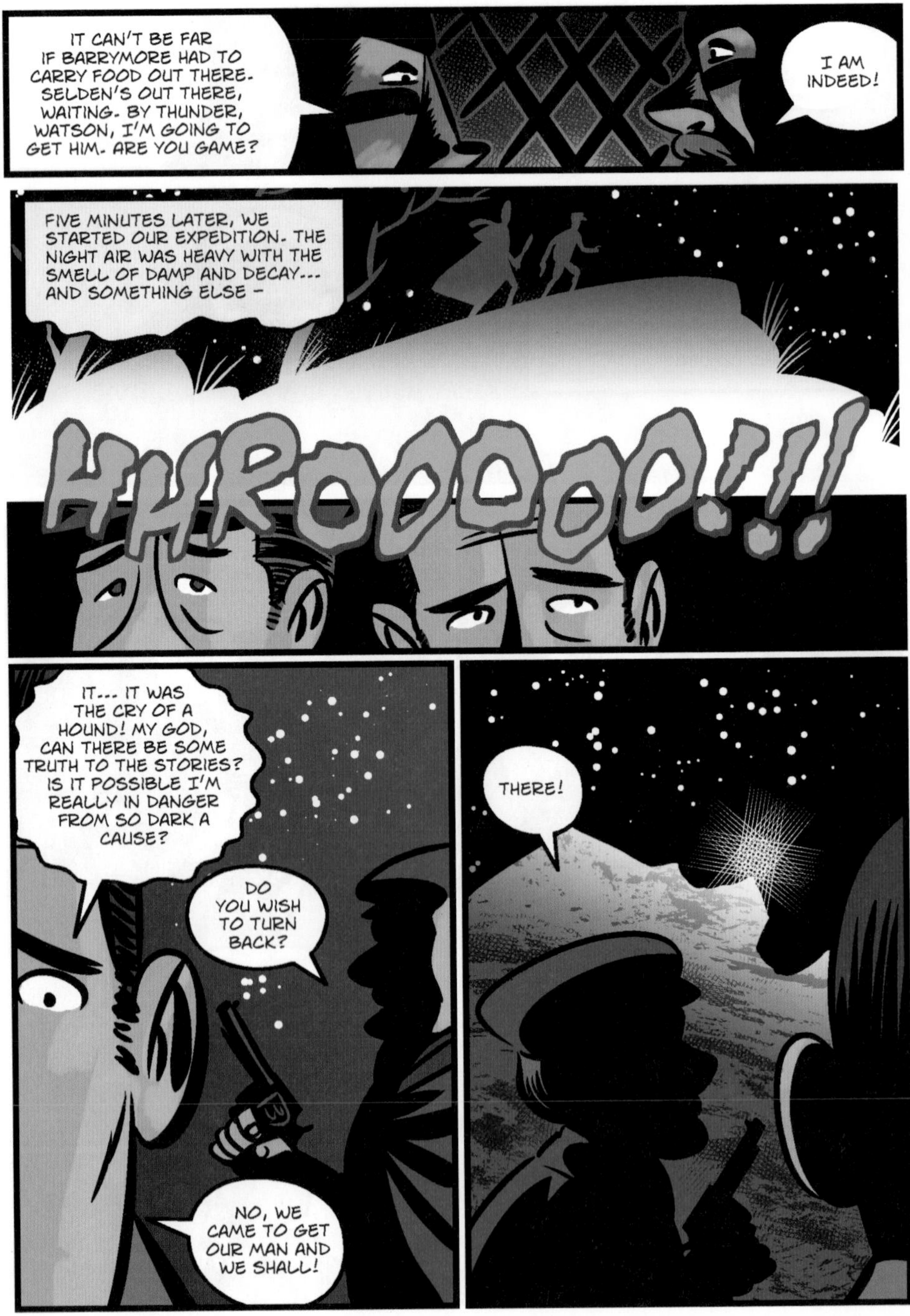
IT CAN'T BE FAR IF BARRYMORE HAD TO CARRY FOOD OUT THERE. SELDEN'S OUT THERE, WAITING. BY THUNDER, WATSON, I'M GOING TO GET HIM. ARE YOU GAME?
I AM INDEED!
FIVE MINUTES LATER, WE STARTED OUR EXPEDITION. THE NIGHT AIR WAS HEAVY WITH THE SMELL OF DAMP AND DECAY... AND SOMETHING ELSE –
HUROOOOO!!!
IT... IT WAS THE CRY OF A HOUND! MY GOD, CAN THERE BE SOME TRUTH TO THE STORIES? IS IT POSSIBLE I'M REALLY IN DANGER FROM SO DARK A CAUSE?
DO YOU WISH TO TURN BACK?
NO, WE CAME TO GET OUR MAN AND WE SHALL!
THERE!

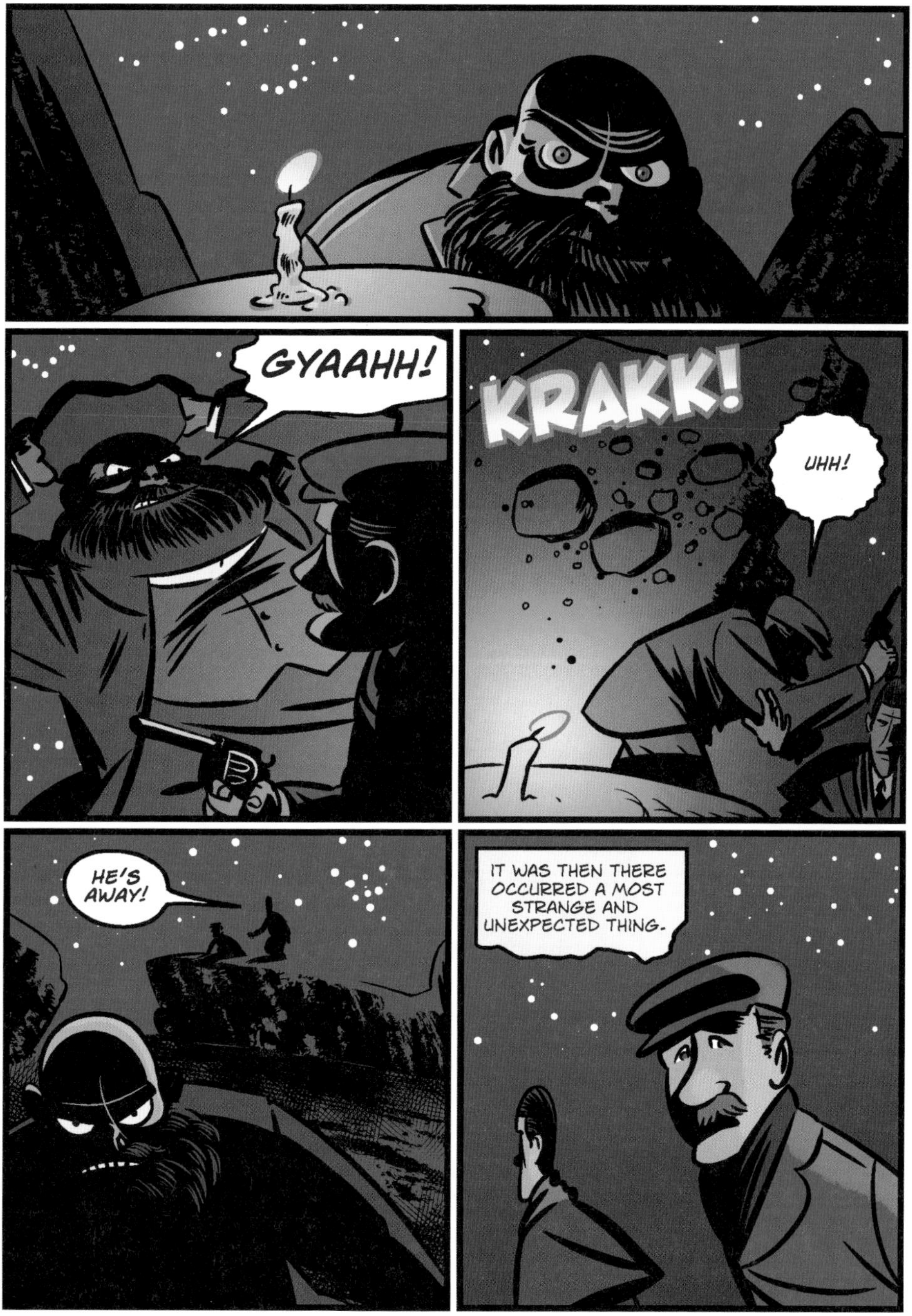
GYAAHH!
KRAKK!
UHH!
HE'S AWAY!
IT WAS THEN THERE OCCURRED A MOST STRANGE AND UNEXPECTED THING.

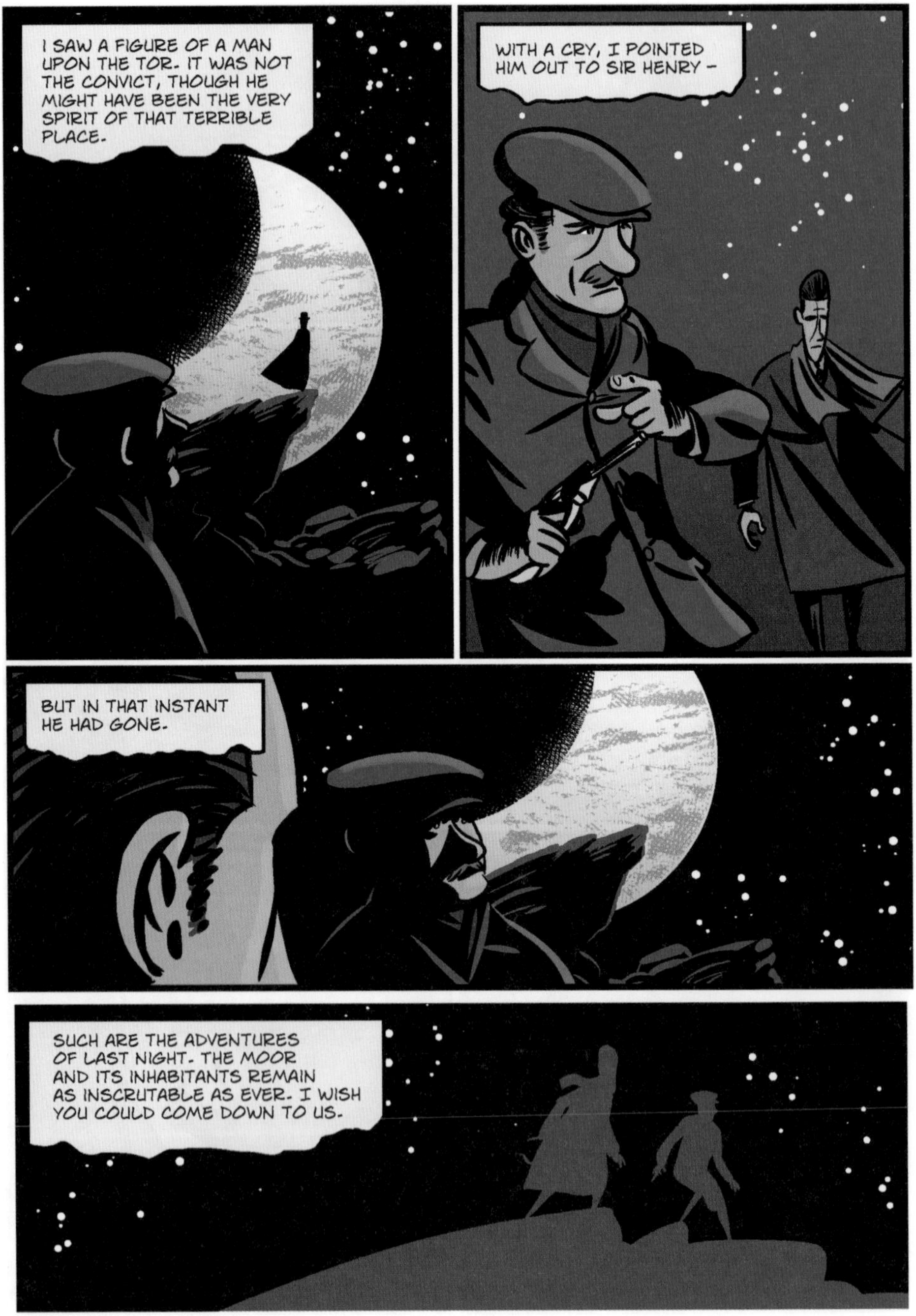
I SAW A FIGURE OF A MAN UPON THE TOR. IT WAS NOT THE CONVICT, THOUGH HE MIGHT HAVE BEEN THE VERY SPIRIT OF THAT TERRIBLE PLACE.
WITH A CRY, I POINTED HIM OUT TO SIR HENRY –
BUT IN THAT INSTANT HE HAD GONE.
SUCH ARE THE ADVENTURES OF LAST NIGHT. THE MOOR AND ITS INHABITANTS REMAIN AS INSCRUTABLE AS EVER. I WISH YOU COULD COME DOWN TO US.

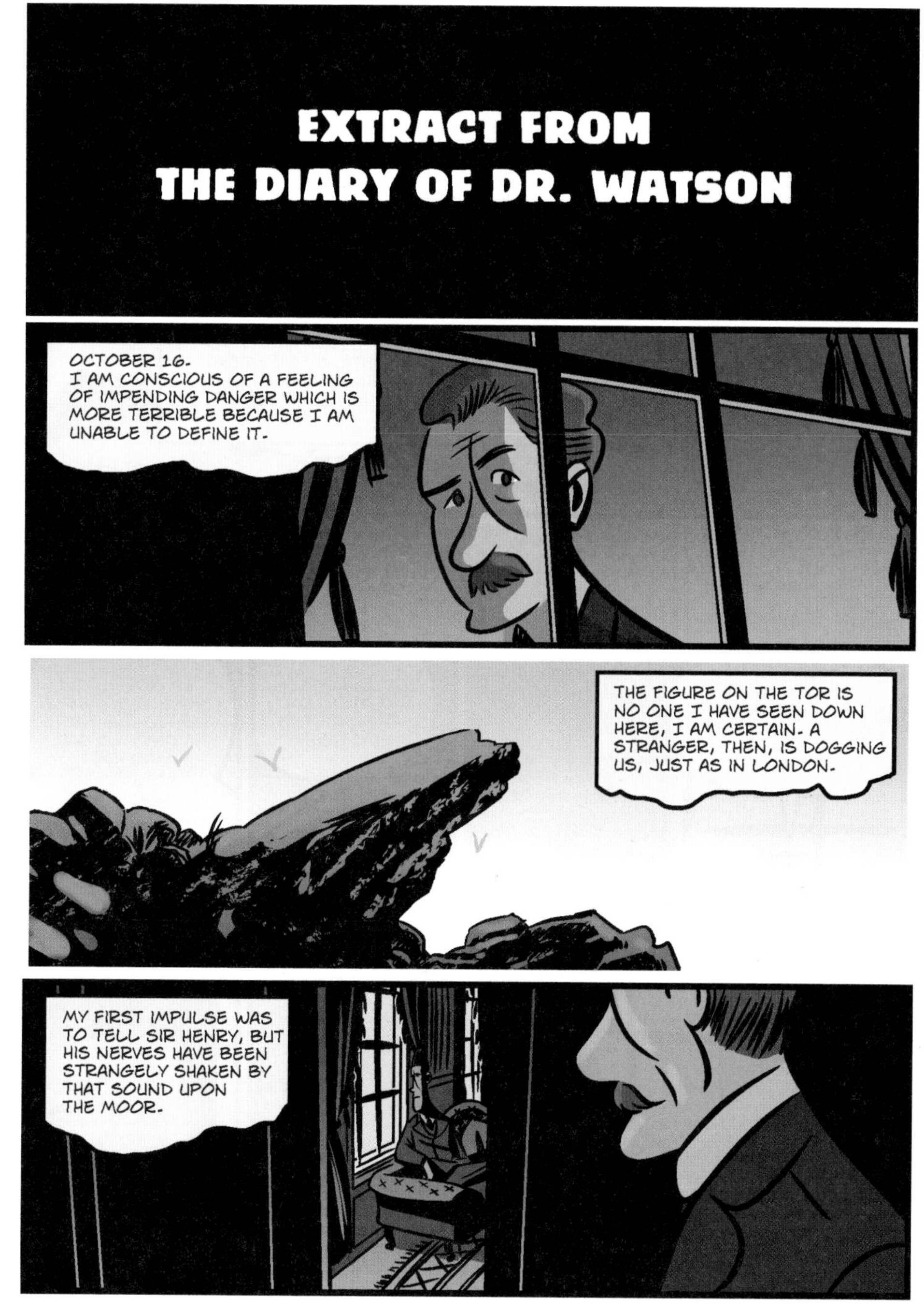
EXTRACT FROM
THE DIARY OF DR. WATSON
OCTOBER 16. I AM CONSCIOUS OF A FEELING OF IMPENDING DANGER WHICH IS MORE TERRIBLE BECAUSE I AM UNABLE TO DEFINE IT.
THE FIGURE ON THE TOR IS NO ONE I HAVE SEEN DOWN HERE, I AM CERTAIN. A STRANGER, THEN, IS DOGGING US, JUST AS IN LONDON.
MY FIRST IMPULSE WAS TO TELL SIR HENRY, BUT HIS NERVES HAVE BEEN STRANGELY SHAKEN BY THAT SOUND UPON THE MOOR.

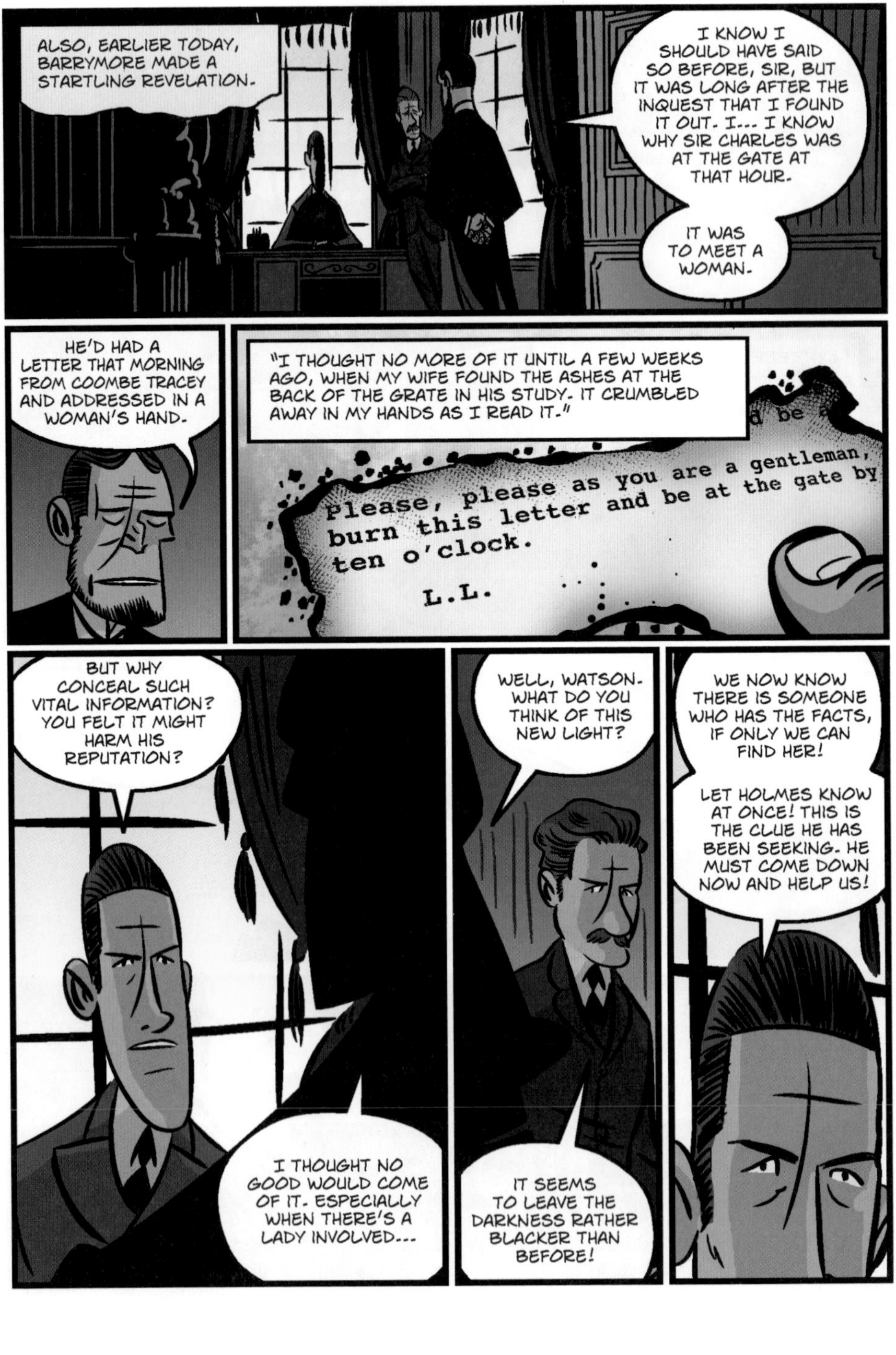
ALSO, EARLIER TODAY, BARRYMORE MADE A STARTLING REVELATION.
I KNOW I SHOULD HAVE SAID SO BEFORE, SIR, BUT IT WAS LONG AFTER THE INQUEST THAT I FOUND IT OUT. I... I KNOW WHY SIR CHARLES WAS AT THE GATE AT THAT HOUR.
IT WAS TO MEET A WOMAN.
HE'D HAD A LETTER THAT MORNING FROM COOMBE TRACEY AND ADDRESSED IN A WOMAN'S HAND.
"I THOUGHT NO MORE OF IT UNTIL A FEW WEEKS AGO, WHEN MY WIFE FOUND THE ASHES AT THE BACK OF THE GRATE IN HIS STUDY. IT CRUMBLED AWAY IN MY HANDS AS I READ IT."
Please, please as you are a gentleman, burn this letter and be at the gate by ten o'clock.
L.L.
BUT WHY CONCEAL SUCH VITAL INFORMATION? YOU FELT IT MIGHT HARM HIS REPUTATION?
I THOUGHT NO GOOD WOULD COME OF IT. ESPECIALLY WHEN THERE'S A LADY INVOLVED...
WELL, WATSON. WHAT DO YOU THINK OF THIS NEW LIGHT?
IT SEEMS TO LEAVE THE DARKNESS RATHER BLACKER THAN BEFORE!
WE NOW KNOW THERE IS SOMEONE WHO HAS THE FACTS, IF ONLY WE CAN FIND HER!
LET HOLMES KNOW AT ONCE! THIS IS THE CLUE HE HAS BEEN SEEKING. HE MUST COME DOWN NOW AND HELP US!

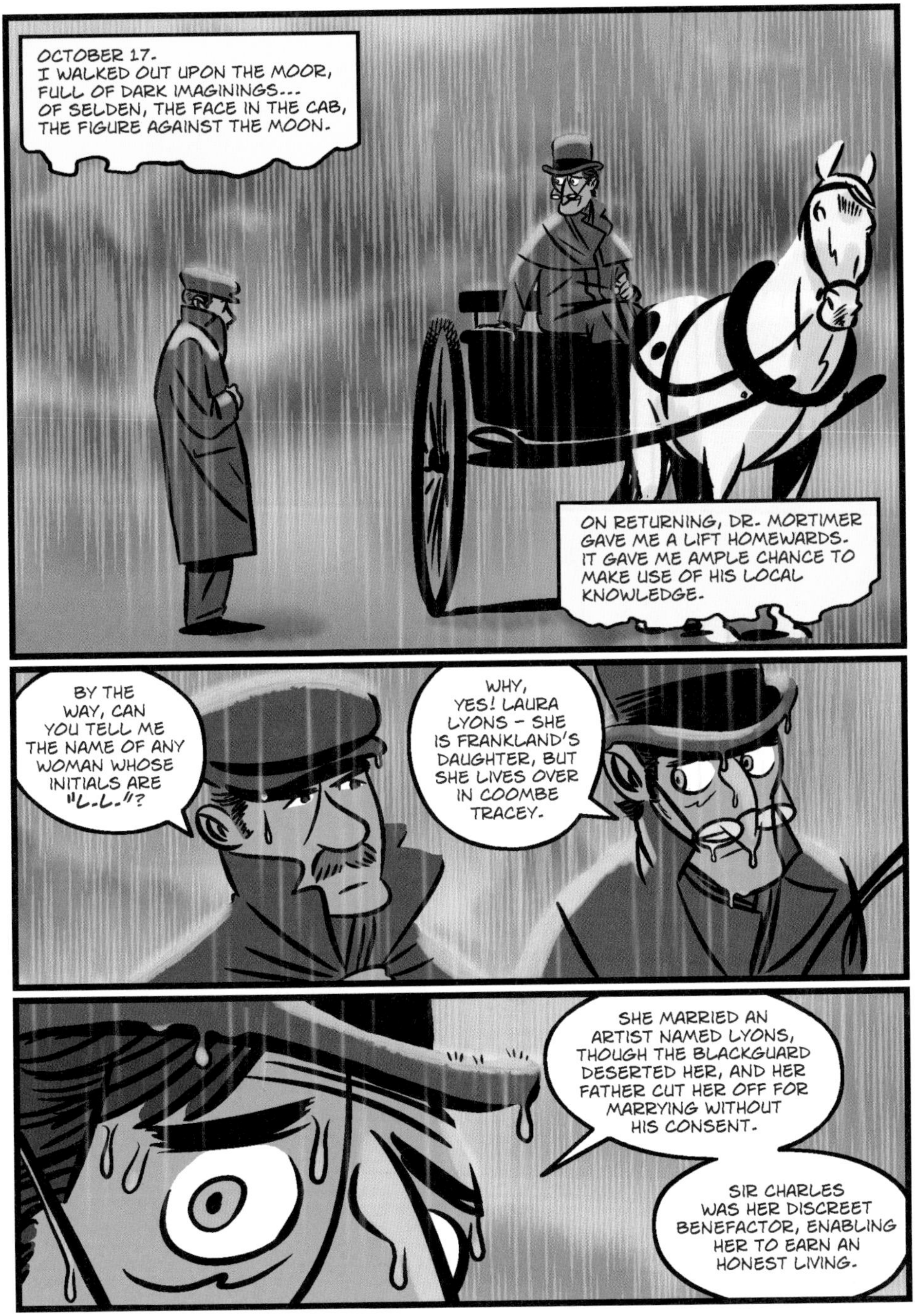
OCTOBER 17.
I WALKED OUT UPON THE MOOR, FULL OF DARK IMAGININGS... OF SELDEN, THE FACE IN THE CAB, THE FIGURE AGAINST THE MOON.
ON RETURNING, DR. MORTIMER GAVE ME A LIFT HOMEWARDS. IT GAVE ME AMPLE CHANCE TO MAKE USE OF HIS LOCAL KNOWLEDGE.
BY THE WAY, CAN YOU TELL ME THE NAME OF ANY WOMAN WHOSE INITIALS ARE "L.L."?
WHY, YES! LAURA LYONS - SHE IS FRANKLAND'S DAUGHTER, BUT SHE LIVES OVER IN COOMBE TRACEY.
SHE MARRIED AN ARTIST NAMED LYONS, THOUGH THE BLACKGUARD DESERTED HER, AND HER FATHER CUT HER OFF FOR MARRYING WITHOUT HIS CONSENT.
SIR CHARLES WAS HER DISCREET BENEFACTOR, ENABLING HER TO EARN AN HONEST LIVING.

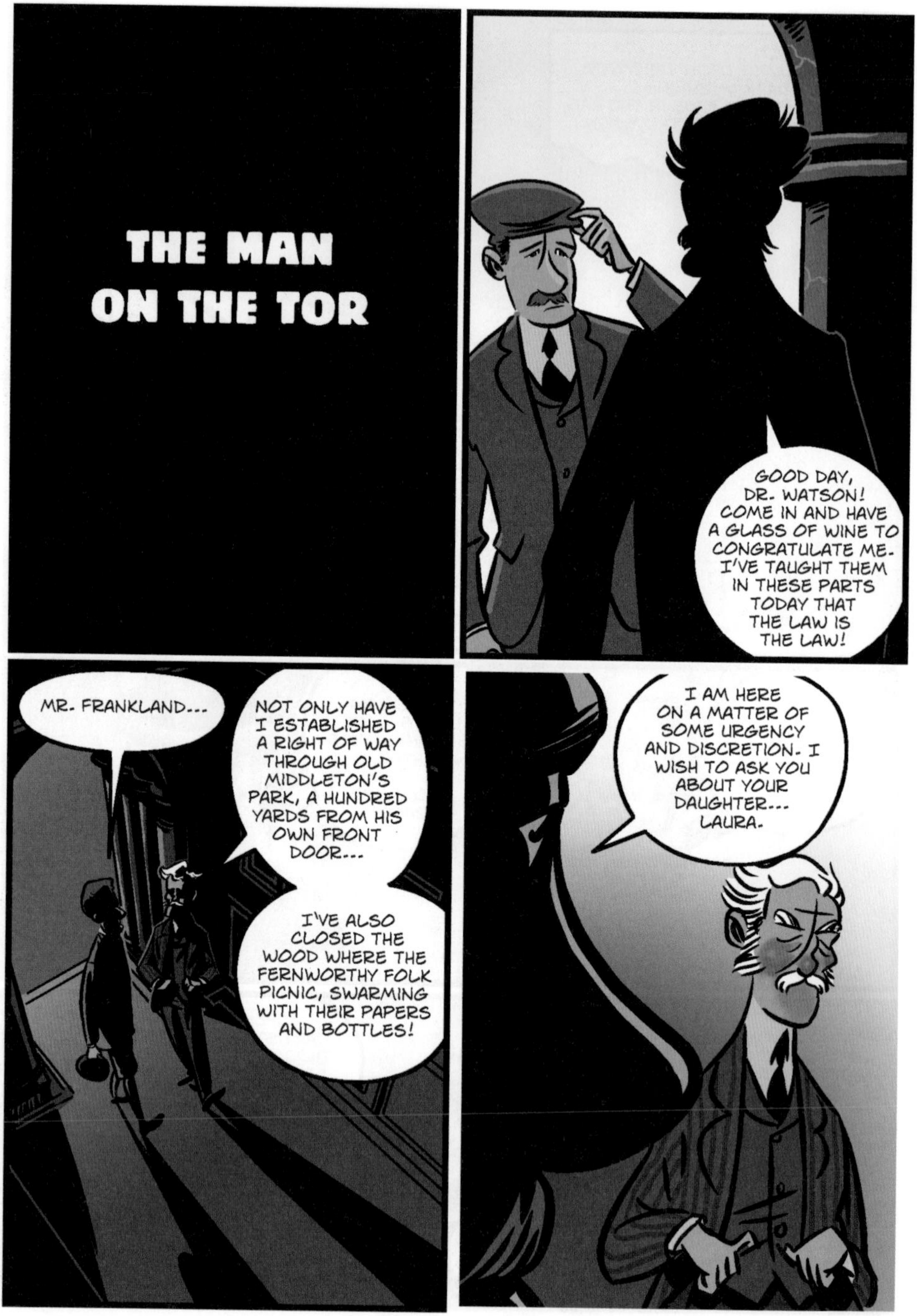
THE MAN ON THE TOR
GOOD DAY, DR. WATSON! COME IN AND HAVE A GLASS OF WINE TO CONGRATULATE ME. I'VE TAUGHT THEM IN THESE PARTS TODAY THAT THE LAW IS THE LAW!
MR. FRANKLAND...
NOT ONLY HAVE I ESTABLISHED A RIGHT OF WAY THROUGH OLD MIDDLETON'S PARK, A HUNDRED YARDS FROM HIS OWN FRONT DOOR...
I'VE ALSO CLOSED THE WOOD WHERE THE FERNWORTHY FOLK PICNIC, SWARMING WITH THEIR PAPERS AND BOTTLES!
I AM HERE ON A MATTER OF SOME URGENCY AND DISCRETION. I WISH TO ASK YOU ABOUT YOUR DAUGHTER... LAURA.

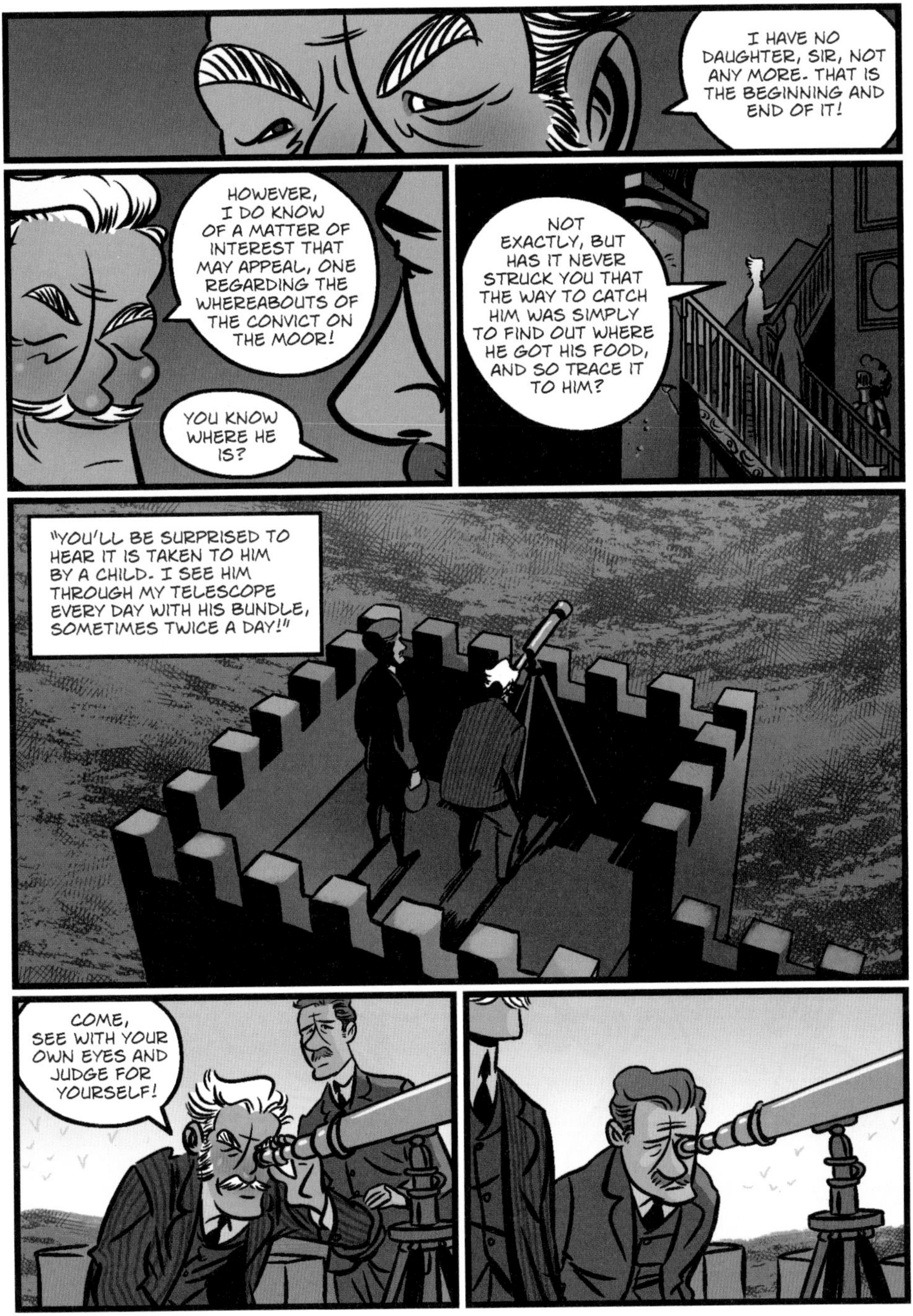
I HAVE NO DAUGHTER, SIR, NOT ANY MORE. THAT IS THE BEGINNING AND END OF IT!
HOWEVER, I DO KNOW OF A MATTER OF INTEREST THAT MAY APPEAL, ONE REGARDING THE WHEREABOUTS OF THE CONVICT ON THE MOOR!
YOU KNOW WHERE HE IS?
NOT EXACTLY, BUT HAS IT NEVER STRUCK YOU THAT THE WAY TO CATCH HIM WAS SIMPLY TO FIND OUT WHERE HE GOT HIS FOOD, AND SO TRACE IT TO HIM?
"YOU'LL BE SURPRISED TO HEAR IT IS TAKEN TO HIM BY A CHILD. I SEE HIM THROUGH MY TELESCOPE EVERY DAY WITH HIS BUNDLE, SOMETIMES TWICE A DAY!"
COME, SEE WITH YOUR OWN EYES AND JUDGE FOR YOURSELF!

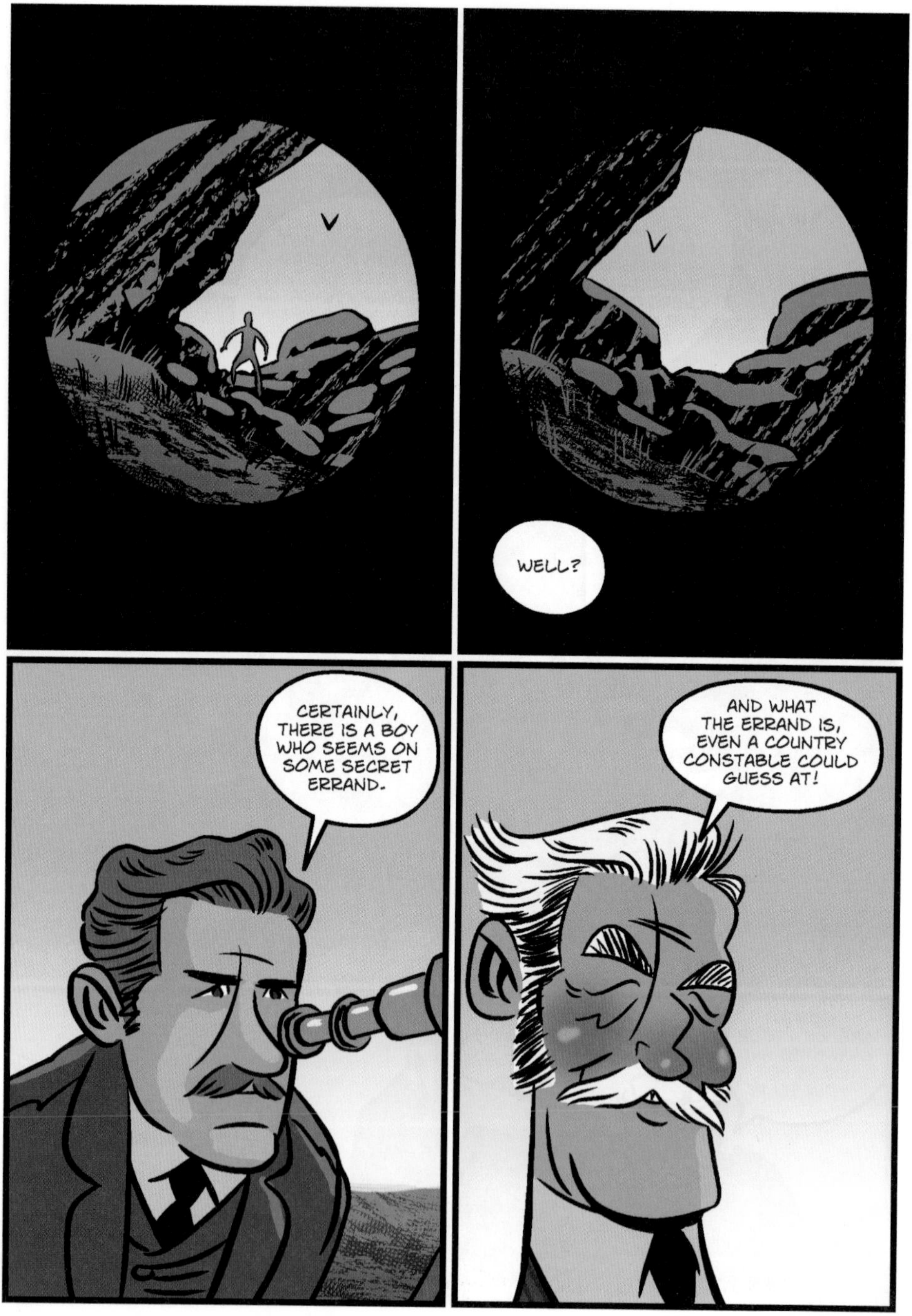
WELL?
CERTAINLY, THERE IS A BOY WHO SEEMS ON SOME SECRET ERRAND.
AND WHAT THE ERRAND IS, EVEN A COUNTRY CONSTABLE COULD GUESS AT!

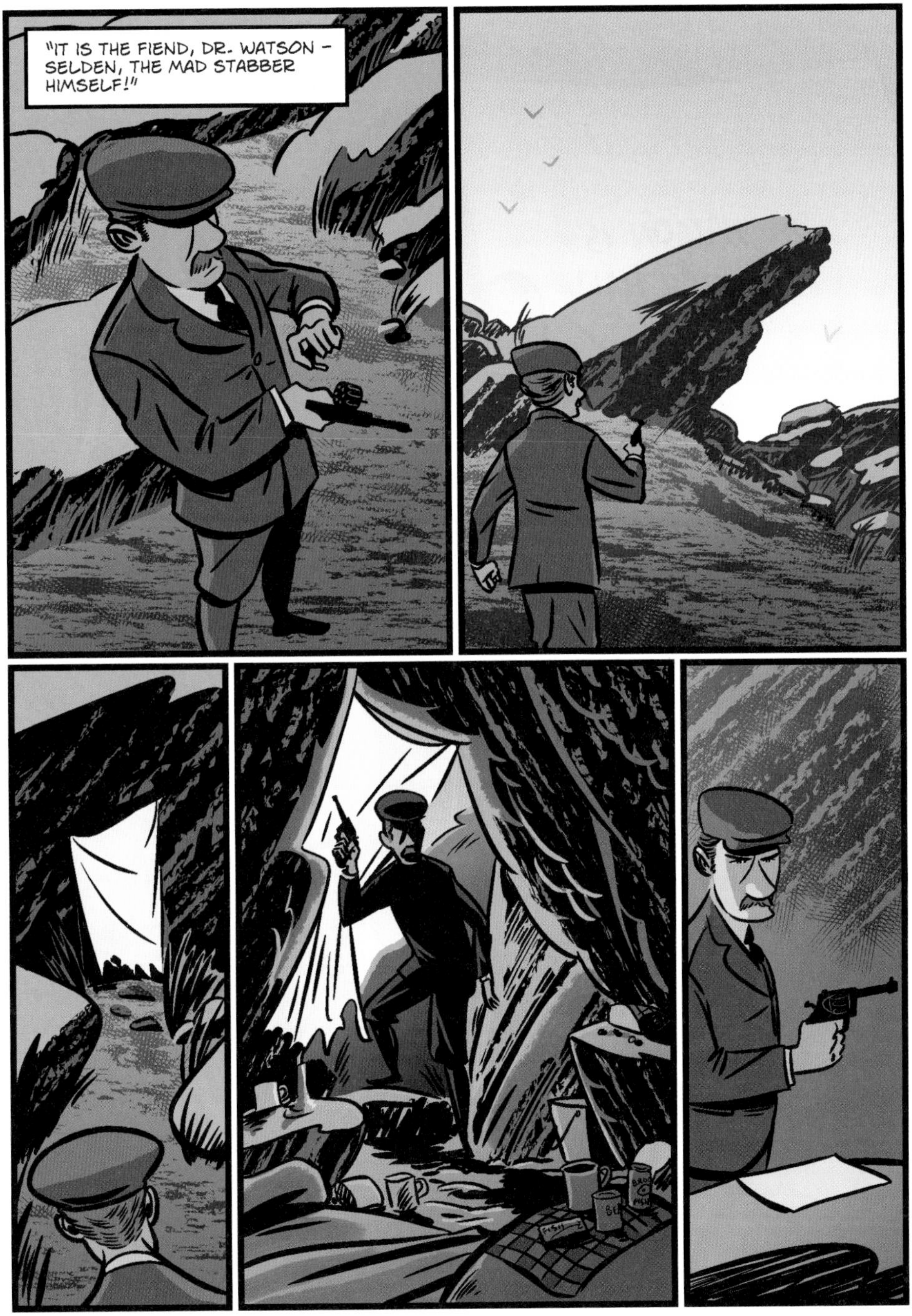
"IT IS THE FIEND, DR. WATSON - SELDEN, THE MAD STABBER HIMSELF!"

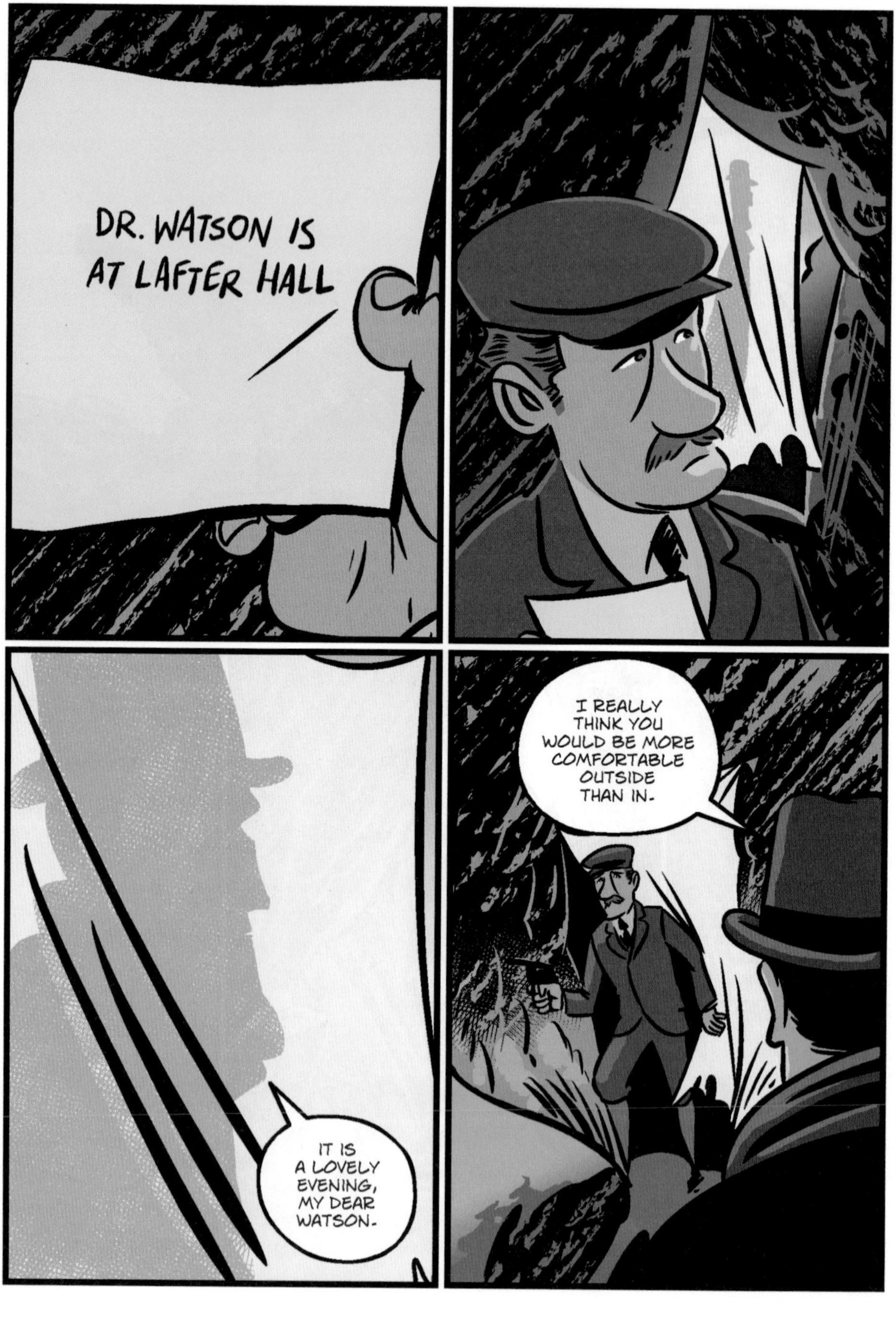
DR. WATSON IS AT LAFTER HALL
IT IS A LOVELY EVENING, MY DEAR WATSON.
I REALLY THINK YOU WOULD BE MORE COMFORTABLE OUTSIDE THAN IN.

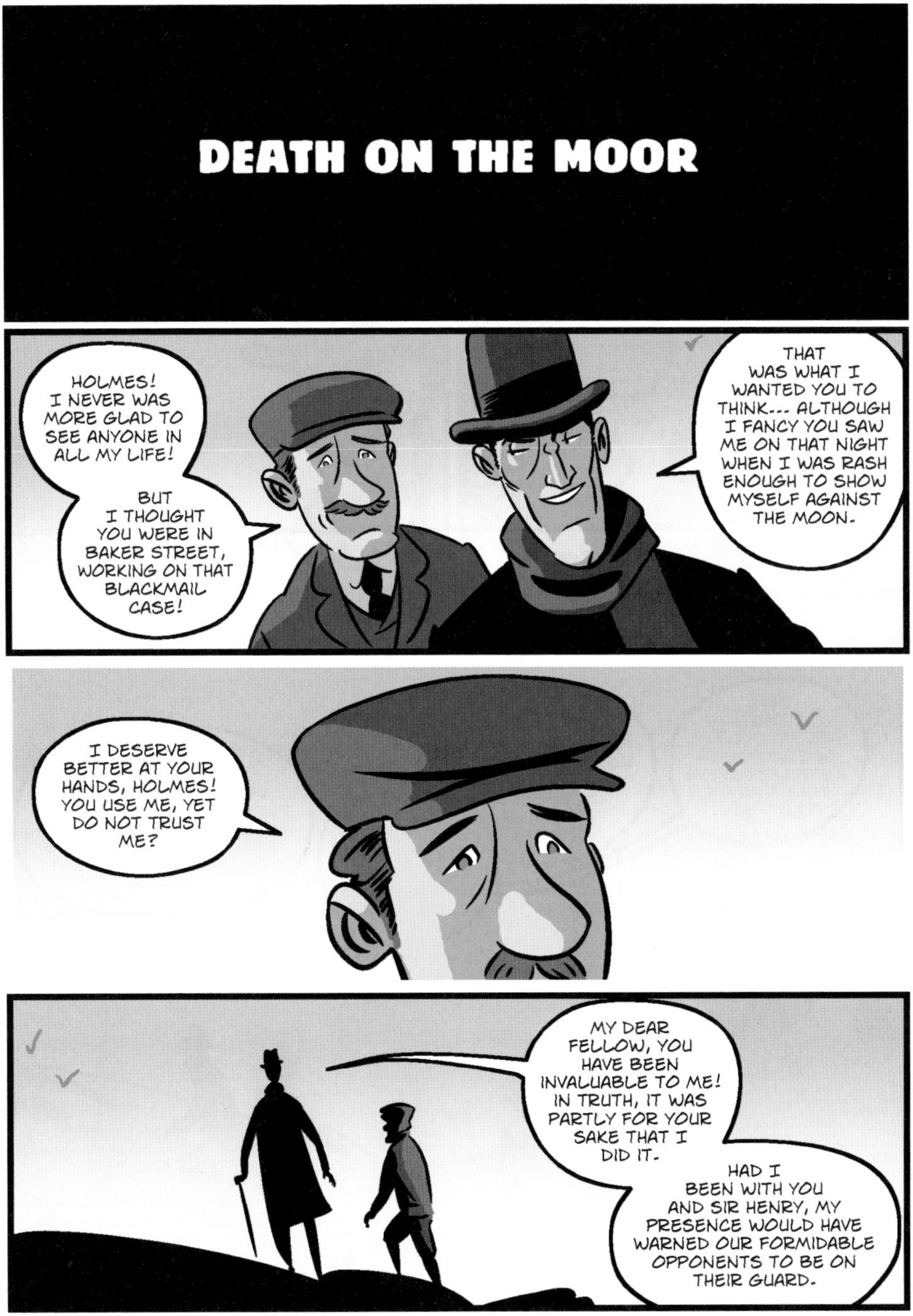
DEATH ON THE MOOR
HOLMES! I NEVER WAS MORE GLAD TO SEE ANYONE IN ALL MY LIFE!
BUT I THOUGHT YOU WERE IN BAKER STREET, WORKING ON THAT BLACKMAIL CASE!
THAT WAS WHAT I WANTED YOU TO THINK... ALTHOUGH I FANCY YOU SAW ME ON THAT NIGHT WHEN I WAS RASH ENOUGH TO SHOW MYSELF AGAINST THE MOON.
I DESERVE BETTER AT YOUR HANDS, HOLMES! YOU USE ME, YET DO NOT TRUST ME?
MY DEAR FELLOW, YOU HAVE BEEN INVALUABLE TO ME! IN TRUTH, IT WAS PARTLY FOR YOUR SAKE THAT I DID IT.
HAD I BEEN WITH YOU AND SIR HENRY, MY PRESENCE WOULD HAVE WARNED OUR FORMIDABLE OPPONENTS TO BE ON THEIR GUARD.

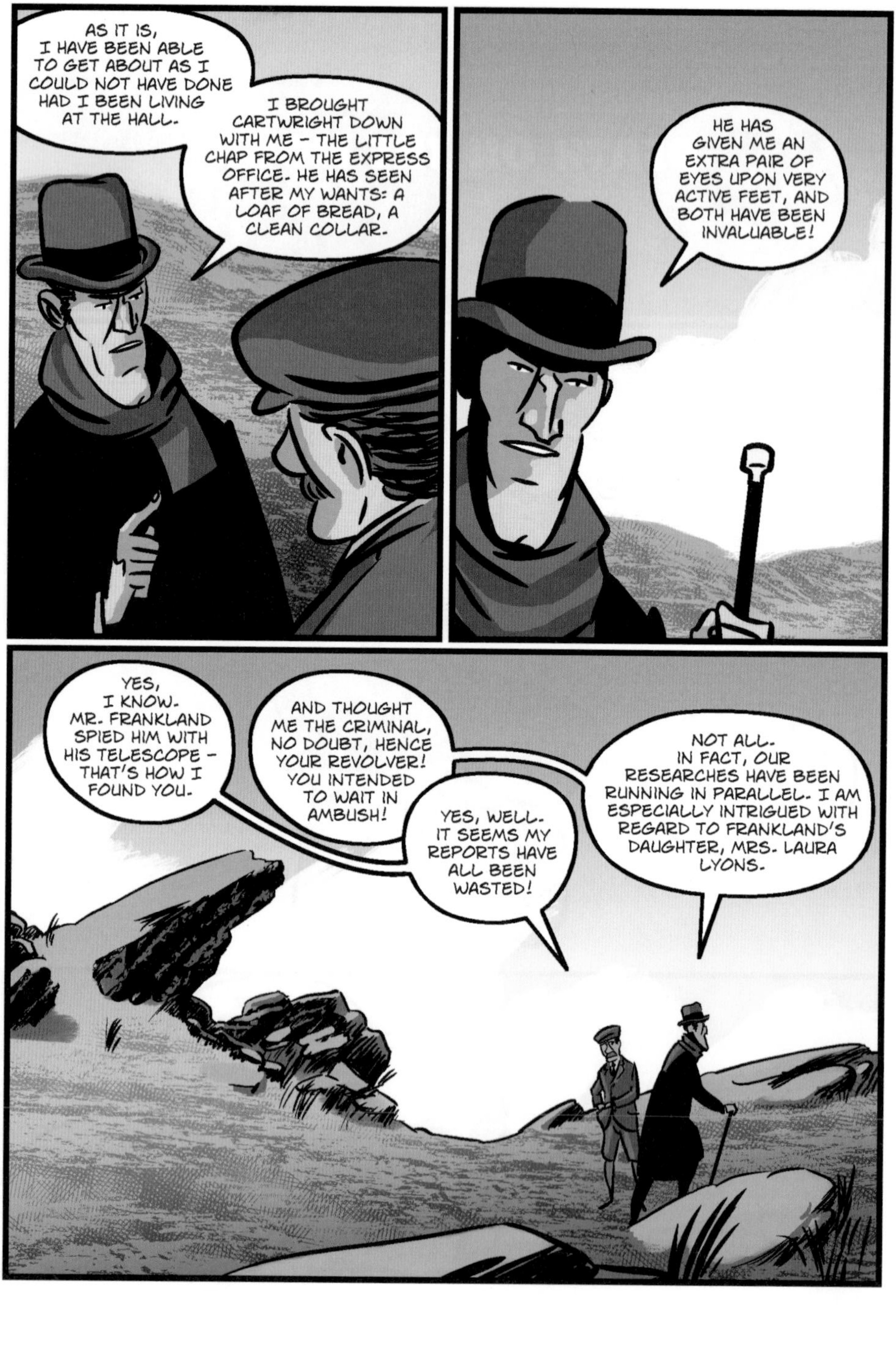
AS IT IS, I HAVE BEEN ABLE TO GET ABOUT AS I COULD NOT HAVE DONE HAD I BEEN LIVING AT THE HALL.
I BROUGHT CARTWRIGHT DOWN WITH ME – THE LITTLE CHAP FROM THE EXPRESS OFFICE. HE HAS SEEN AFTER MY WANTS: A LOAF OF BREAD, A CLEAN COLLAR.
HE HAS GIVEN ME AN EXTRA PAIR OF EYES UPON VERY ACTIVE FEET, AND BOTH HAVE BEEN INVALUABLE!
YES, I KNOW. MR. FRANKLAND SPIED HIM WITH HIS TELESCOPE – THAT'S HOW I FOUND YOU.
AND THOUGHT ME THE CRIMINAL, NO DOUBT, HENCE YOUR REVOLVER! YOU INTENDED TO WAIT IN AMBUSH!
YES, WELL. IT SEEMS MY REPORTS HAVE ALL BEEN WASTED!
NOT ALL. IN FACT, OUR RESEARCHES HAVE BEEN RUNNING IN PARALLEL. I AM ESPECIALLY INTRIGUED WITH REGARD TO FRANKLAND'S DAUGHTER, MRS. LAURA LYONS.

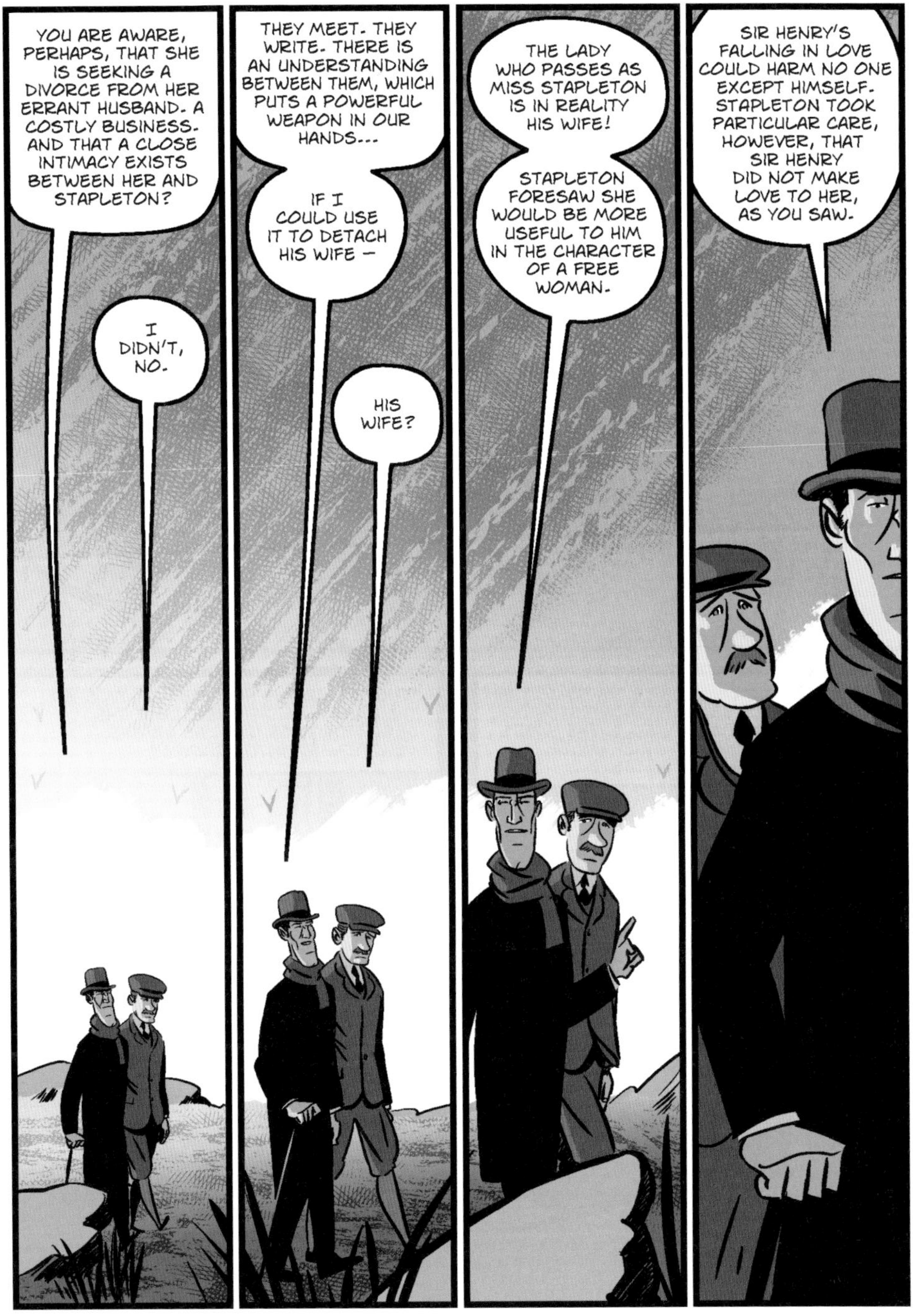
YOU ARE AWARE, PERHAPS, THAT SHE IS SEEKING A DIVORCE FROM HER ERRANT HUSBAND. A COSTLY BUSINESS. AND THAT A CLOSE INTIMACY EXISTS BETWEEN HER AND STAPLETON?
I DIDN'T, NO.
THEY MEET. THEY WRITE. THERE IS AN UNDERSTANDING BETWEEN THEM, WHICH PUTS A POWERFUL WEAPON IN OUR HANDS...
IF I COULD USE IT TO DETACH HIS WIFE —
HIS WIFE?
THE LADY WHO PASSES AS MISS STAPLETON IS IN REALITY HIS WIFE!
STAPLETON FORESAW SHE WOULD BE MORE USEFUL TO HIM IN THE CHARACTER OF A FREE WOMAN.
SIR HENRY'S FALLING IN LOVE COULD HARM NO ONE EXCEPT HIMSELF. STAPLETON TOOK PARTICULAR CARE, HOWEVER, THAT SIR HENRY DID NOT MAKE LOVE TO HER, AS YOU SAW.

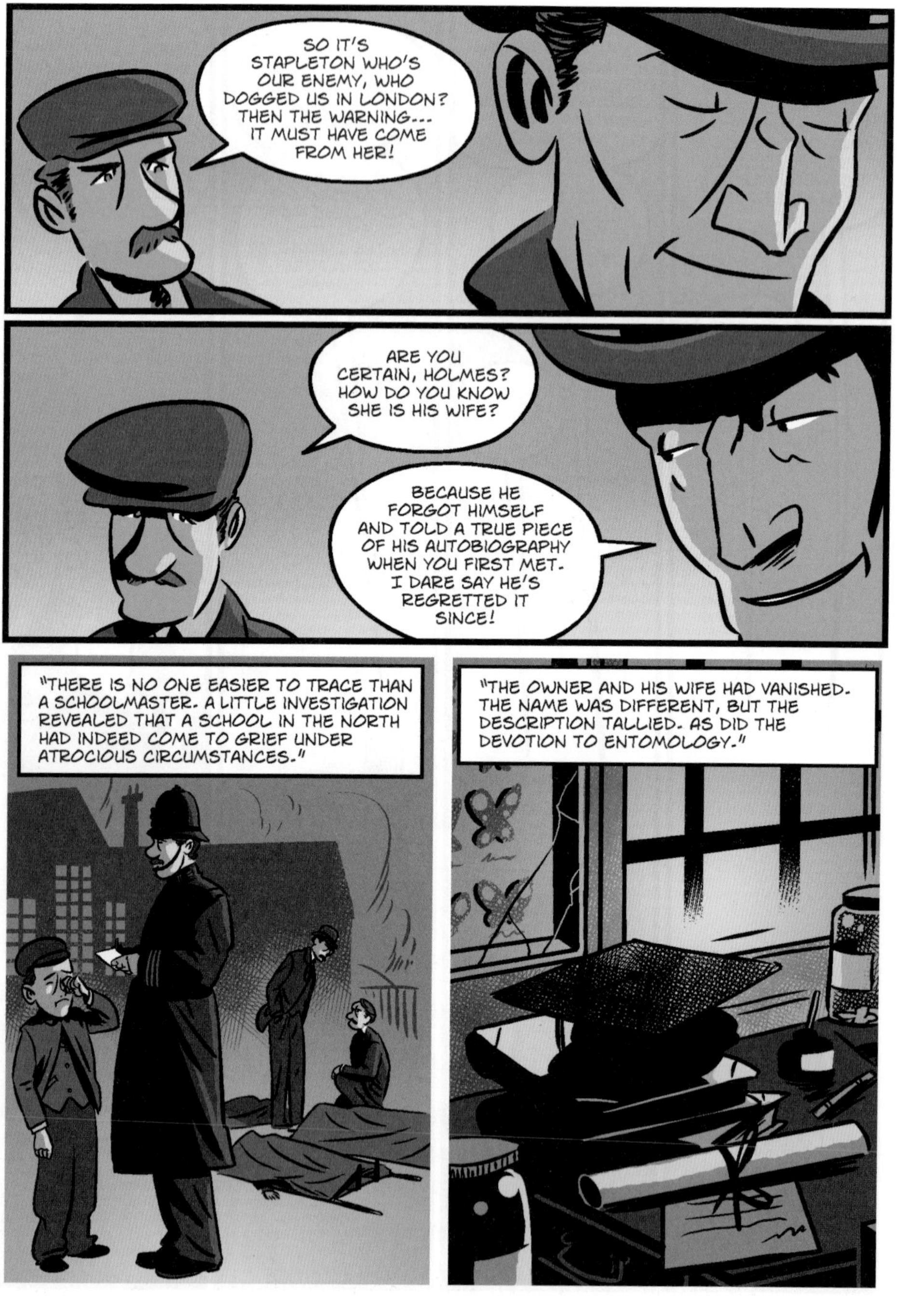
SO IT'S STAPLETON WHO'S OUR ENEMY, WHO DOGGED US IN LONDON? THEN THE WARNING... IT MUST HAVE COME FROM HER!
ARE YOU CERTAIN, HOLMES? HOW DO YOU KNOW SHE IS HIS WIFE?
BECAUSE HE FORGOT HIMSELF AND TOLD A TRUE PIECE OF HIS AUTOBIOGRAPHY WHEN YOU FIRST MET. I DARE SAY HE'S REGRETTED IT SINCE!
"THERE IS NO ONE EASIER TO TRACE THAN A SCHOOLMASTER. A LITTLE INVESTIGATION REVEALED THAT A SCHOOL IN THE NORTH HAD INDEED COME TO GRIEF UNDER ATROCIOUS CIRCUMSTANCES."
"THE OWNER AND HIS WIFE HAD VANISHED. THE NAME WAS DIFFERENT, BUT THE DESCRIPTION TALLIED. AS DID THE DEVOTION TO ENTOMOLOGY."

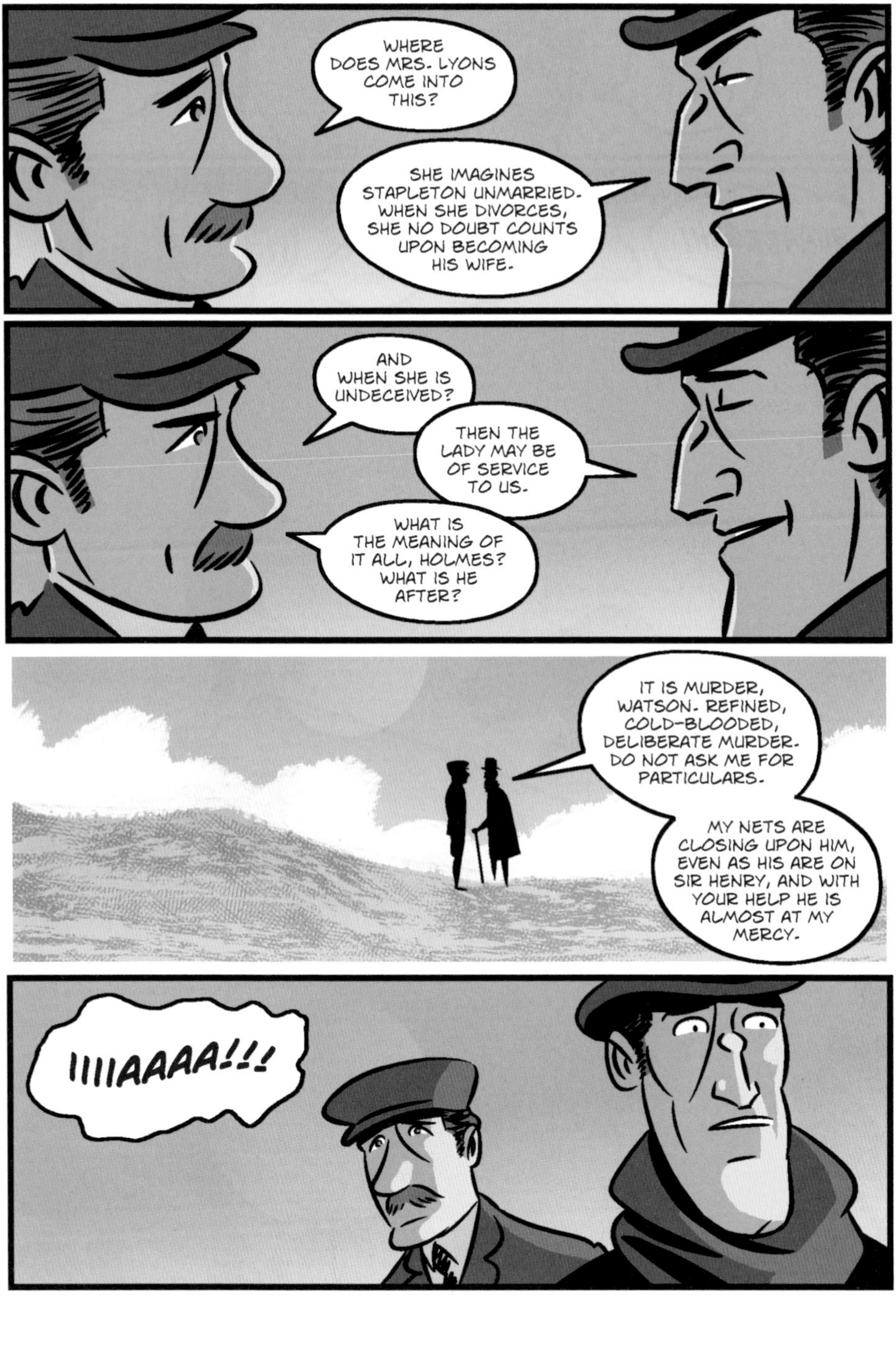
WHERE DOES MRS. LYONS COME INTO THIS?
SHE IMAGINES STAPLETON UNMARRIED. WHEN SHE DIVORCES, SHE NO DOUBT COUNTS UPON BECOMING HIS WIFE.
AND WHEN SHE IS UNDECEIVED?
THEN THE LADY MAY BE OF SERVICE TO US.
WHAT IS THE MEANING OF IT ALL, HOLMES? WHAT IS HE AFTER?
IT IS MURDER, WATSON. REFINED, COLD-BLOODED, DELIBERATE MURDER. DO NOT ASK ME FOR PARTICULARS.
MY NETS ARE CLOSING UPON HIM, EVEN AS HIS ARE ON SIR HENRY, AND WITH YOUR HELP HE IS ALMOST AT MY MERCY.
IIIIAAAA!!!

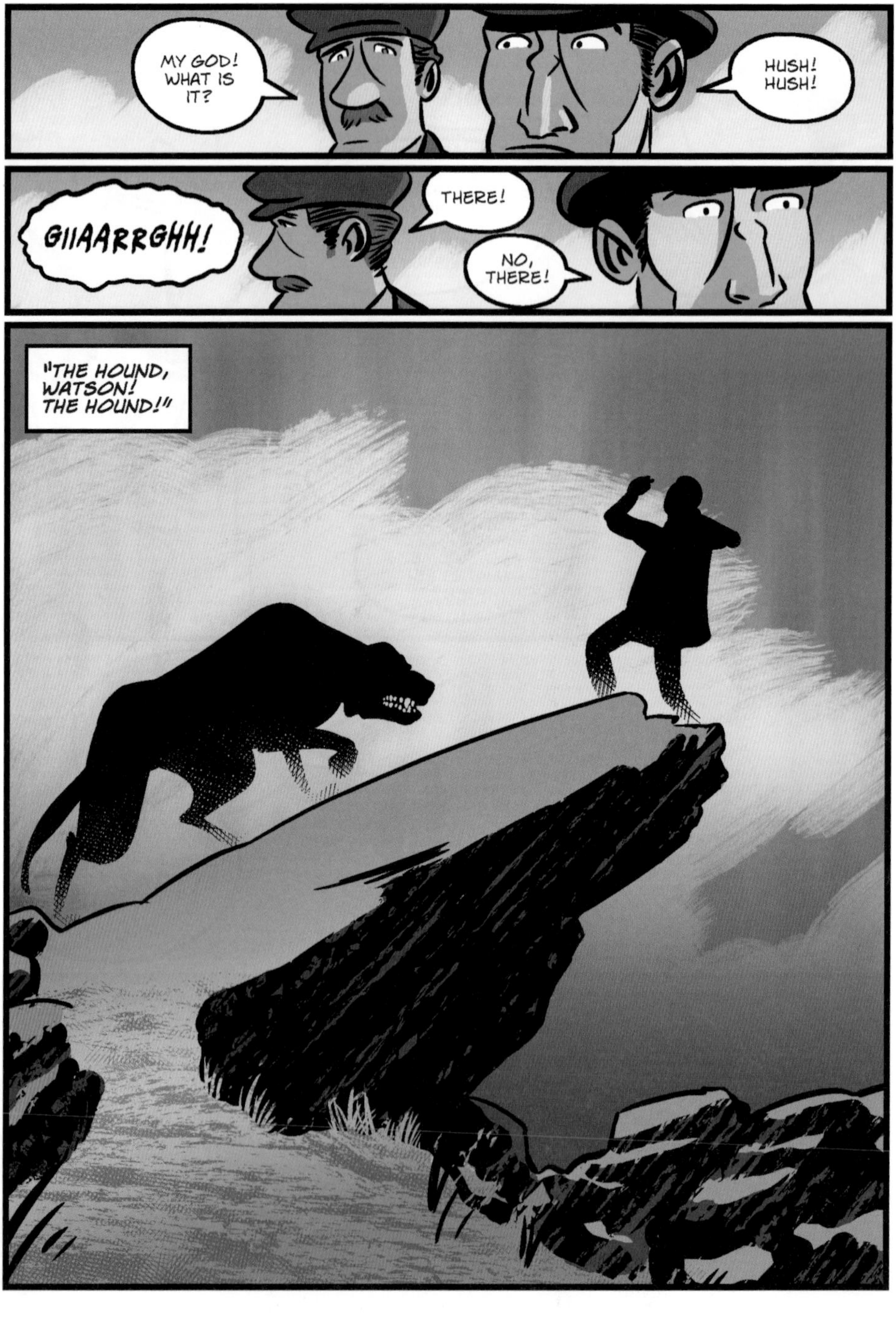
MY GOD! WHAT IS IT?
HUSH! HUSH!
GIIAARRGHH!
THERE!
NO, THERE!
"THE HOUND, WATSON! THE HOUND!"

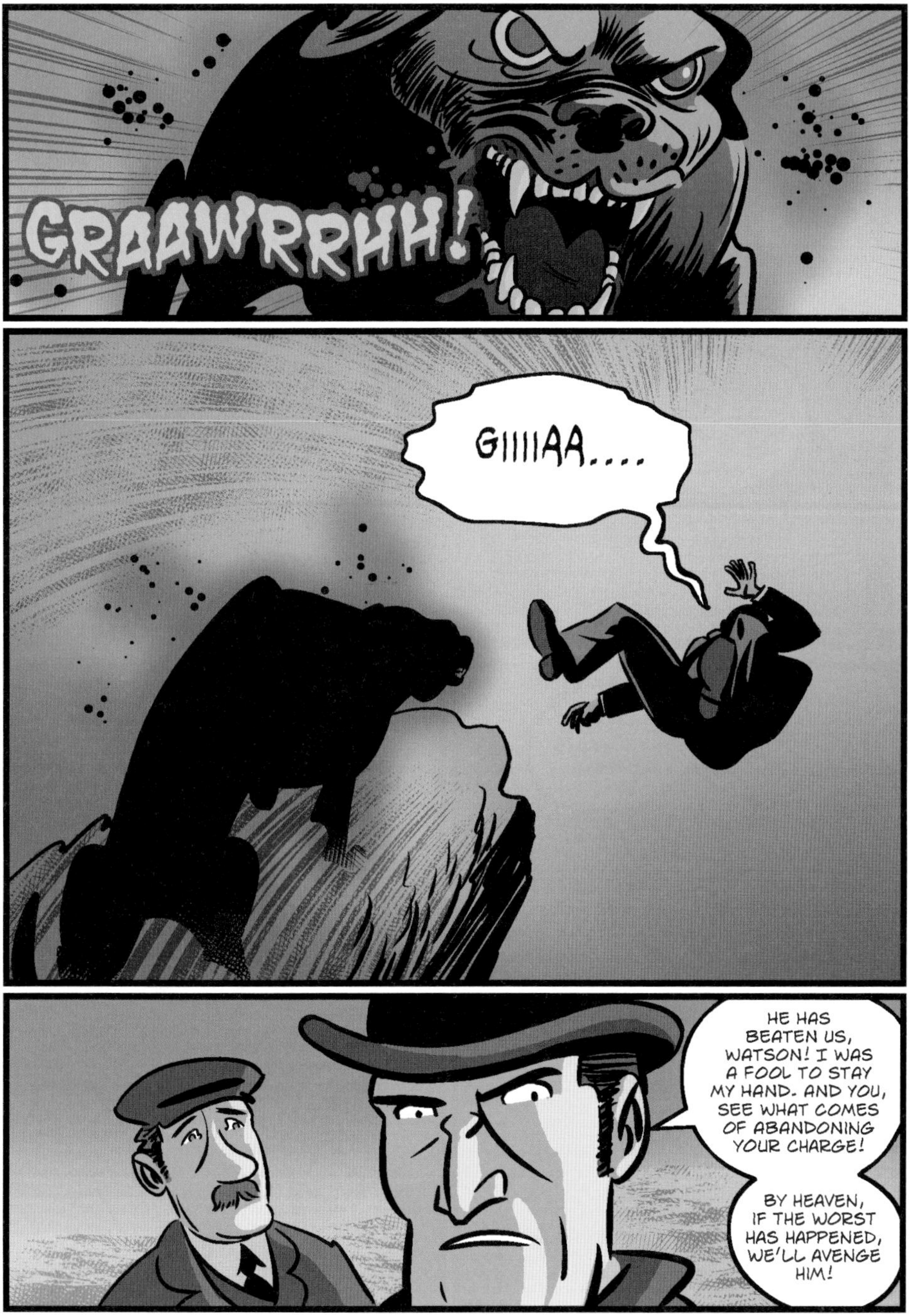
GRAAWRRHH!
GIIIIAA....
HE HAS BEATEN US, WATSON! I WAS A FOOL TO STAY MY HAND. AND YOU, SEE WHAT COMES OF ABANDONING YOUR CHARGE!
BY HEAVEN, IF THE WORST HAS HAPPENED, WE'LL AVENGE HIM!

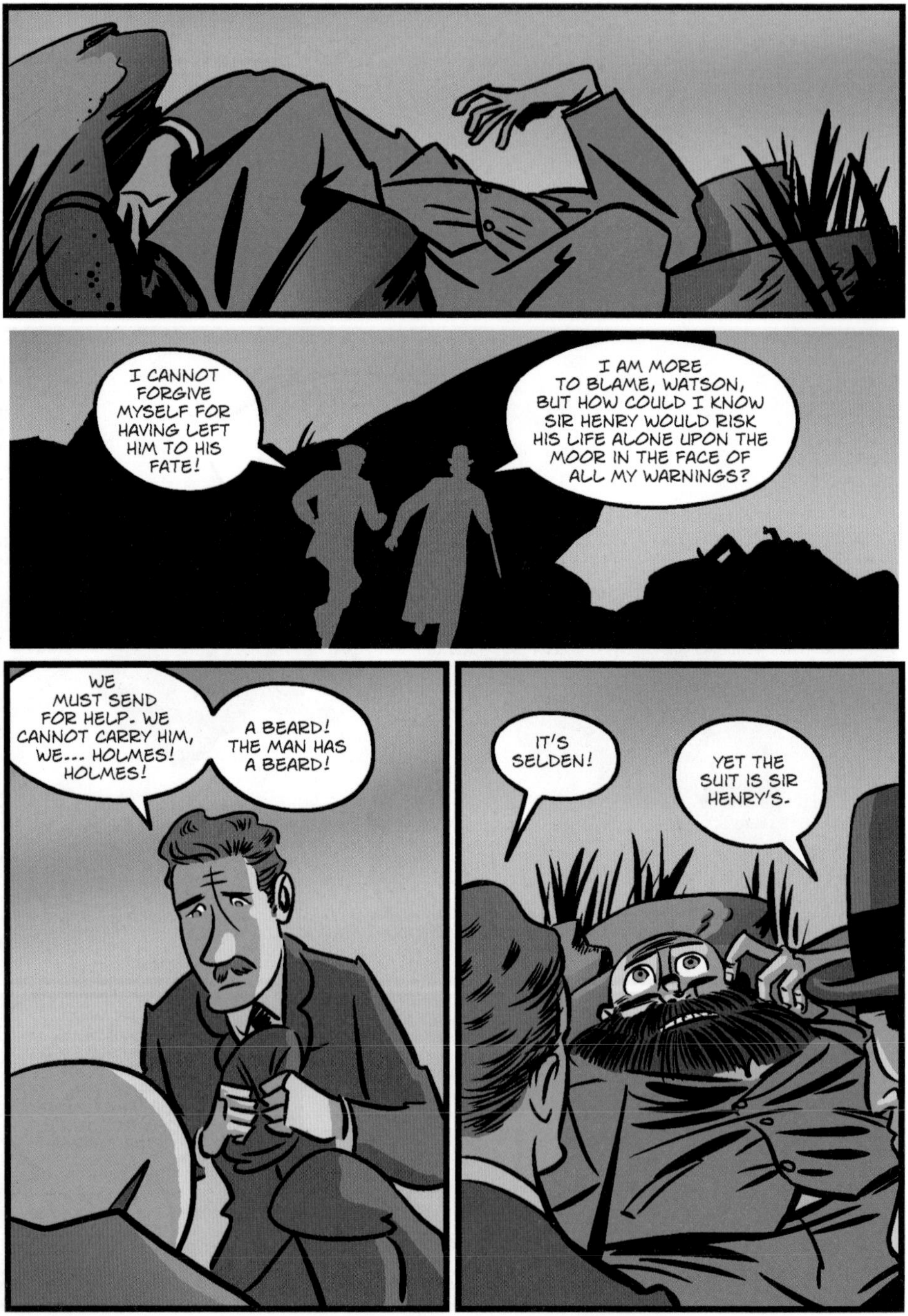
I CANNOT FORGIVE MYSELF FOR HAVING LEFT HIM TO HIS FATE!
I AM MORE TO BLAME, WATSON, BUT HOW COULD I KNOW SIR HENRY WOULD RISK HIS LIFE ALONE UPON THE MOOR IN THE FACE OF ALL MY WARNINGS?
WE MUST SEND FOR HELP. WE CANNOT CARRY HIM, WE... HOLMES! HOLMES!
A BEARD! THE MAN HAS A BEARD!
IT'S SELDEN!
YET THE SUIT IS SIR HENRY'S.

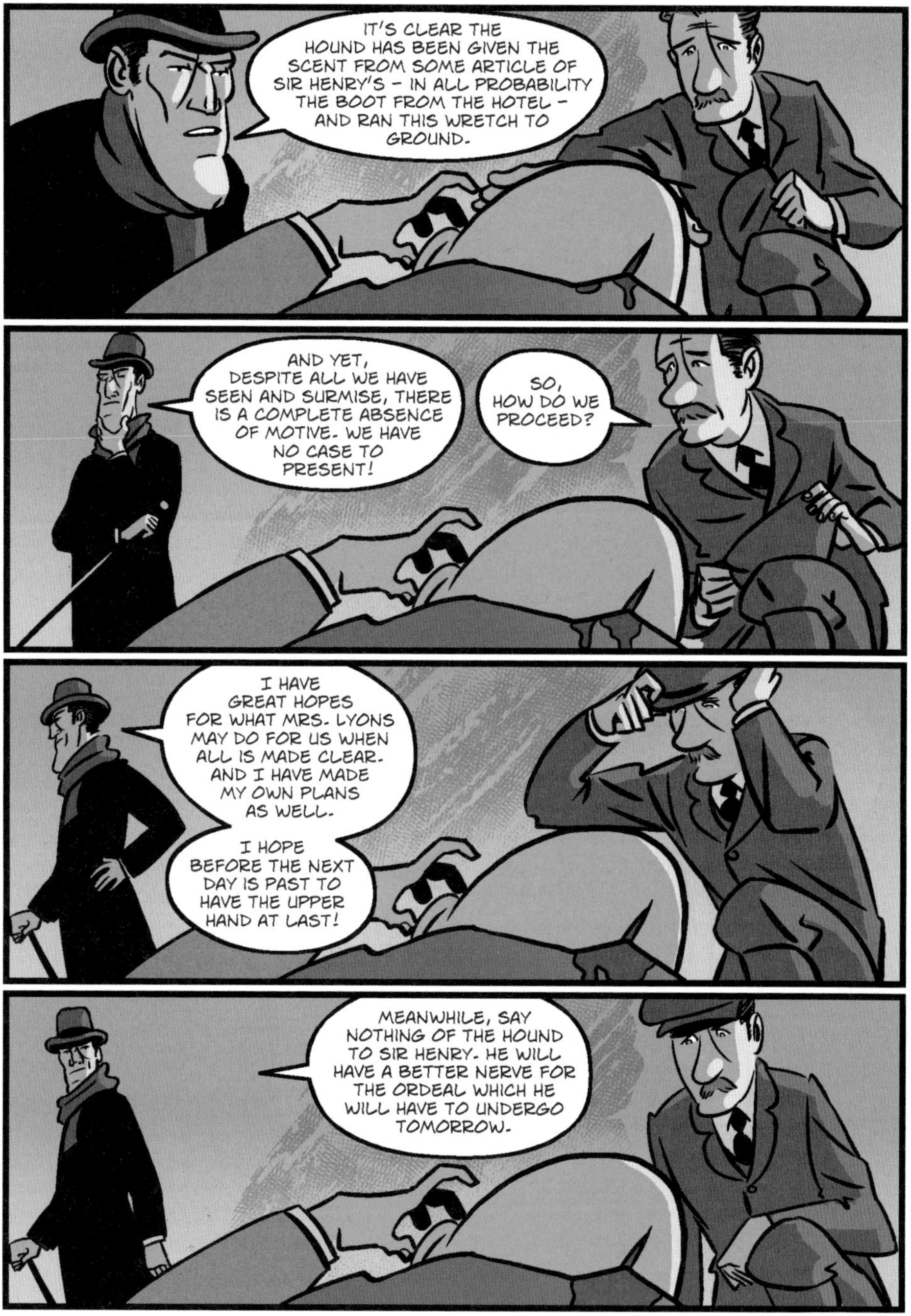
IT'S CLEAR THE HOUND HAS BEEN GIVEN THE SCENT FROM SOME ARTICLE OF SIR HENRY'S – IN ALL PROBABILITY THE BOOT FROM THE HOTEL – AND RAN THIS WRETCH TO GROUND.
AND YET, DESPITE ALL WE HAVE SEEN AND SURMISE, THERE IS A COMPLETE ABSENCE OF MOTIVE. WE HAVE NO CASE TO PRESENT!
SO, HOW DO WE PROCEED?
I HAVE GREAT HOPES FOR WHAT MRS. LYONS MAY DO FOR US WHEN ALL IS MADE CLEAR. AND I HAVE MADE MY OWN PLANS AS WELL.
I HOPE BEFORE THE NEXT DAY IS PAST TO HAVE THE UPPER HAND AT LAST!
MEANWHILE, SAY NOTHING OF THE HOUND TO SIR HENRY. HE WILL HAVE A BETTER NERVE FOR THE ORDEAL WHICH HE WILL HAVE TO UNDERGO TOMORROW.

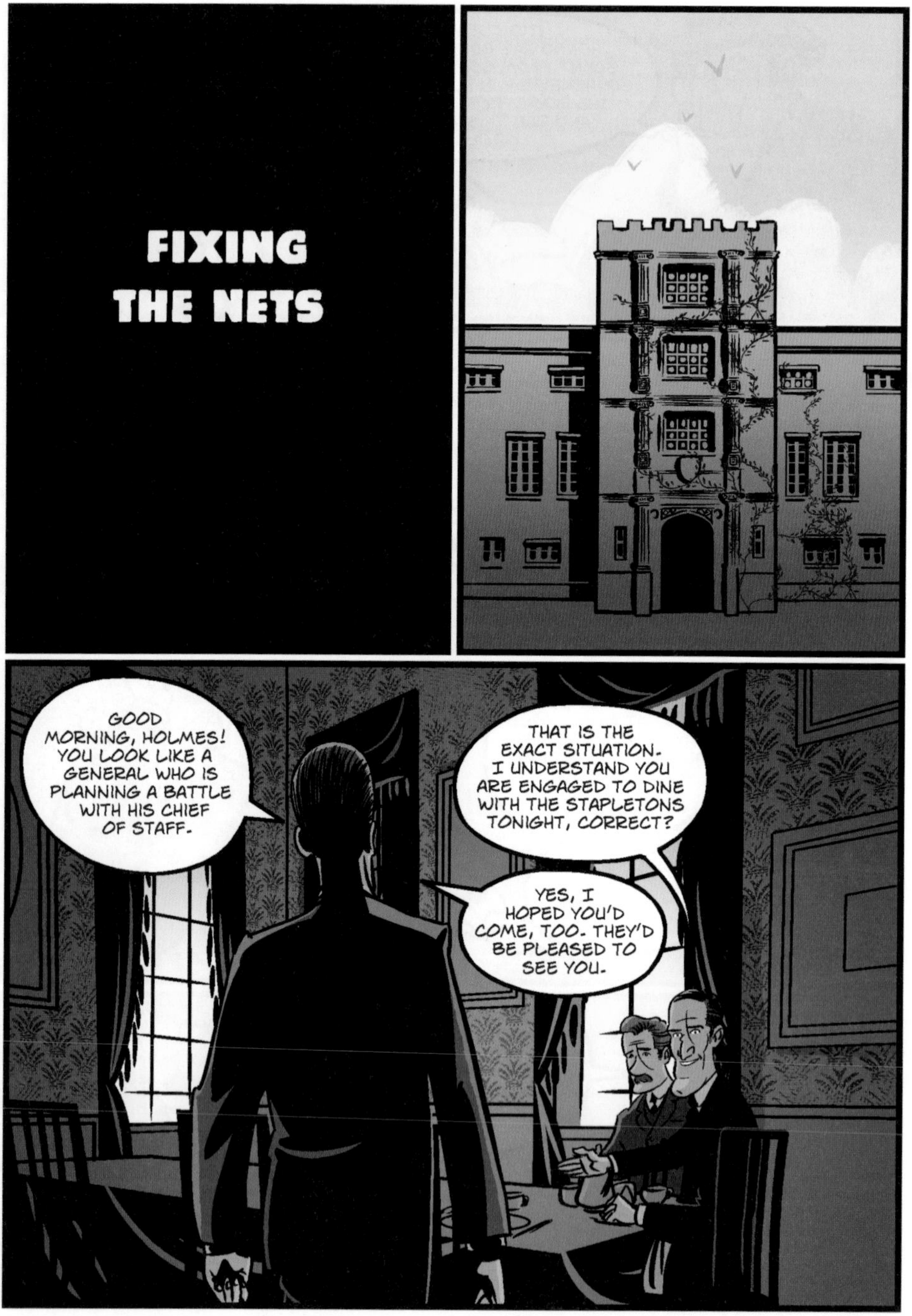
FIXING THE NETS
GOOD MORNING, HOLMES! YOU LOOK LIKE A GENERAL WHO IS PLANNING A BATTLE WITH HIS CHIEF OF STAFF.
THAT IS THE EXACT SITUATION. I UNDERSTAND YOU ARE ENGAGED TO DINE WITH THE STAPLETONS TONIGHT, CORRECT?
YES, I HOPED YOU'D COME, TOO. THEY'D BE PLEASED TO SEE YOU.

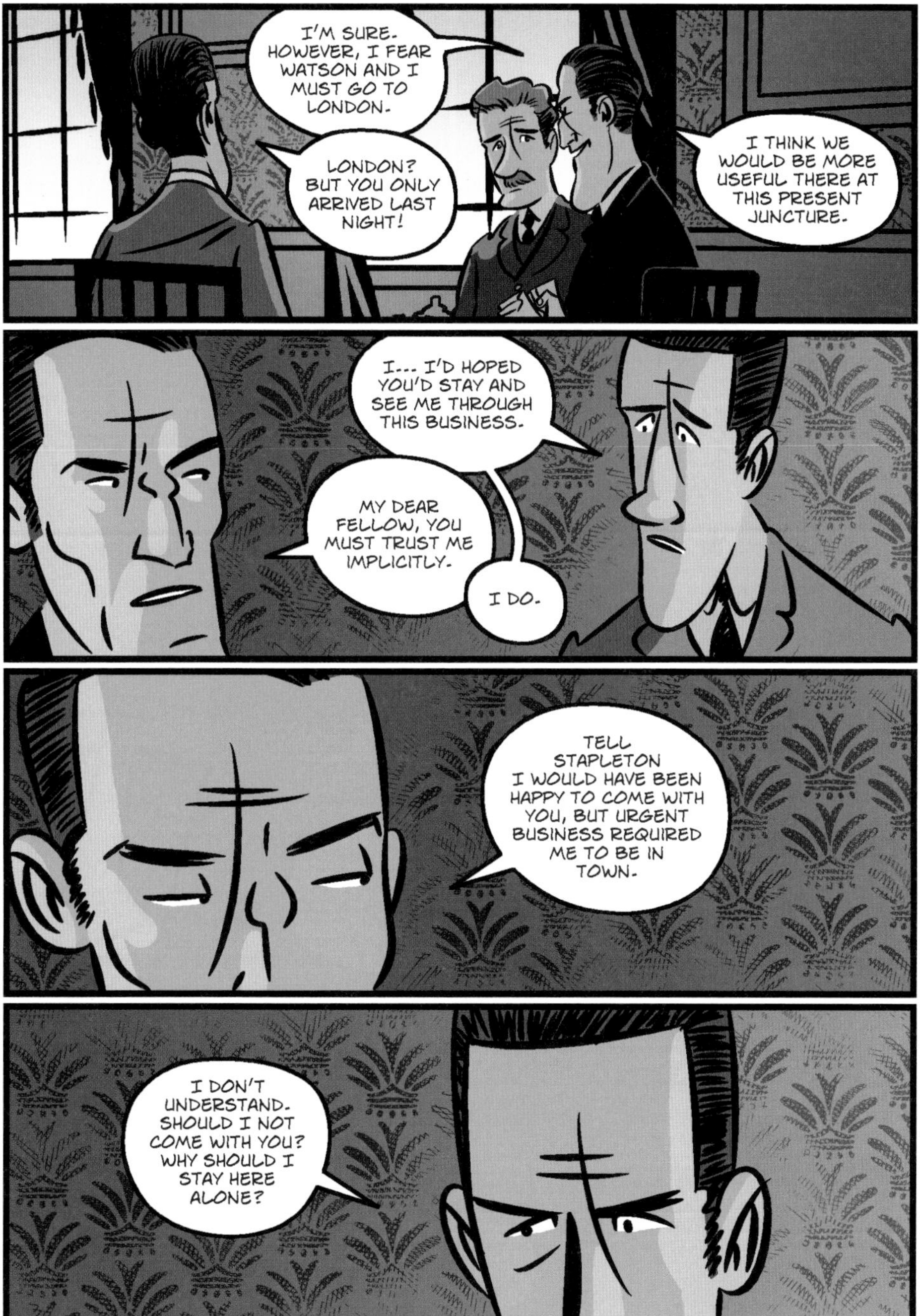
I'M SURE. HOWEVER, I FEAR WATSON AND I MUST GO TO LONDON.
LONDON? BUT YOU ONLY ARRIVED LAST NIGHT!
I THINK WE WOULD BE MORE USEFUL THERE AT THIS PRESENT JUNCTURE.
I... I'D HOPED YOU'D STAY AND SEE ME THROUGH THIS BUSINESS.
MY DEAR FELLOW, YOU MUST TRUST ME IMPLICITLY.
I DO.
TELL STAPLETON I WOULD HAVE BEEN HAPPY TO COME WITH YOU, BUT URGENT BUSINESS REQUIRED ME TO BE IN TOWN.
I DON'T UNDERSTAND. SHOULD I NOT COME WITH YOU? WHY SHOULD I STAY HERE ALONE?

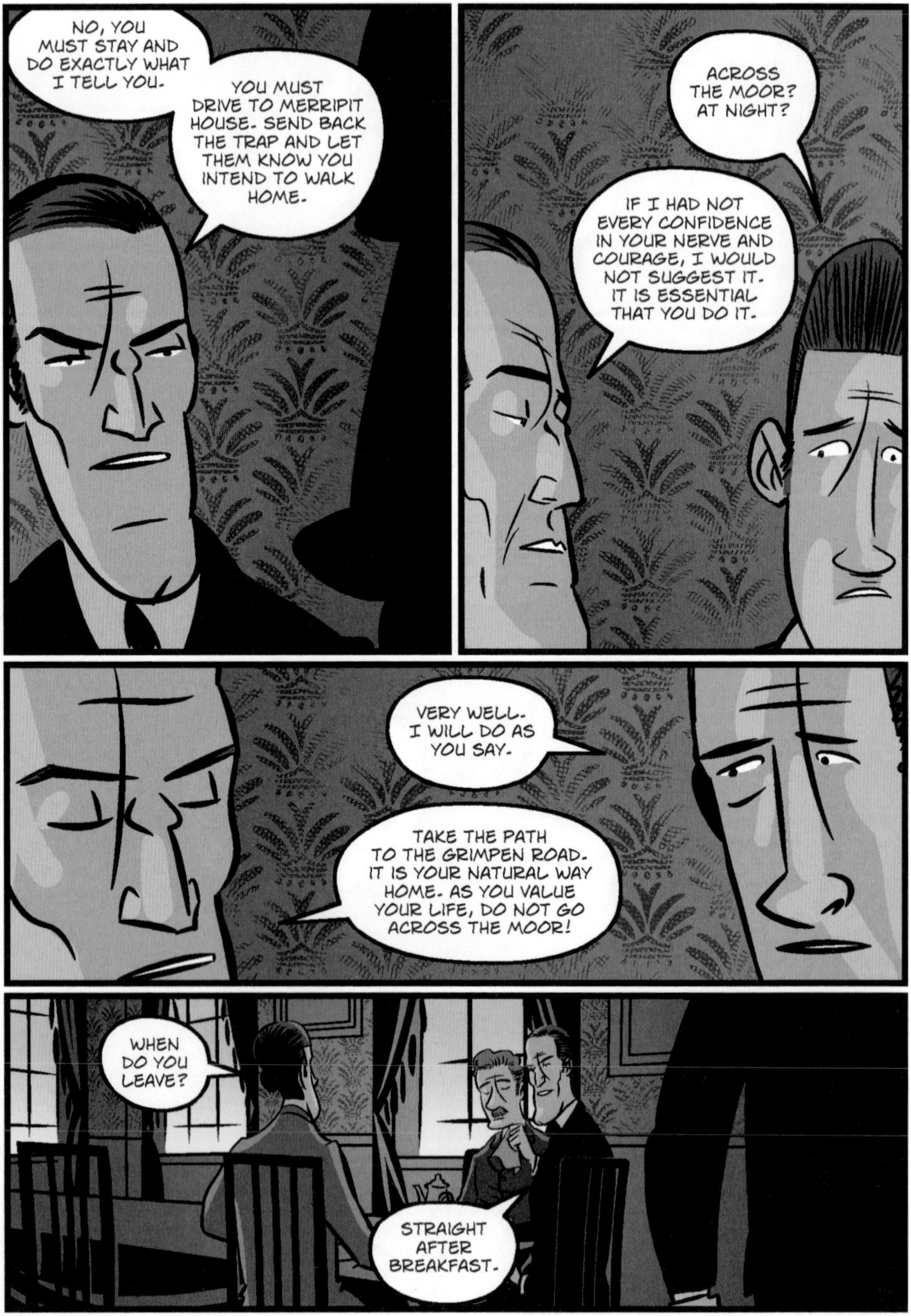
NO, YOU MUST STAY AND DO EXACTLY WHAT I TELL YOU.
YOU MUST DRIVE TO MERRIPIT HOUSE. SEND BACK THE TRAP AND LET THEM KNOW YOU INTEND TO WALK HOME.
ACROSS THE MOOR? AT NIGHT?
IF I HAD NOT EVERY CONFIDENCE IN YOUR NERVE AND COURAGE, I WOULD NOT SUGGEST IT. IT IS ESSENTIAL THAT YOU DO IT.
VERY WELL. I WILL DO AS YOU SAY.
TAKE THE PATH TO THE GRIMPEN ROAD. IT IS YOUR NATURAL WAY HOME. AS YOU VALUE YOUR LIFE, DO NOT GO ACROSS THE MOOR!
WHEN DO YOU LEAVE?
STRAIGHT AFTER BREAKFAST.

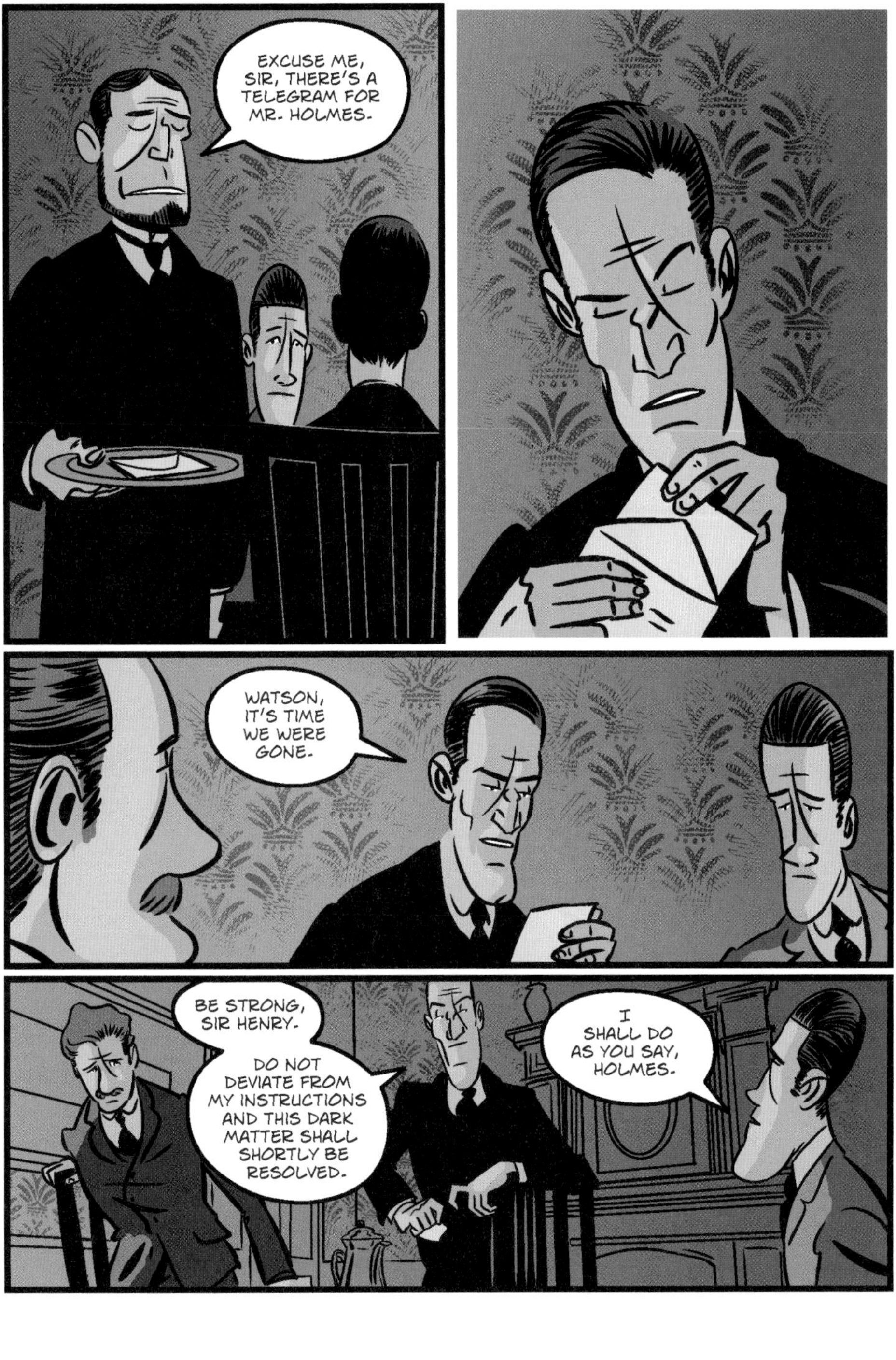
EXCUSE ME, SIR, THERE'S A TELEGRAM FOR MR. HOLMES.
WATSON, IT'S TIME WE WERE GONE.
BE STRONG, SIR HENRY.
DO NOT DEVIATE FROM MY INSTRUCTIONS AND THIS DARK MATTER SHALL SHORTLY BE RESOLVED.
I SHALL DO AS YOU SAY, HOLMES.

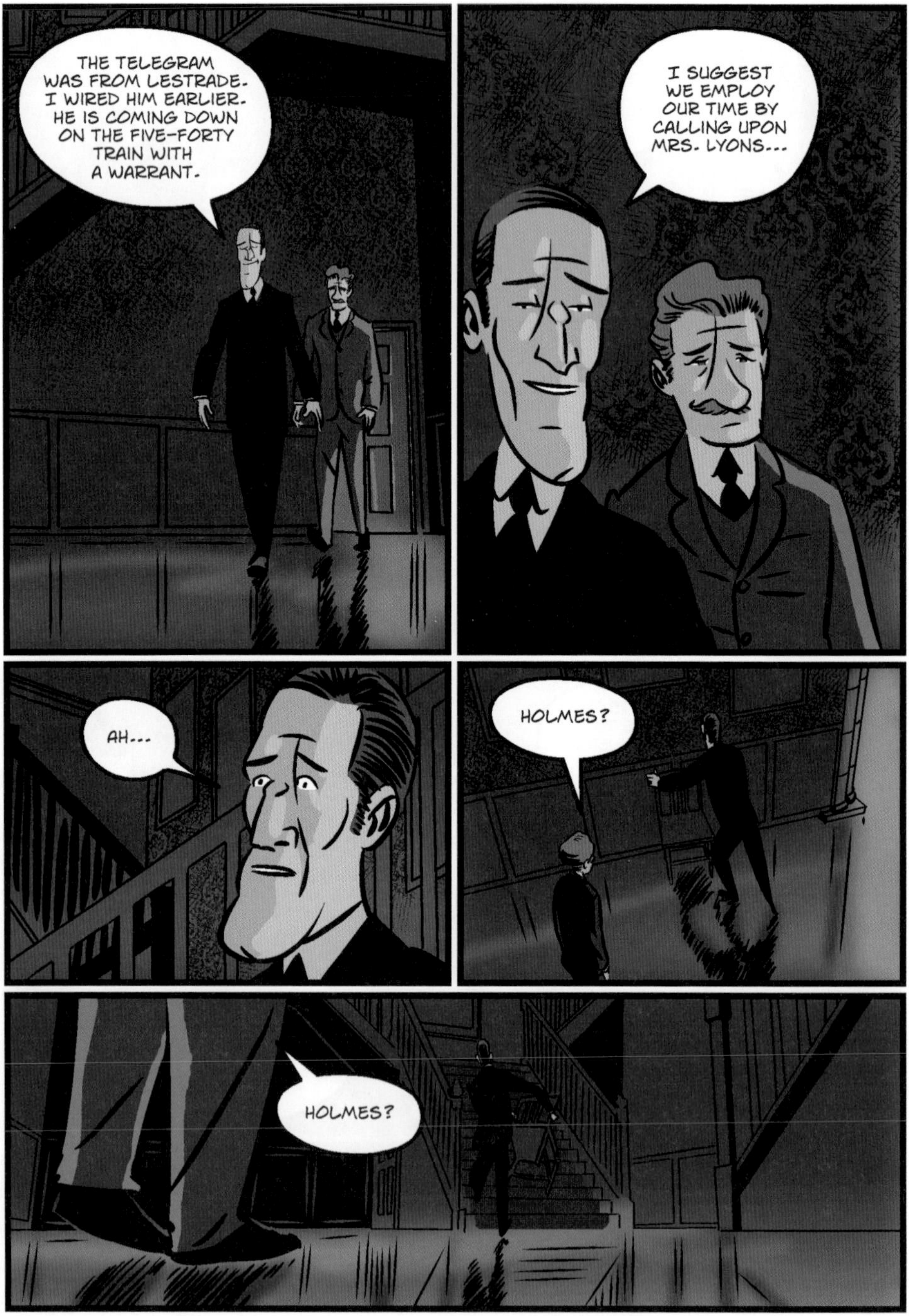
THE TELEGRAM WAS FROM LESTRADE. I WIRED HIM EARLIER. HE IS COMING DOWN ON THE FIVE-FORTY TRAIN WITH A WARRANT.
I SUGGEST WE EMPLOY OUR TIME BY CALLING UPON MRS. LYONS...
AH...
HOLMES?
HOLMES?

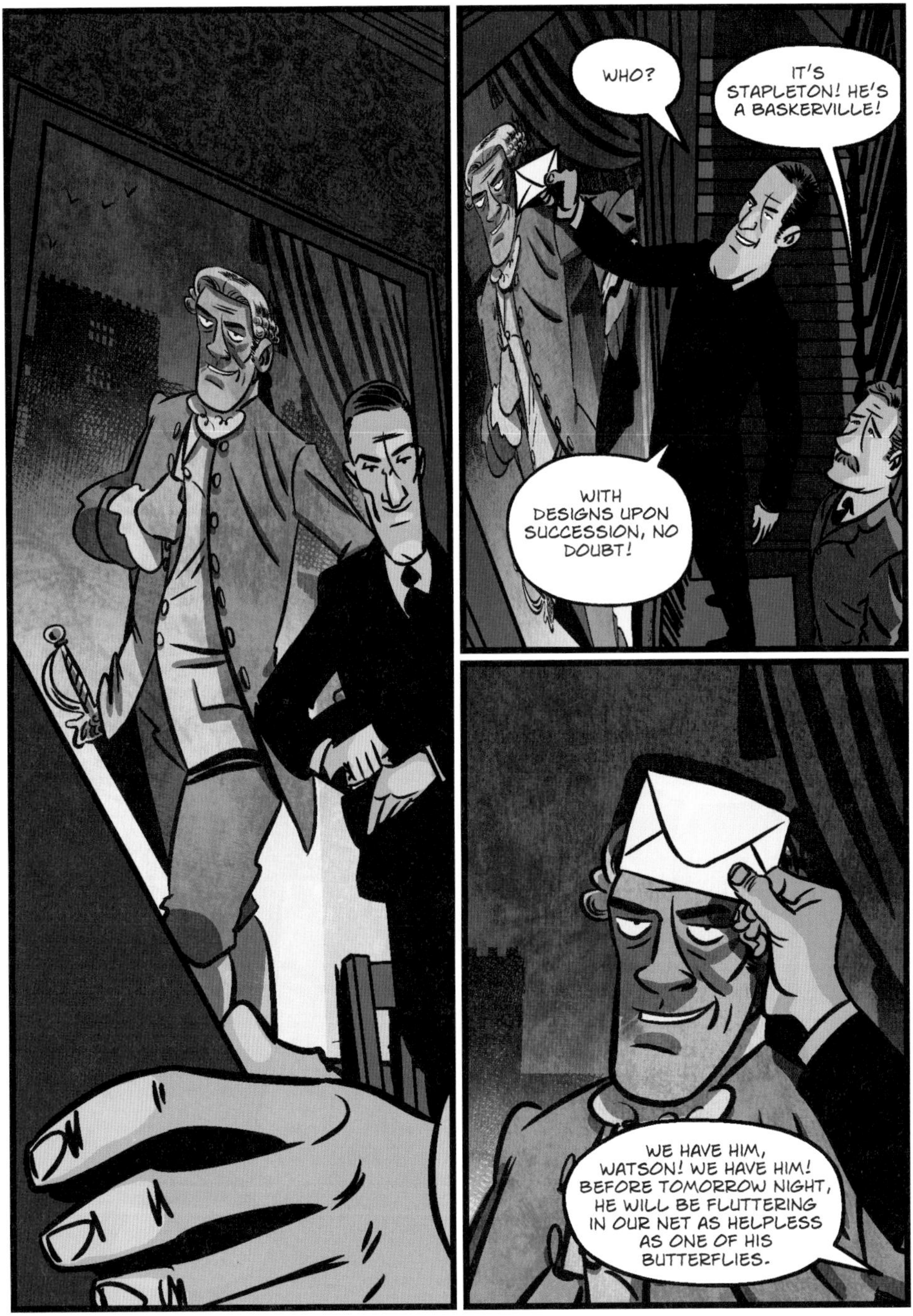
WHO?
IT'S STAPLETON! HE'S A BASKERVILLE!
WITH DESIGNS UPON SUCCESSION, NO DOUBT!
WE HAVE HIM, WATSON! WE HAVE HIM! BEFORE TOMORROW NIGHT, HE WILL BE FLUTTERING IN OUR NET AS HELPLESS AS ONE OF HIS BUTTERFLIES.

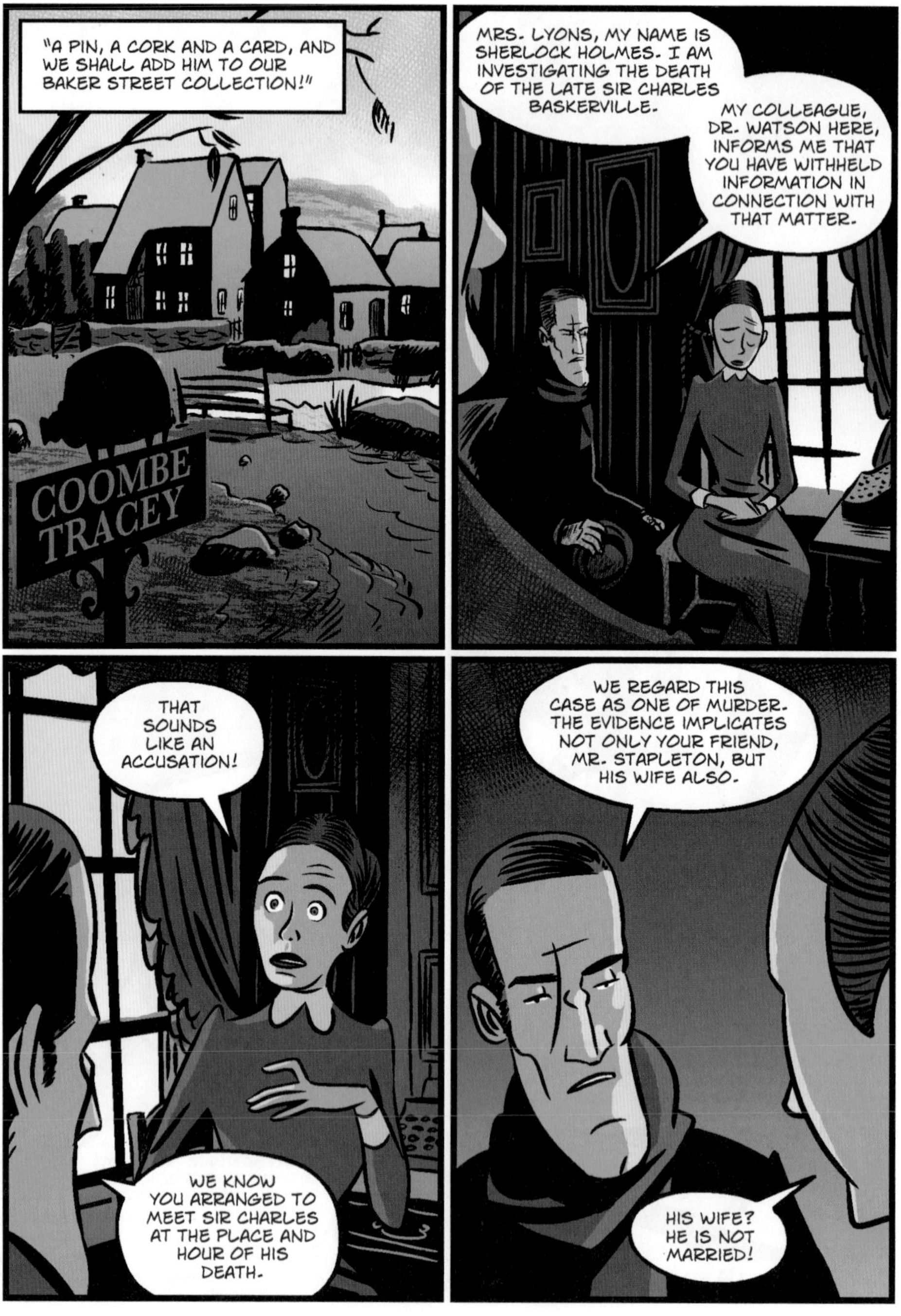
"A PIN, A CORK AND A CARD, AND WE SHALL ADD HIM TO OUR BAKER STREET COLLECTION!"
COOMBE TRACEY
MRS. LYONS, MY NAME IS SHERLOCK HOLMES. I AM INVESTIGATING THE DEATH OF THE LATE SIR CHARLES BASKERVILLE.
MY COLLEAGUE, DR. WATSON HERE, INFORMS ME THAT YOU HAVE WITHHELD INFORMATION IN CONNECTION WITH THAT MATTER.
THAT SOUNDS LIKE AN ACCUSATION!
WE KNOW YOU ARRANGED TO MEET SIR CHARLES AT THE PLACE AND HOUR OF HIS DEATH.
WE REGARD THIS CASE AS ONE OF MURDER. THE EVIDENCE IMPLICATES NOT ONLY YOUR FRIEND, MR. STAPLETON, BUT HIS WIFE ALSO.
HIS WIFE? HE IS NOT MARRIED!

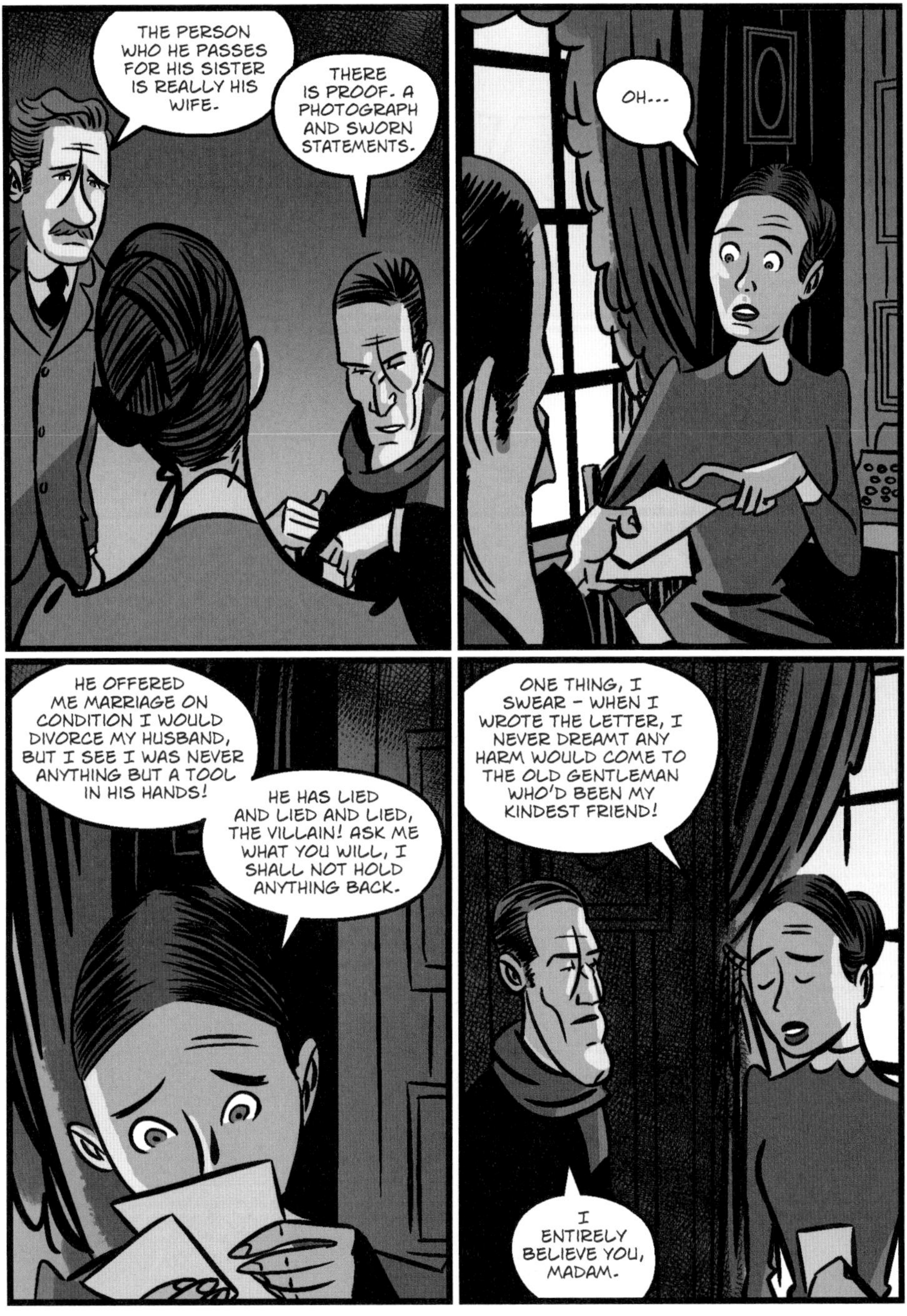
THE PERSON WHO HE PASSES FOR HIS SISTER IS REALLY HIS WIFE.
THERE IS PROOF. A PHOTOGRAPH AND SWORN STATEMENTS.
OH...
HE OFFERED ME MARRIAGE ON CONDITION I WOULD DIVORCE MY HUSBAND, BUT I SEE I WAS NEVER ANYTHING BUT A TOOL IN HIS HANDS!
HE HAS LIED AND LIED AND LIED, THE VILLAIN! ASK ME WHAT YOU WILL, I SHALL NOT HOLD ANYTHING BACK.
ONE THING, I SWEAR - WHEN I WROTE THE LETTER, I NEVER DREAMT ANY HARM WOULD COME TO THE OLD GENTLEMAN WHO'D BEEN MY KINDEST FRIEND!
I ENTIRELY BELIEVE YOU, MADAM.

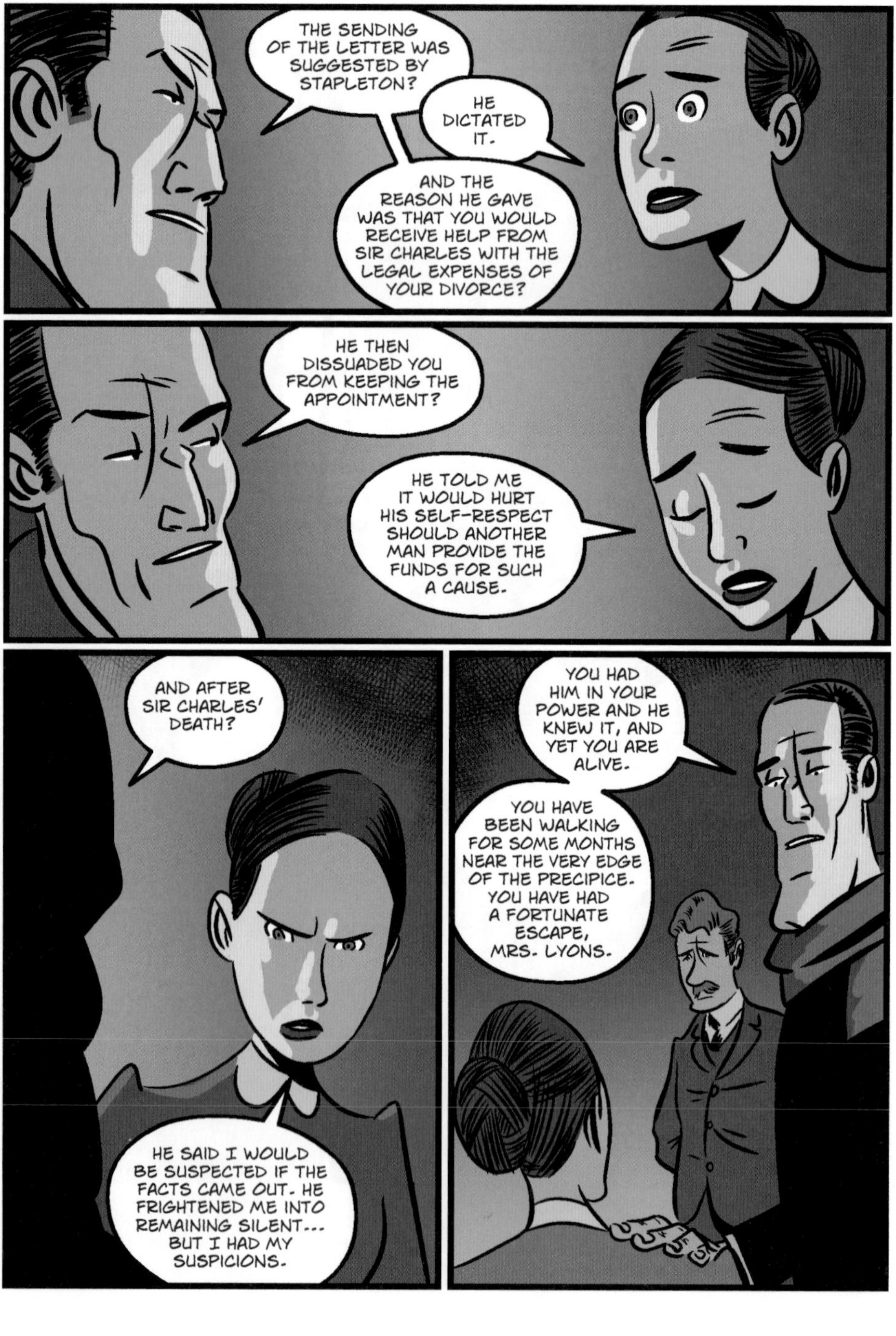
THE SENDING OF THE LETTER WAS SUGGESTED BY STAPLETON?
HE DICTATED IT.
AND THE REASON HE GAVE WAS THAT YOU WOULD RECEIVE HELP FROM SIR CHARLES WITH THE LEGAL EXPENSES OF YOUR DIVORCE?
HE THEN DISSUADED YOU FROM KEEPING THE APPOINTMENT?
HE TOLD ME IT WOULD HURT HIS SELF-RESPECT SHOULD ANOTHER MAN PROVIDE THE FUNDS FOR SUCH A CAUSE.
AND AFTER SIR CHARLES' DEATH?
HE SAID I WOULD BE SUSPECTED IF THE FACTS CAME OUT. HE FRIGHTENED ME INTO REMAINING SILENT... BUT I HAD MY SUSPICIONS.
YOU HAD HIM IN YOUR POWER AND HE KNEW IT, AND YET YOU ARE ALIVE.
YOU HAVE BEEN WALKING FOR SOME MONTHS NEAR THE VERY EDGE OF THE PRECIPICE. YOU HAVE HAD A FORTUNATE ESCAPE, MRS. LYONS.

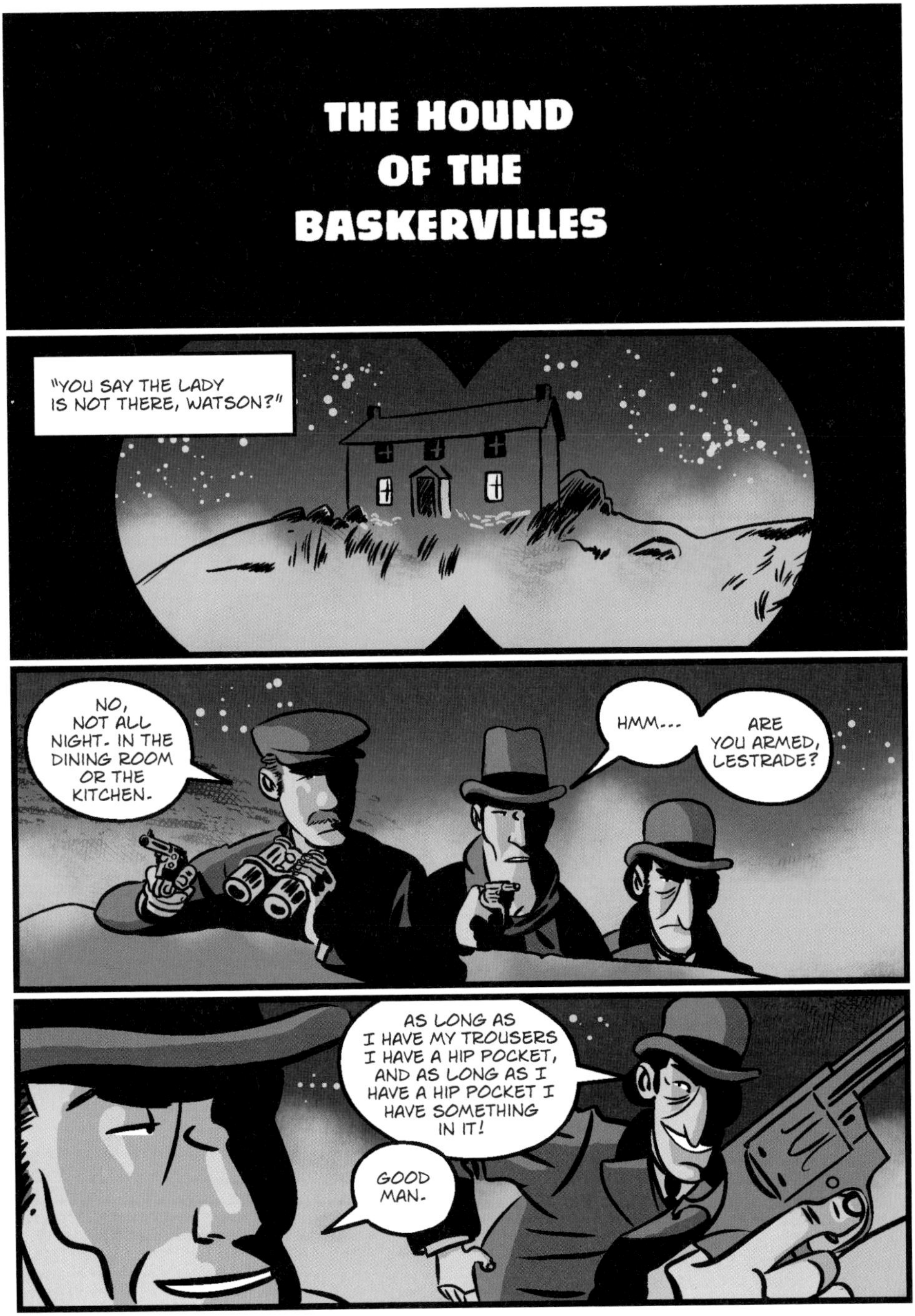
THE HOUND OF THE BASKERVILLES
"YOU SAY THE LADY IS NOT THERE, WATSON?"
NO, NOT ALL NIGHT. IN THE DINING ROOM OR THE KITCHEN.
HMM...
ARE YOU ARMED, LESTRADE?
AS LONG AS I HAVE MY TROUSERS I HAVE A HIP POCKET, AND AS LONG AS I HAVE A HIP POCKET I HAVE SOMETHING IN IT!
GOOD MAN.

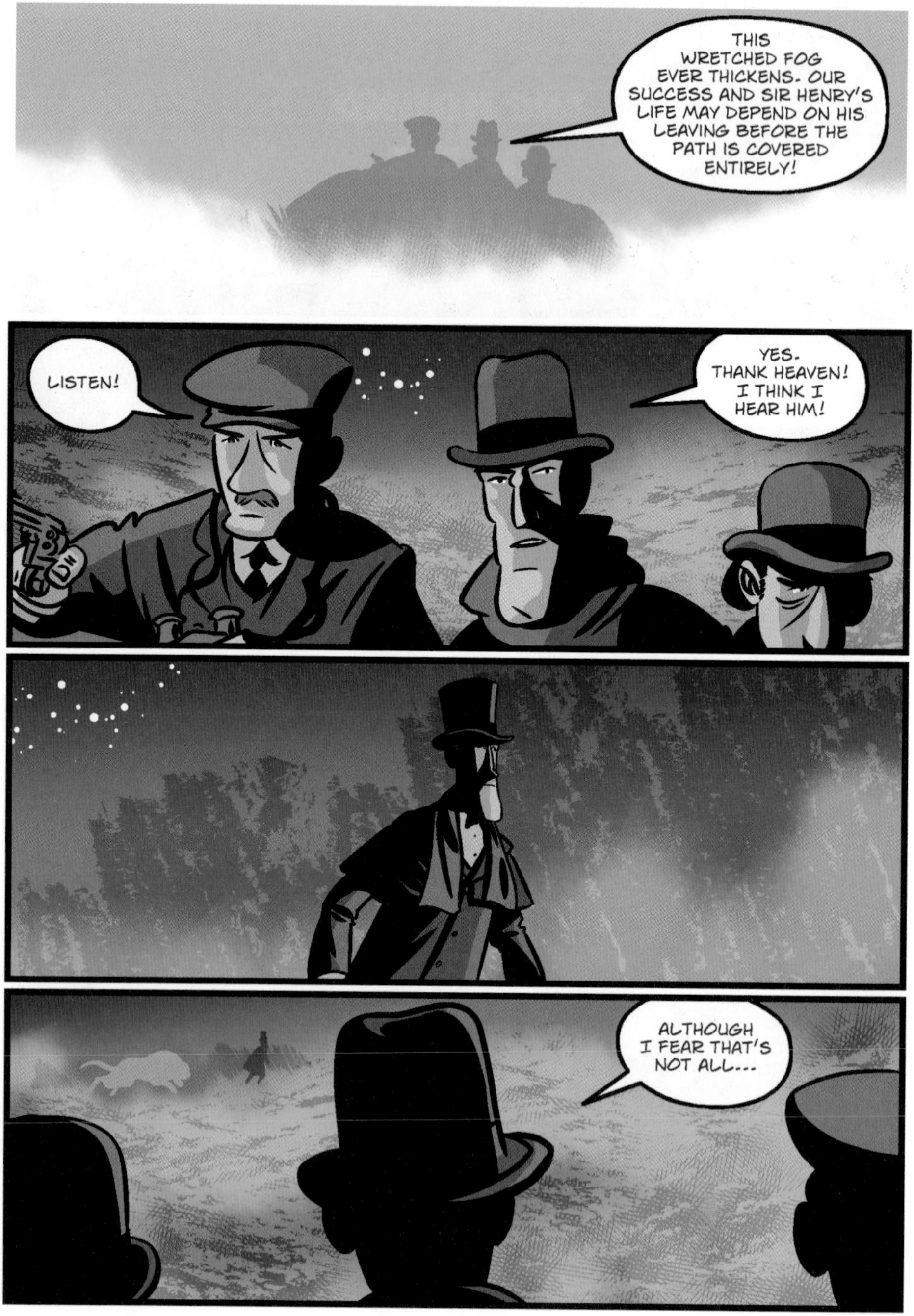
THIS WRETCHED FOG EVER THICKENS. OUR SUCCESS AND SIR HENRY'S LIFE MAY DEPEND ON HIS LEAVING BEFORE THE PATH IS COVERED ENTIRELY!
LISTEN!
YES. THANK HEAVEN! I THINK I HEAR HIM!
ALTHOUGH I FEAR THAT'S NOT ALL...

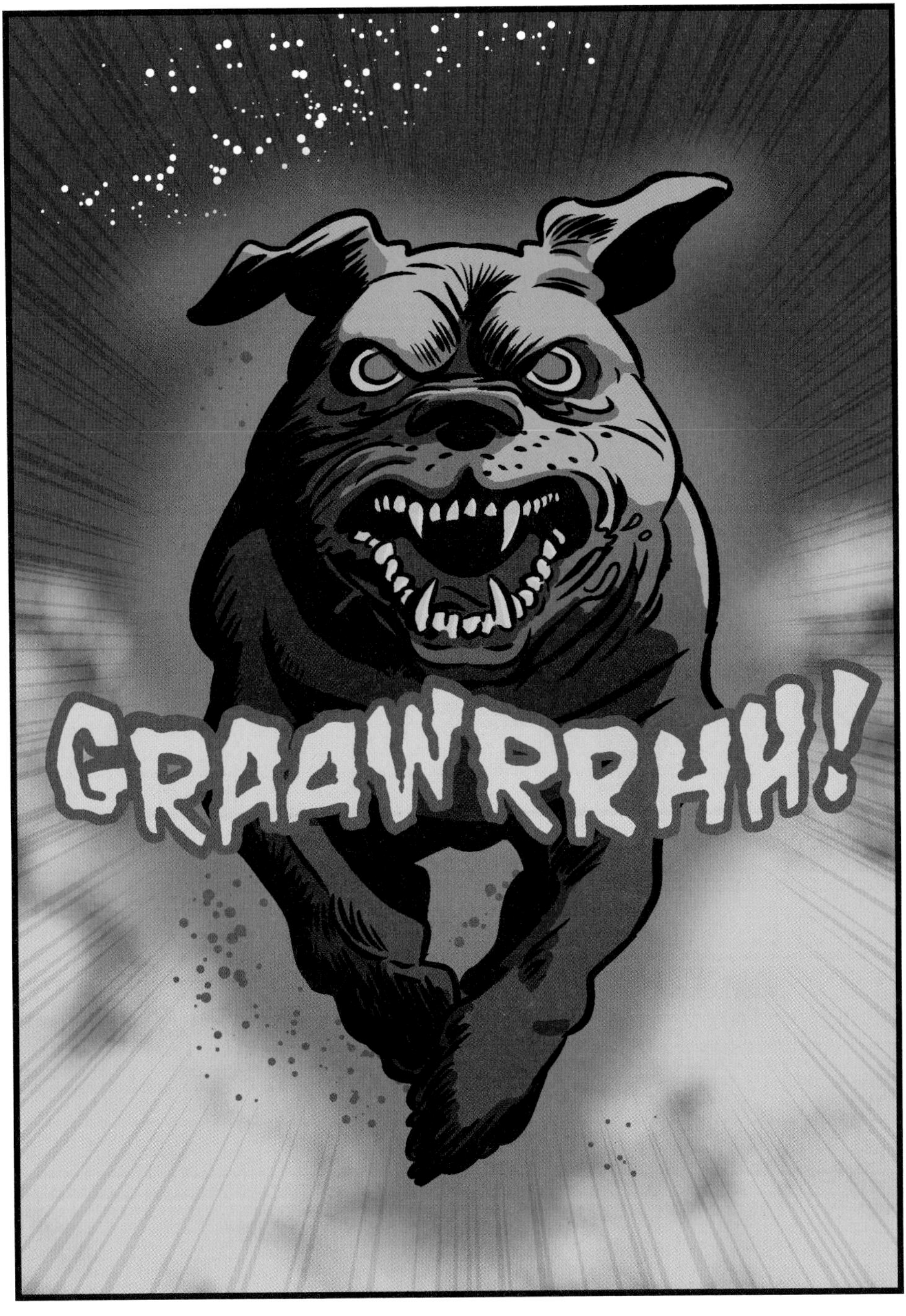
GRAAWRRHH!

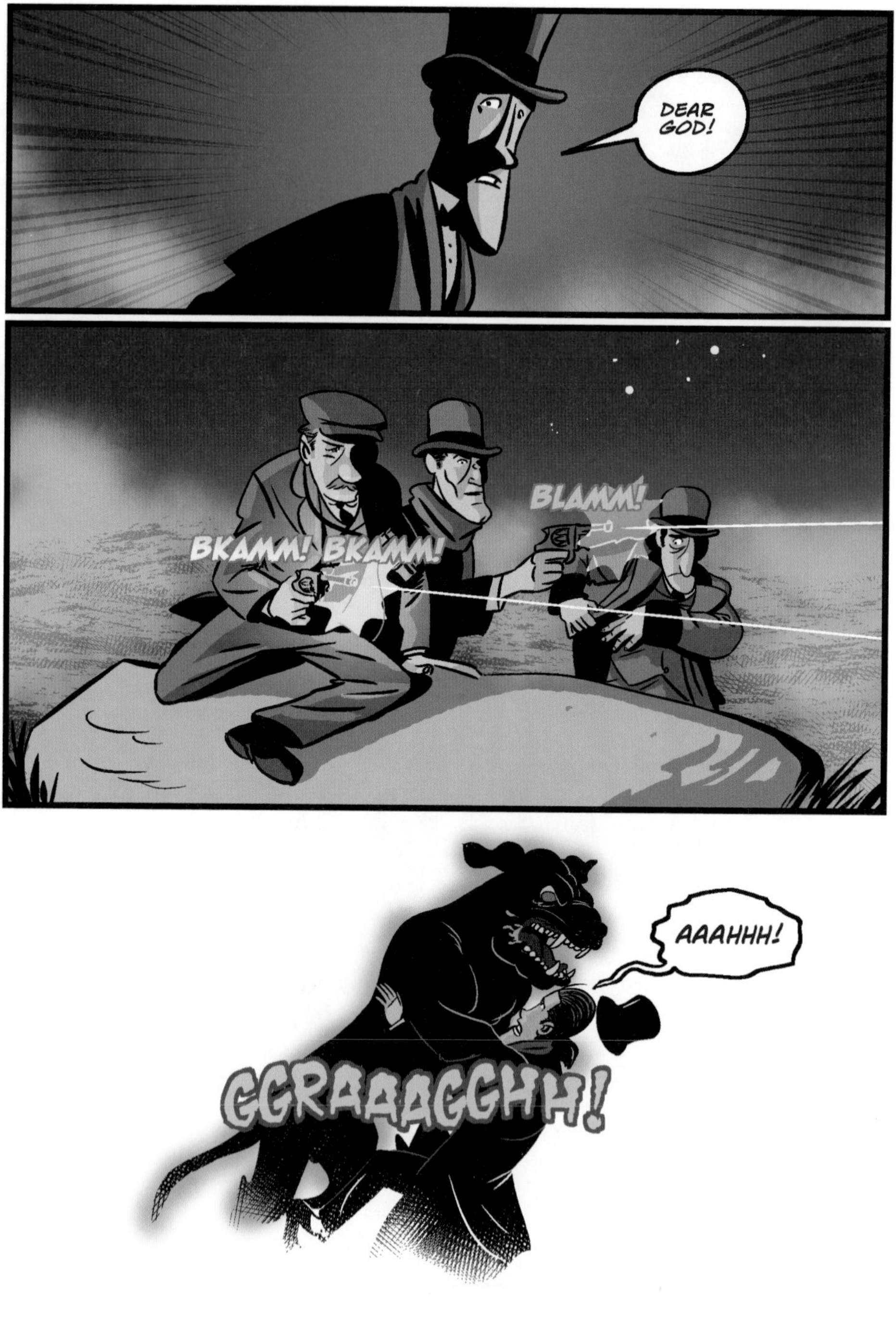
DEAR GOD!
BLAMM!
BKAMM! BKAMM!
AAAHHH!
GGRAAAGGHH!

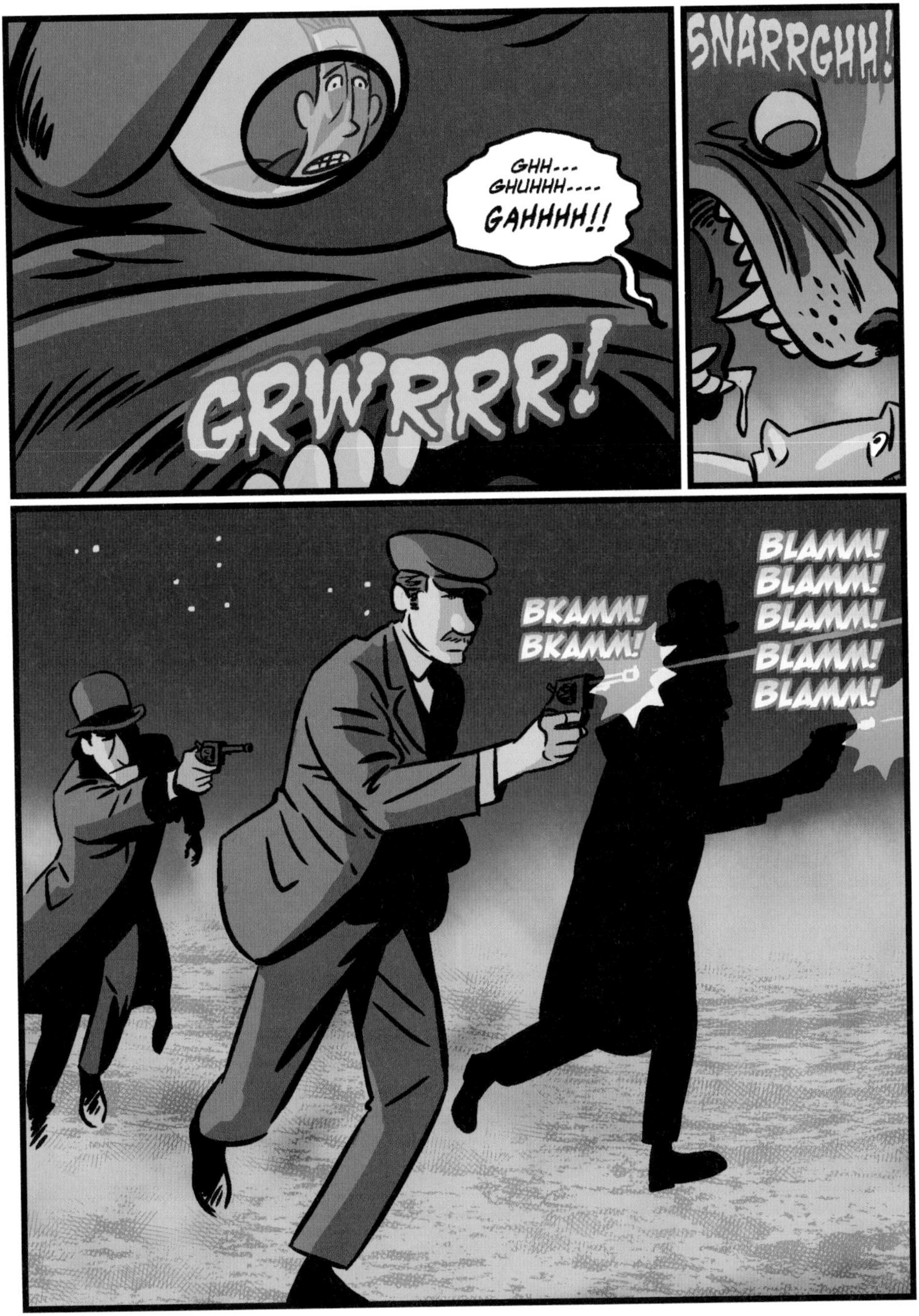
GHH...
GHUHHH....
GAHHHH!!
GRWRRR!
SNARRGHH!
BKAMM!
BKAMM!
BLAMM!
BLAMM!
BLAMM!
BLAMM!
BLAMM!

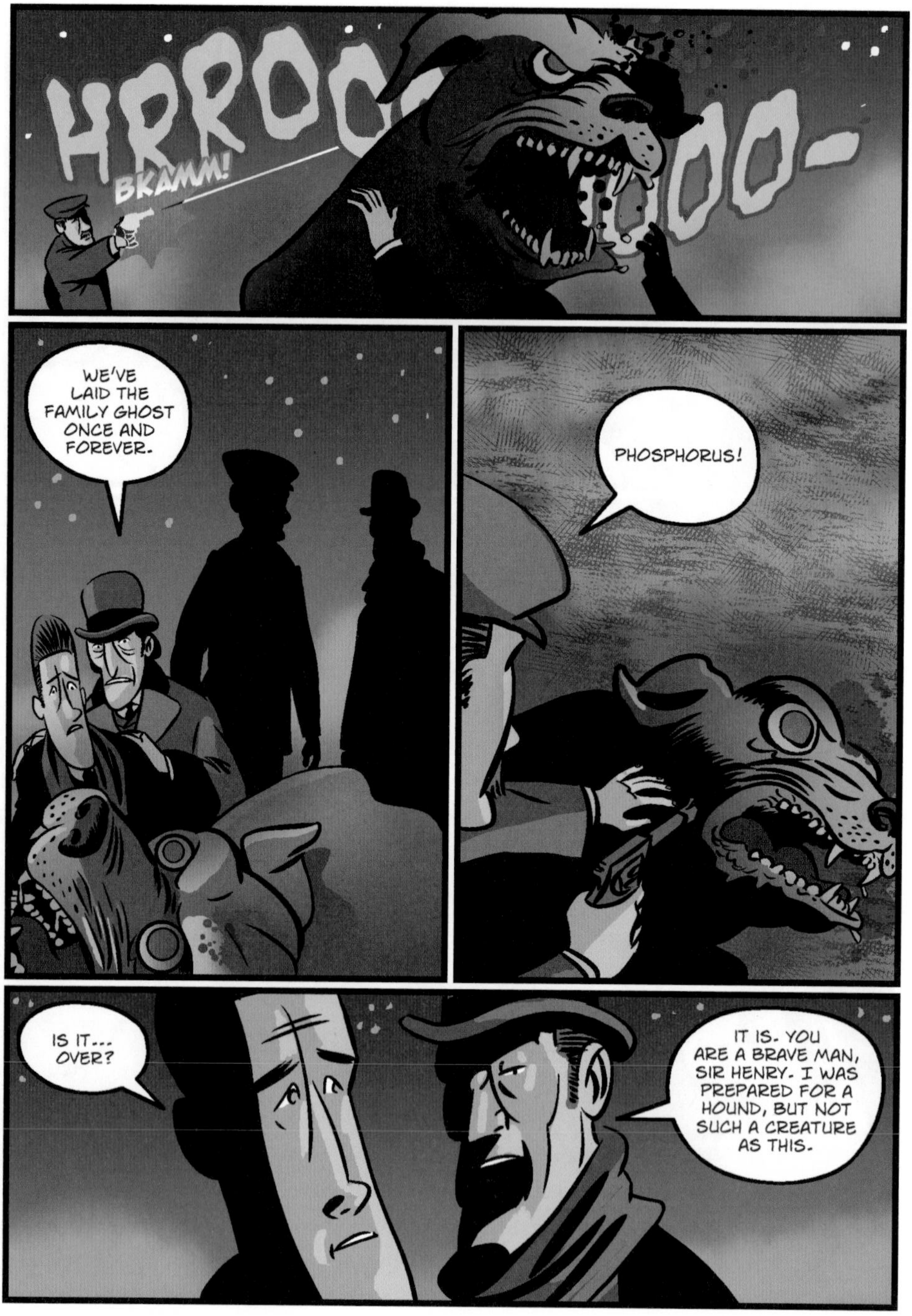
HRROOOOOOO-
BKAMM!
WE'VE LAID THE FAMILY GHOST ONCE AND FOREVER.
PHOSPHORUS!
IS IT... OVER?
IT IS. YOU ARE A BRAVE MAN, SIR HENRY. I WAS PREPARED FOR A HOUND, BUT NOT SUCH A CREATURE AS THIS.

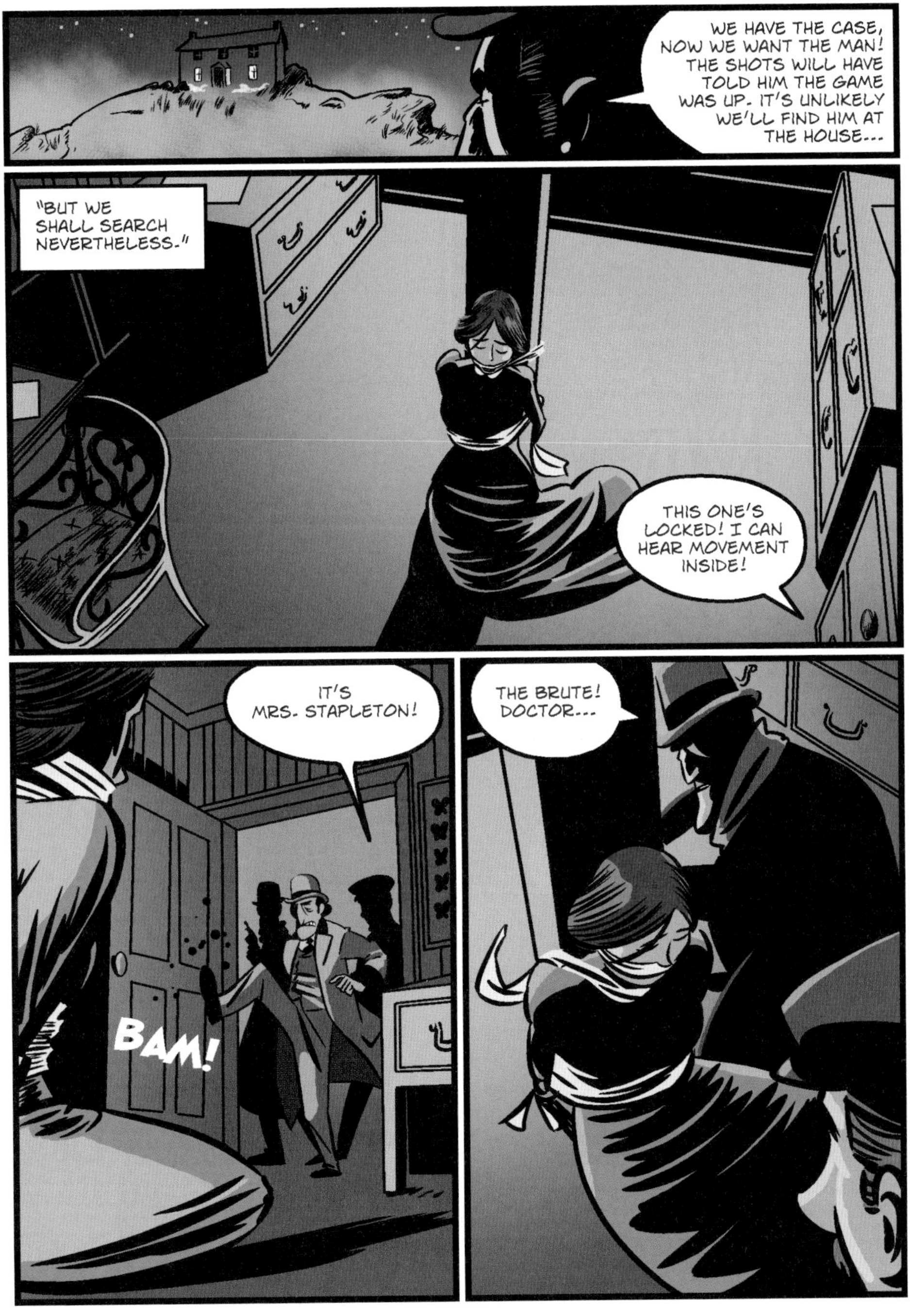
WE HAVE THE CASE, NOW WE WANT THE MAN! THE SHOTS WILL HAVE TOLD HIM THE GAME WAS UP. IT'S UNLIKELY WE'LL FIND HIM AT THE HOUSE...
"BUT WE SHALL SEARCH NEVERTHELESS."
THIS ONE'S LOCKED! I CAN HEAR MOVEMENT INSIDE!
IT'S MRS. STAPLETON!
BAM!
THE BRUTE! DOCTOR...

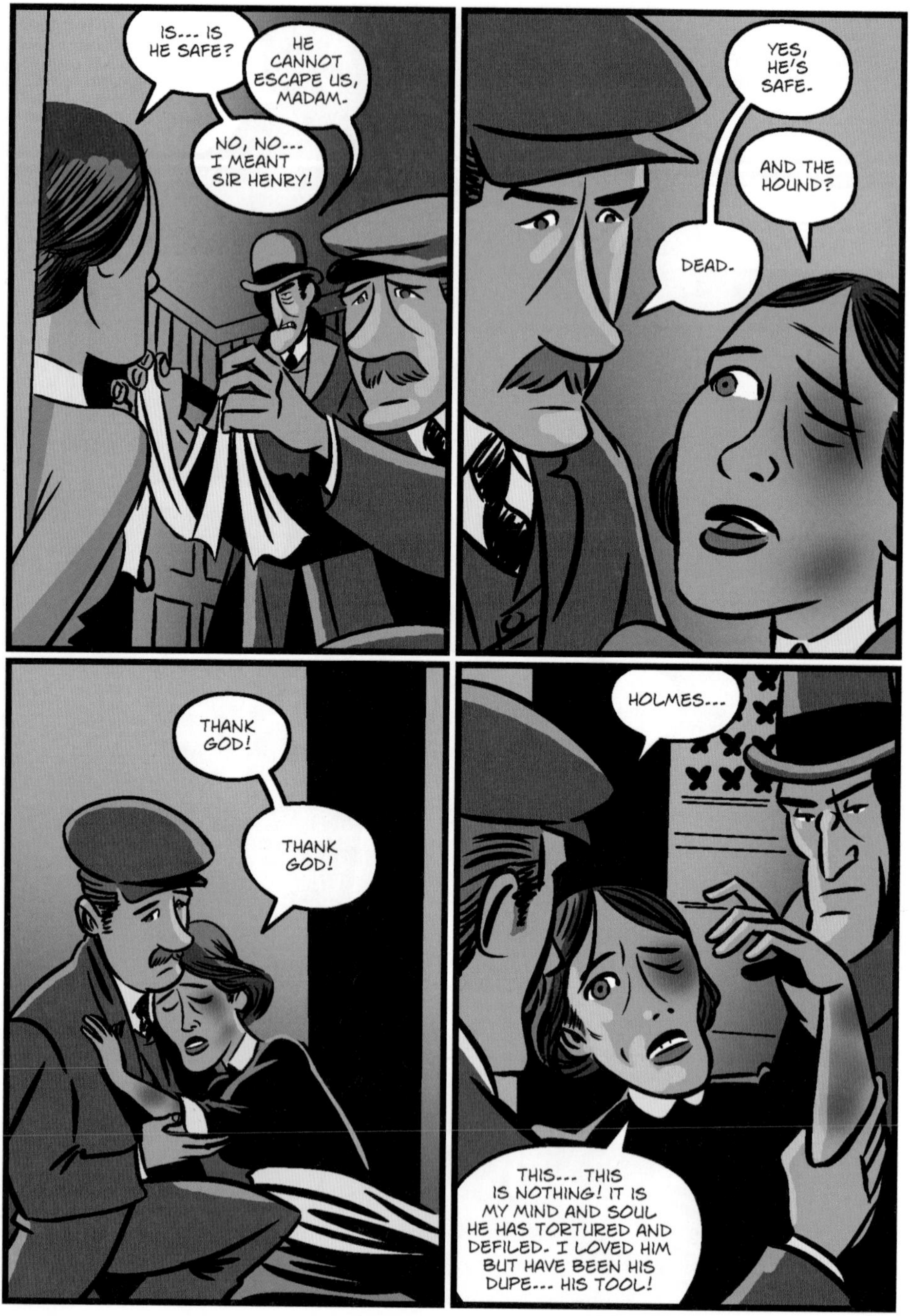
IS... IS HE SAFE?
HE CANNOT ESCAPE US, MADAM.
NO, NO... I MEANT SIR HENRY!
YES, HE'S SAFE.
AND THE HOUND?
DEAD.
THANK GOD!
THANK GOD!
HOLMES...
THIS... THIS IS NOTHING! IT IS MY MIND AND SOUL HE HAS TORTURED AND DEFILED. I LOVED HIM BUT HAVE BEEN HIS DUPE... HIS TOOL!

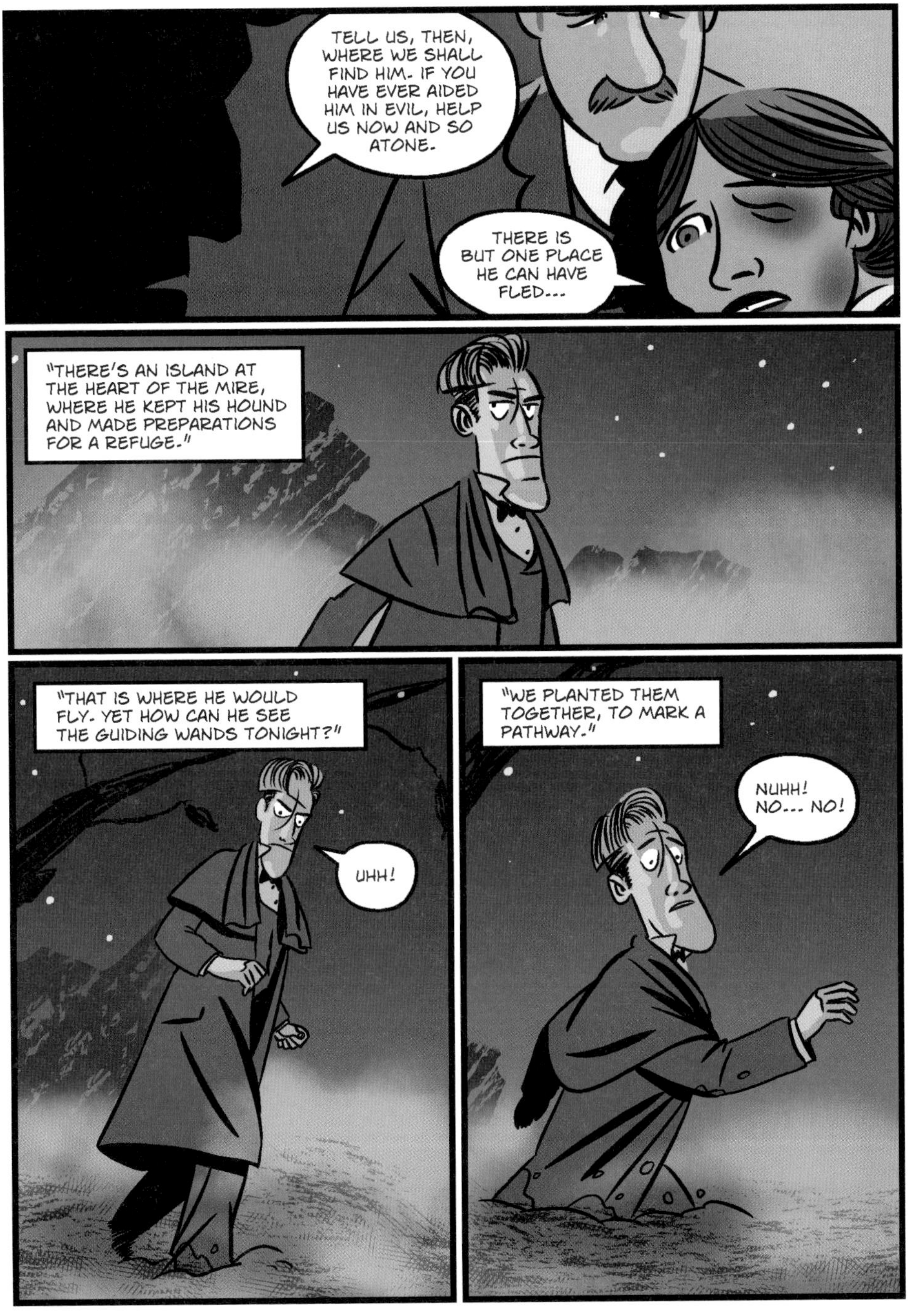
TELL US, THEN, WHERE WE SHALL FIND HIM. IF YOU HAVE EVER AIDED HIM IN EVIL, HELP US NOW AND SO ATONE.
THERE IS BUT ONE PLACE HE CAN HAVE FLED...
"THERE'S AN ISLAND AT THE HEART OF THE MIRE, WHERE HE KEPT HIS HOUND AND MADE PREPARATIONS FOR A REFUGE."
"THAT IS WHERE HE WOULD FLY. YET HOW CAN HE SEE THE GUIDING WANDS TONIGHT?"
UHH!
"WE PLANTED THEM TOGETHER, TO MARK A PATHWAY."
NUHH! NO... NO!

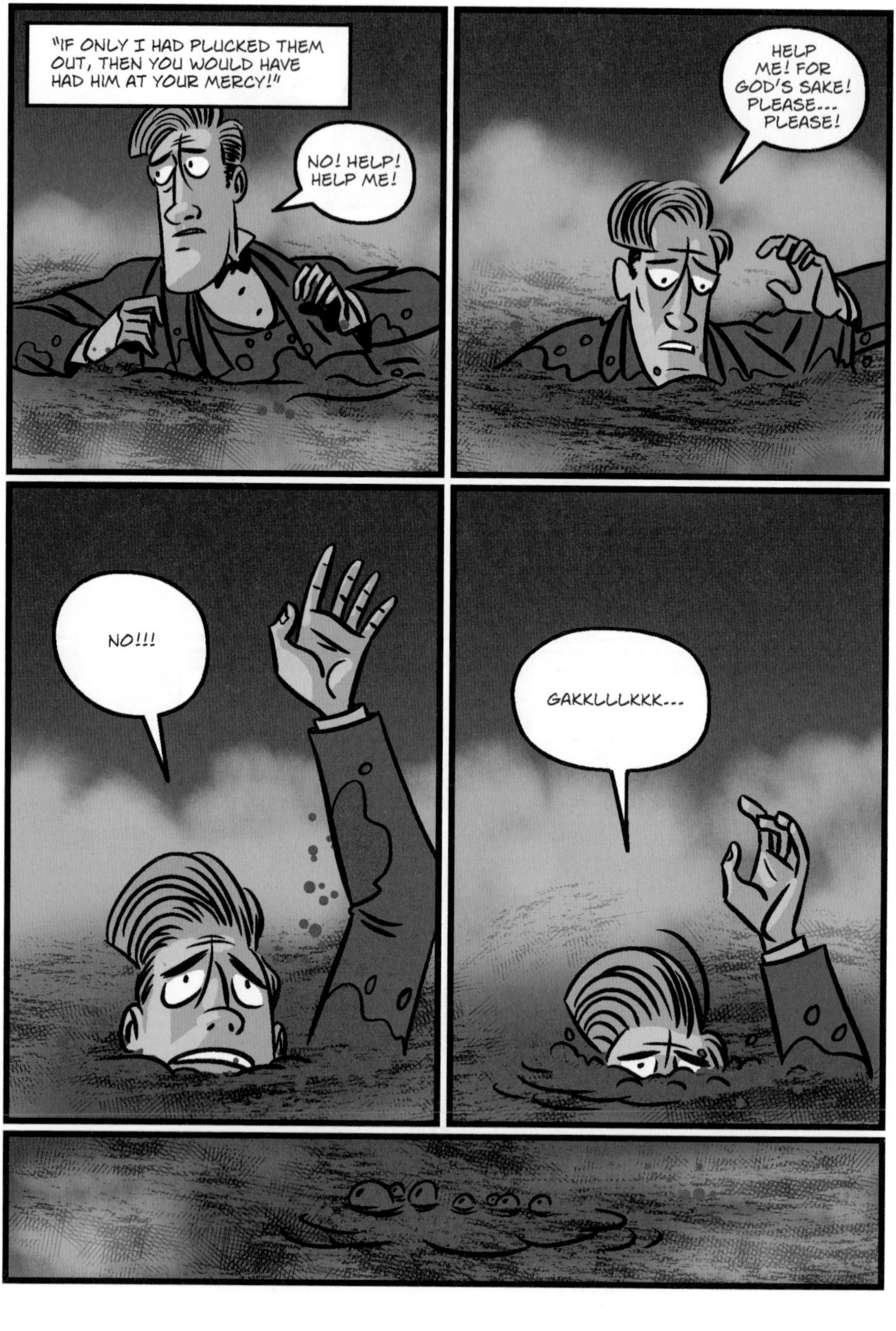
"IF ONLY I HAD PLUCKED THEM OUT, THEN YOU WOULD HAVE HAD HIM AT YOUR MERCY!"
NO! HELP! HELP ME!
HELP ME! FOR GOD'S SAKE! PLEASE... PLEASE!
NO!!!
GAKKLLLKKK...

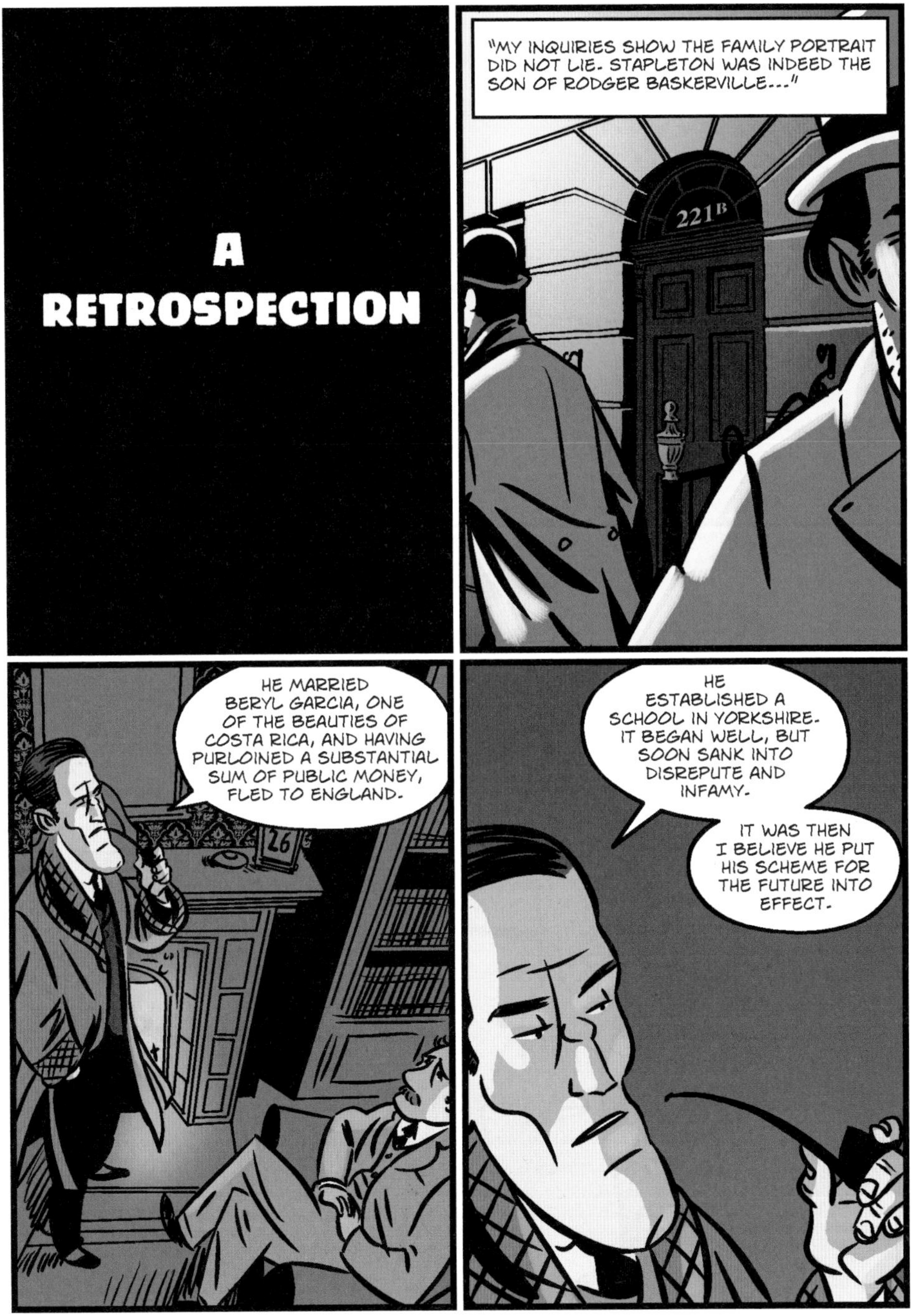
A RETROSPECTION
"MY INQUIRIES SHOW THE FAMILY PORTRAIT DID NOT LIE. STAPLETON WAS INDEED THE SON OF RODGER BASKERVILLE..."
221B
HE MARRIED BERYL GARCIA, ONE OF THE BEAUTIES OF COSTA RICA, AND HAVING PURLOINED A SUBSTANTIAL SUM OF PUBLIC MONEY, FLED TO ENGLAND.
26
HE ESTABLISHED A SCHOOL IN YORKSHIRE. IT BEGAN WELL, BUT SOON SANK INTO DISREPUTE AND INFAMY.
IT WAS THEN I BELIEVE HE PUT HIS SCHEME FOR THE FUTURE INTO EFFECT.

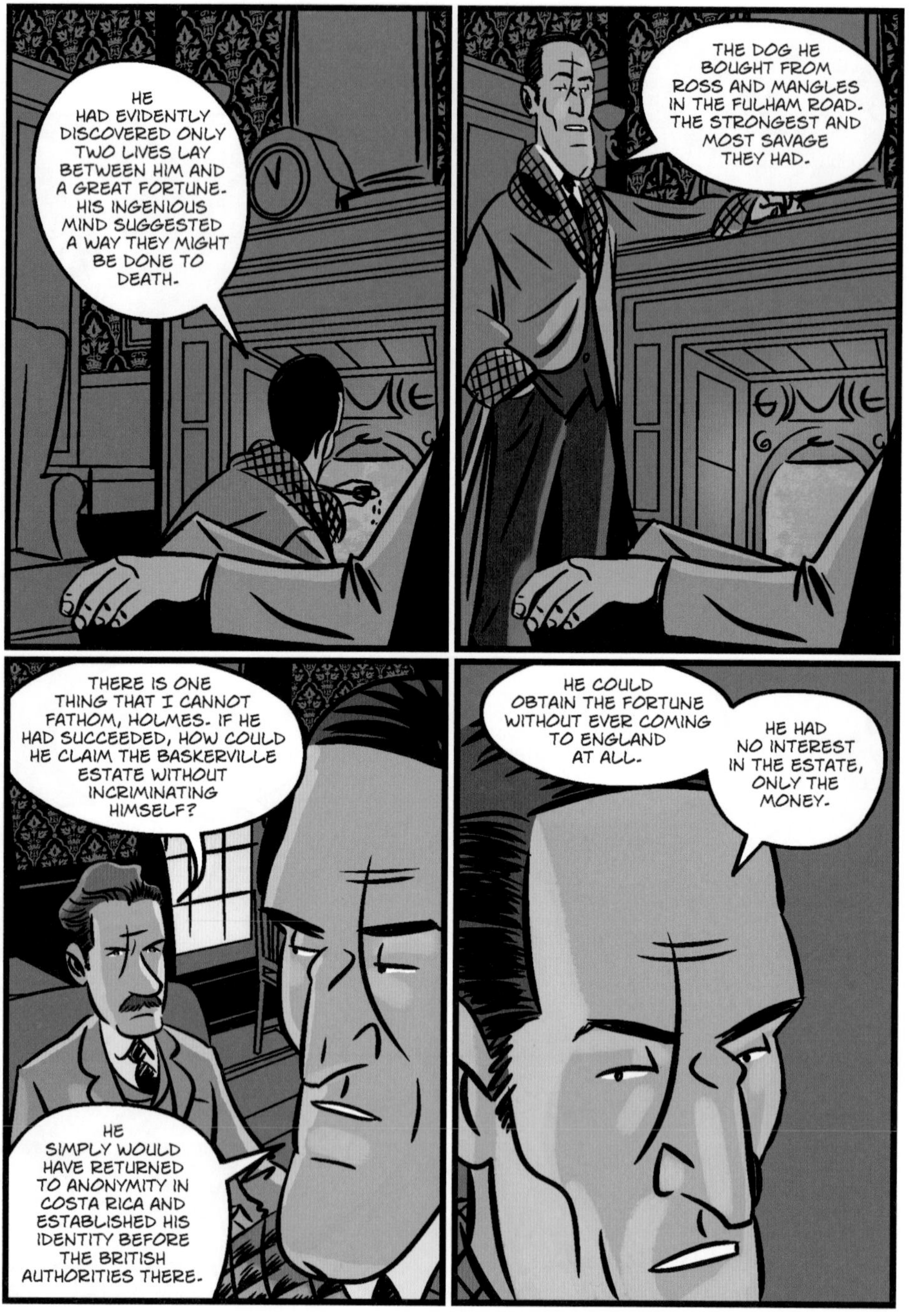
HE HAD EVIDENTLY DISCOVERED ONLY TWO LIVES LAY BETWEEN HIM AND A GREAT FORTUNE. HIS INGENIOUS MIND SUGGESTED A WAY THEY MIGHT BE DONE TO DEATH.
THE DOG HE BOUGHT FROM ROSS AND MANGLES IN THE FULHAM ROAD. THE STRONGEST AND MOST SAVAGE THEY HAD.
THERE IS ONE THING THAT I CANNOT FATHOM, HOLMES. IF HE HAD SUCCEEDED, HOW COULD HE CLAIM THE BASKERVILLE ESTATE WITHOUT INCRIMINATING HIMSELF?
HE SIMPLY WOULD HAVE RETURNED TO ANONYMITY IN COSTA RICA AND ESTABLISHED HIS IDENTITY BEFORE THE BRITISH AUTHORITIES THERE.
HE COULD OBTAIN THE FORTUNE WITHOUT EVER COMING TO ENGLAND AT ALL.
HE HAD NO INTEREST IN THE ESTATE, ONLY THE MONEY.

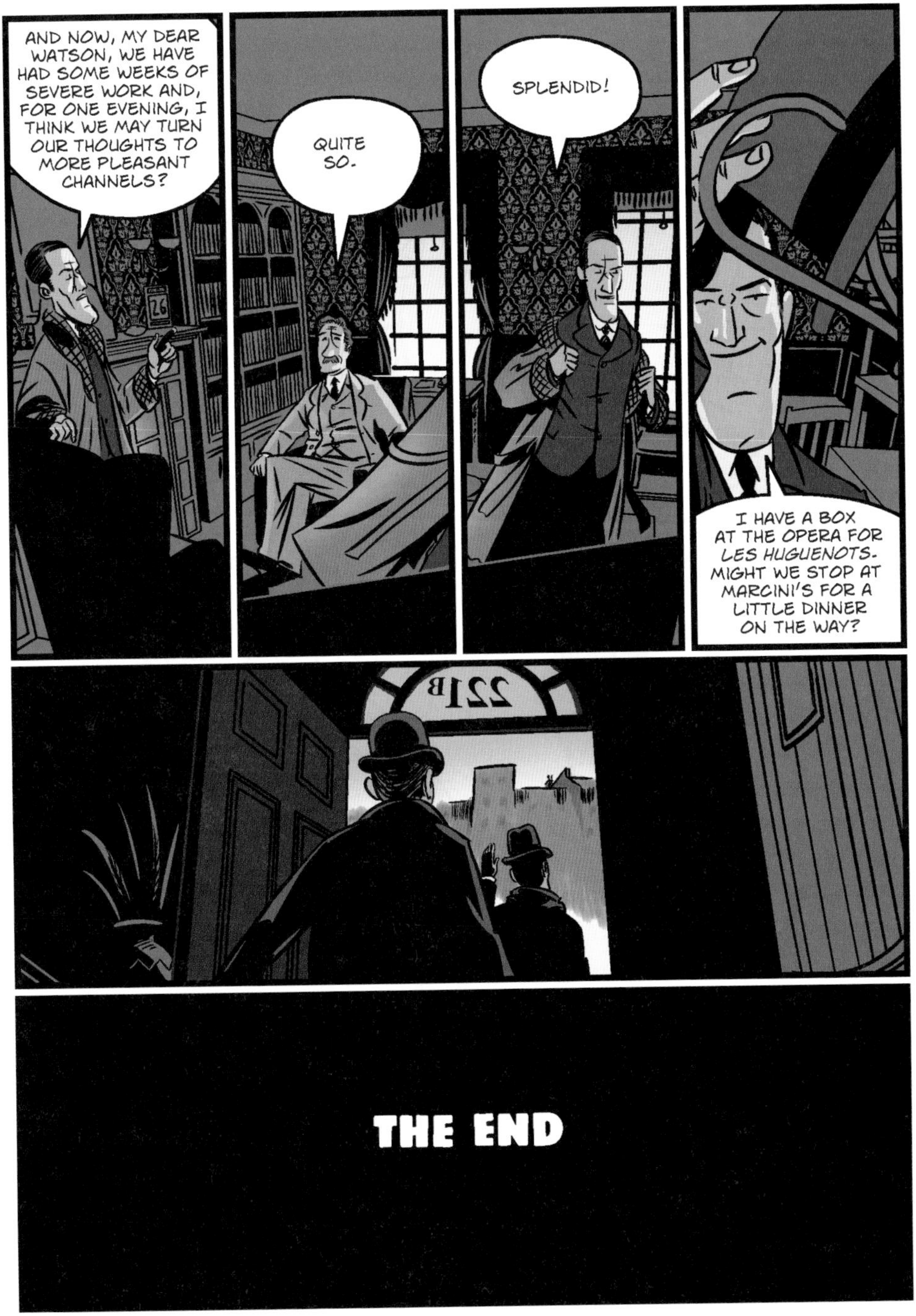
AND NOW, MY DEAR WATSON, WE HAVE HAD SOME WEEKS OF SEVERE WORK AND, FOR ONE EVENING, I THINK WE MAY TURN OUR THOUGHTS TO MORE PLEASANT CHANNELS?
26
QUITE SO.
SPLENDID!
I HAVE A BOX AT THE OPERA FOR *LES HUGUENOTS*. MIGHT WE STOP AT MARCINI'S FOR A LITTLE DINNER ON THE WAY?
221B
THE END

SKETCHBOOK

WITH NOTES BY I.N.J. CULBARD

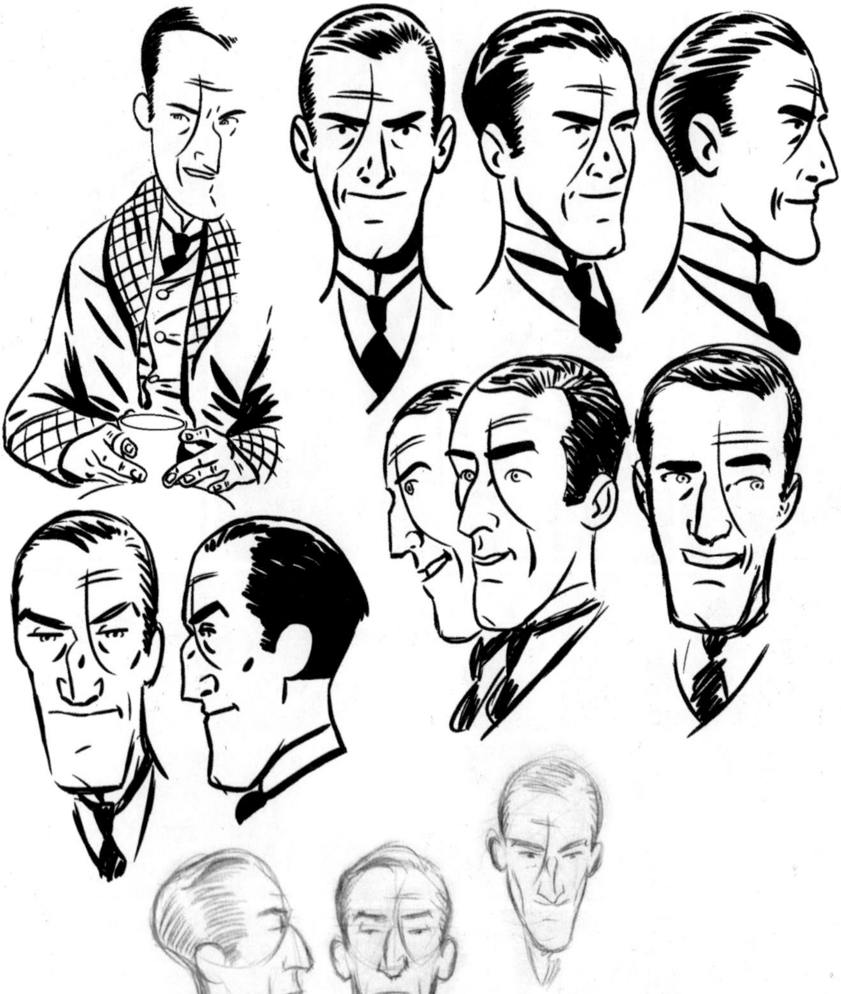

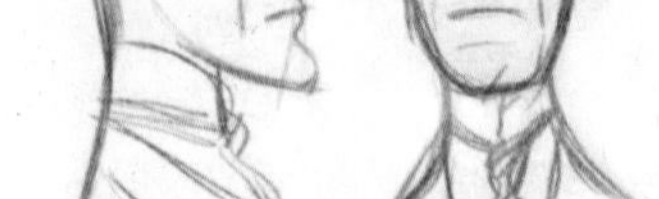

HOLMES IS IN HIS MID-THIRTIES WHEN *THE HOUND OF THE BASKERVILLES* TAKES PLACE. THE DESCRIPTION OF HIM GIVEN BY DR. WATSON IN *A STUDY IN SCARLET* PROVIDED ME WITH A FEW POINTERS. HIS EYES WERE "SHARP AND PIERCING" AND HIS NOSE "THIN" AND "HAWK-LIKE", WITH A CHIN THAT HAD "THE PROMINENCE AND SQUARENESS WHICH MARK THE MAN OF DETERMINATION". THESE ARE SOME EARLY DESIGNS.

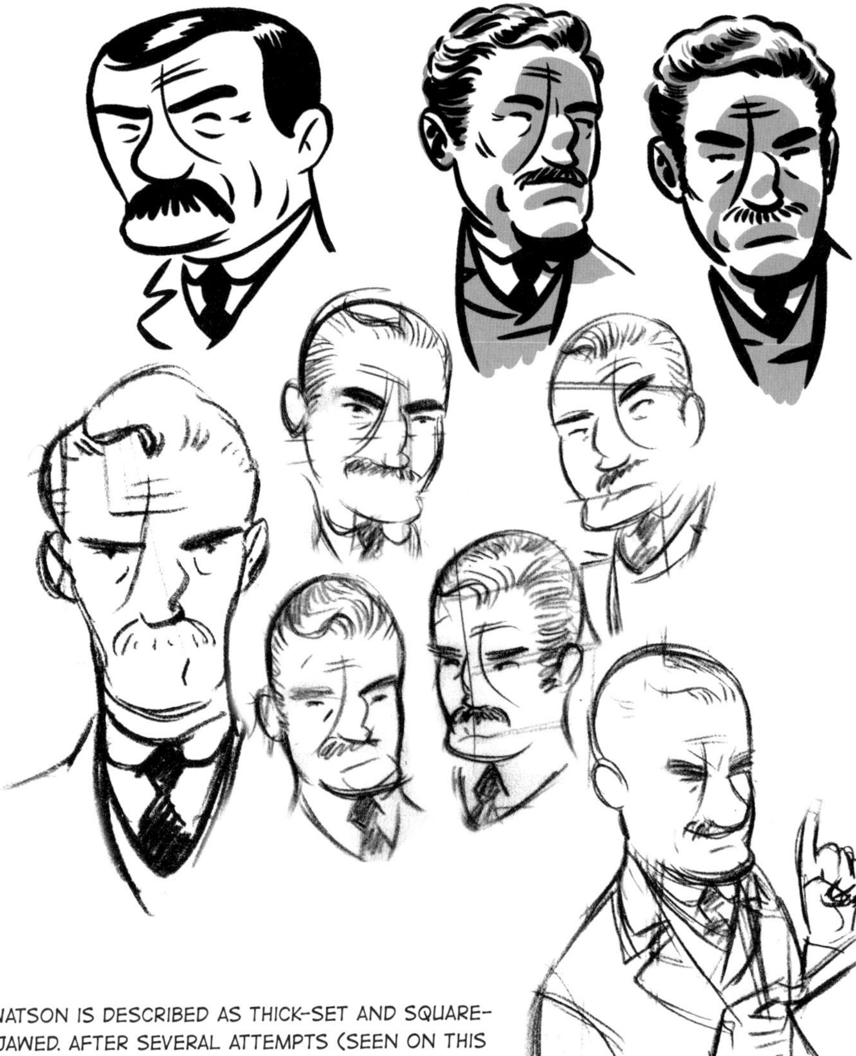

WATSON IS DESCRIBED AS THICK-SET AND SQUARE-JAWED. AFTER SEVERAL ATTEMPTS (SEEN ON THIS PAGE), I CONCLUDED THAT WATSON'S APPEARANCE OUGHT TO COMPLEMENT HOLMES' BY BEING QUITE CONTRARY. SO WHILE HOLMES' HAIR WAS SLICK AND STRAIGHT, IT SEEMED SENSIBLE TO HAVE WATSON'S BE THICKER AND WAVY. HOLMES' NOSE IS ANGULAR WITH A PROMINENT BRIDGE, SO WATSON'S IS FLAT ACROSS THE BRIDGE AND SMOOTH, AND SO ON...

WITH BOTH THESE EARLY JACKET COVER DESIGNS I WANTED TO CAPTURE THE PULP ADVENTURE FEEL TO THE SHERLOCK HOLMES STORIES, SO I WENT FOR AGED-LOOKING CREASED COVERS. HERE (RIGHT) WE HAVE A ROUGH EARLY DESIGN OF HOLMES AND WATSON SET AGAINST THE BLEAK BACKDROP OF THE MOOR, AND THE HOUND FRAMED BY MOONLIGHT ON THE TOR. I BASED THE HOUND'S SILHOUETTE ON THE IMAGE OF THE HOUND WHICH APPEARED ON THE COVER OF THE BOOK'S FIRST EDITION.

THE HOUND OF THE BASKERVILLES
A GRAPHIC NOVEL
Doyle - Edginton - Culbard

The HOUND of the BASKERVILLES
Doyle-Edginton-Culbard
IN JC 08
A GRAPHIC NOVEL

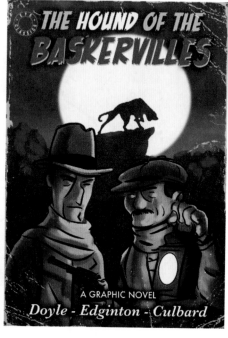

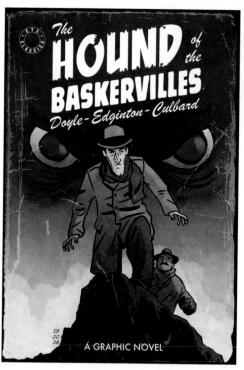

HERE'S A JACKET DESIGN PRODUCED LATER ON ONCE I'D ESTABLISHED HOLMES' APPEARANCE, BUT AS YOU CAN SEE FROM THIS PICTURE I WAS STILL TRYING TO FIGURE OUT WHAT MY VERSION OF WATSON WOULD LOOK LIKE.

The VALLEY of FEAR

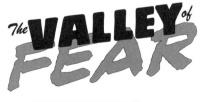

PREVIEW...

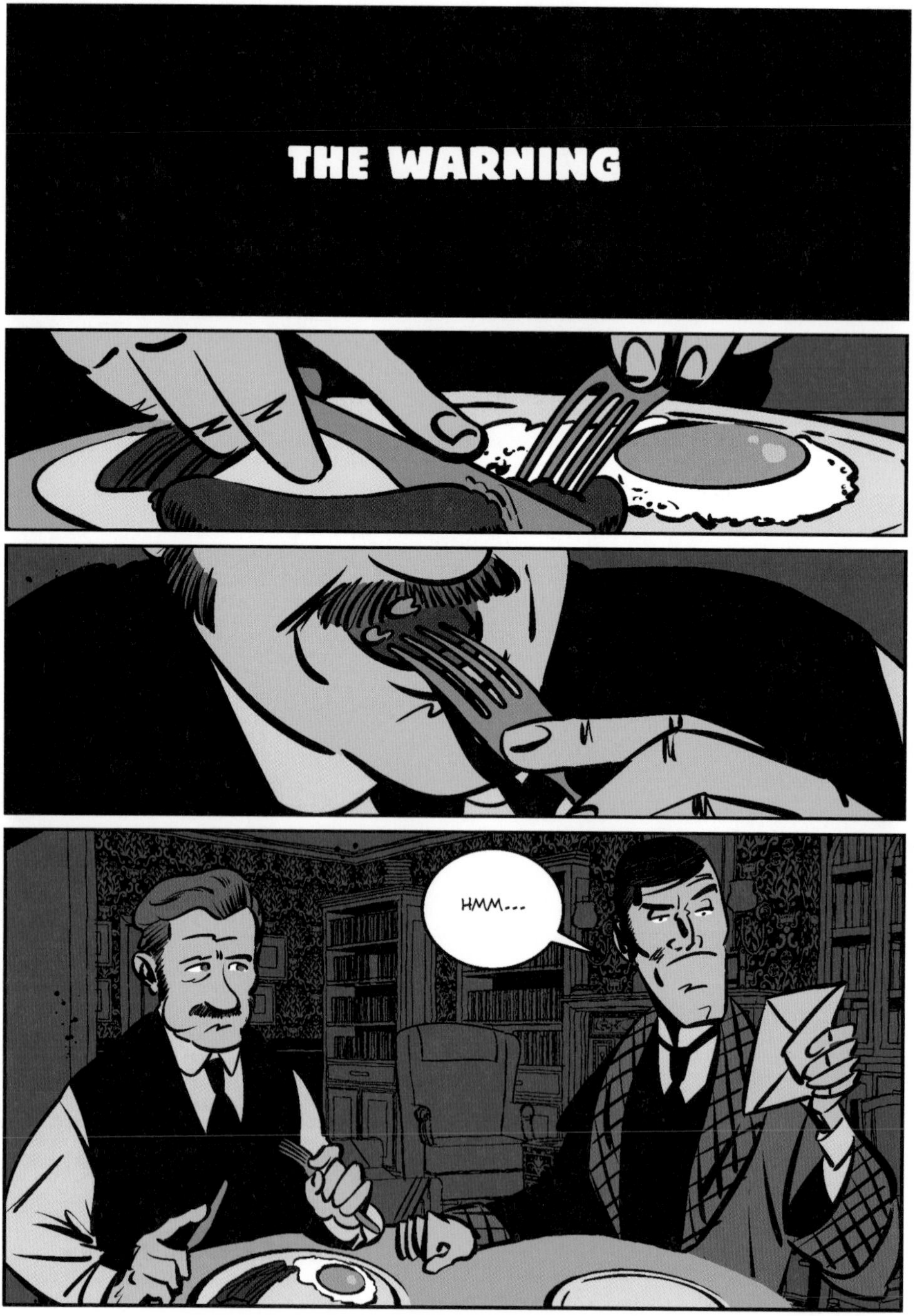
THE WARNING
HMM...

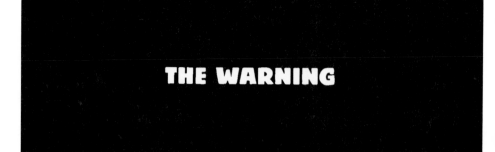

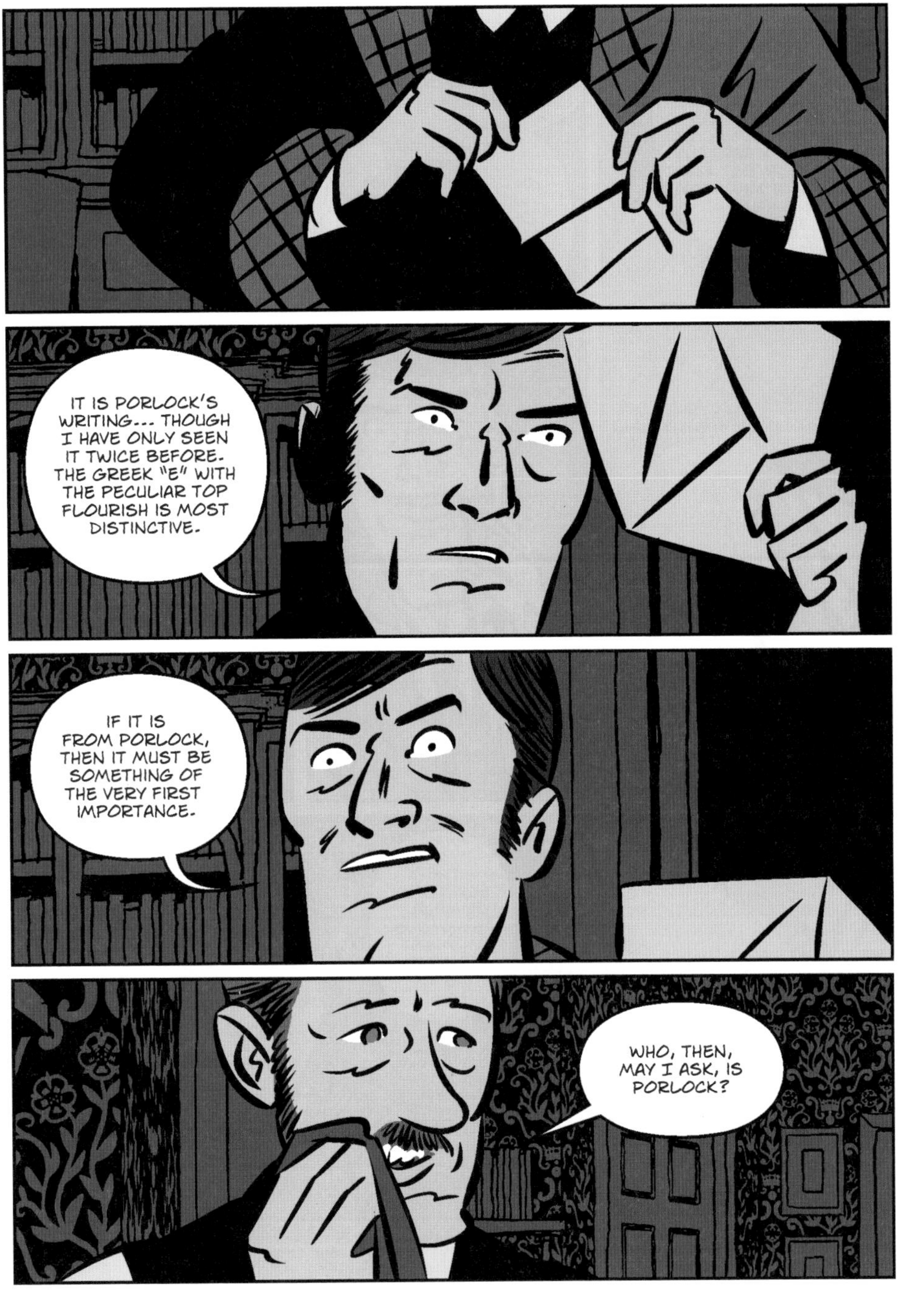
IT IS PORLOCK'S WRITING... THOUGH I HAVE ONLY SEEN IT TWICE BEFORE. THE GREEK "E" WITH THE PECULIAR TOP FLOURISH IS MOST DISTINCTIVE.
IF IT IS FROM PORLOCK, THEN IT MUST BE SOMETHING OF THE VERY FIRST IMPORTANCE.
WHO, THEN, MAY I ASK, IS PORLOCK?

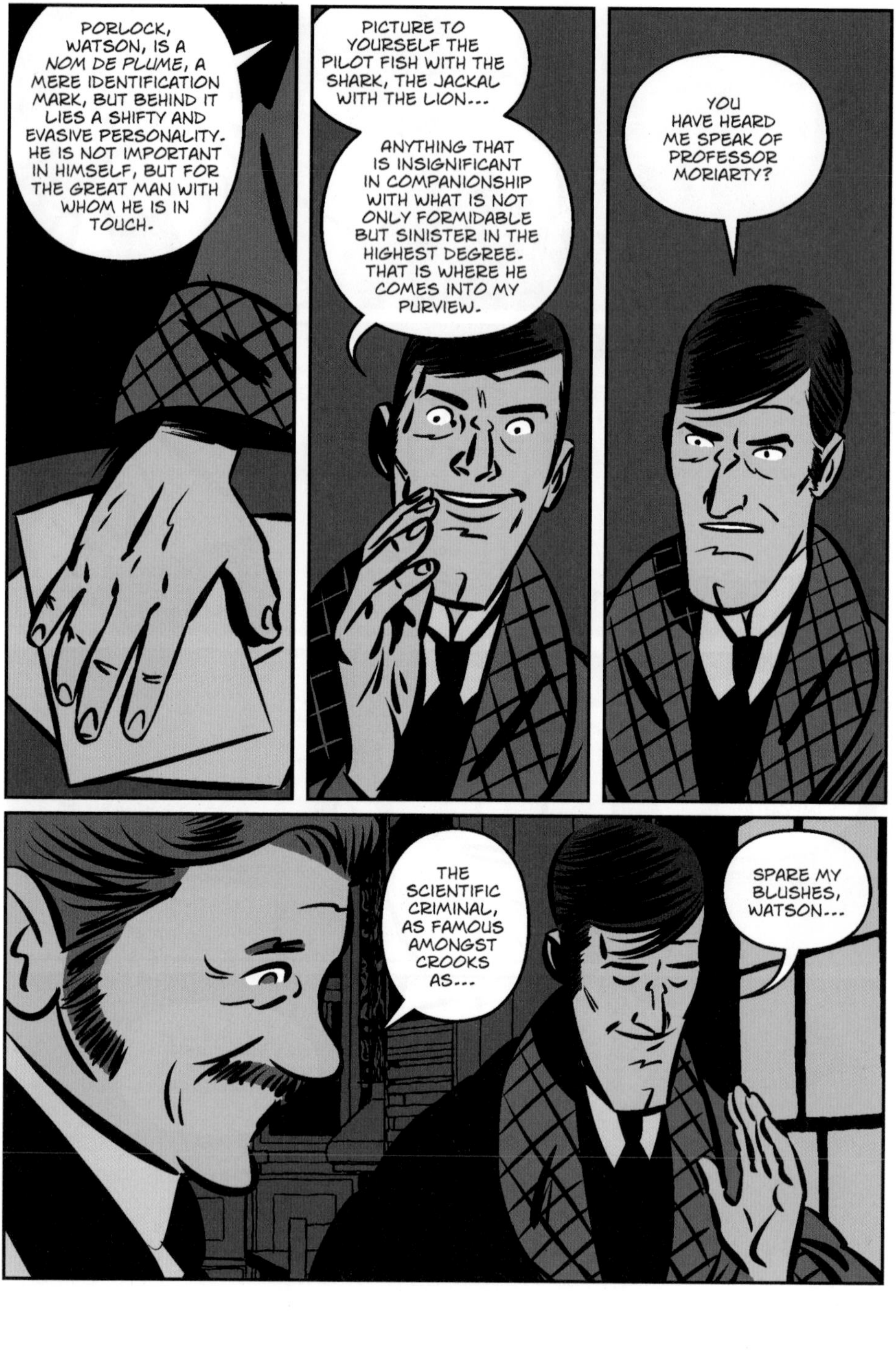
PORLOCK, WATSON, IS A *NOM DE PLUME*, A MERE IDENTIFICATION MARK, BUT BEHIND IT LIES A SHIFTY AND EVASIVE PERSONALITY. HE IS NOT IMPORTANT IN HIMSELF, BUT FOR THE GREAT MAN WITH WHOM HE IS IN TOUCH.
PICTURE TO YOURSELF THE PILOT FISH WITH THE SHARK, THE JACKAL WITH THE LION...
ANYTHING THAT IS INSIGNIFICANT IN COMPANIONSHIP WITH WHAT IS NOT ONLY FORMIDABLE BUT SINISTER IN THE HIGHEST DEGREE. THAT IS WHERE HE COMES INTO MY PURVIEW.
YOU HAVE HEARD ME SPEAK OF PROFESSOR MORIARTY?
THE SCIENTIFIC CRIMINAL, AS FAMOUS AMONGST CROOKS AS...
SPARE MY BLUSHES, WATSON...

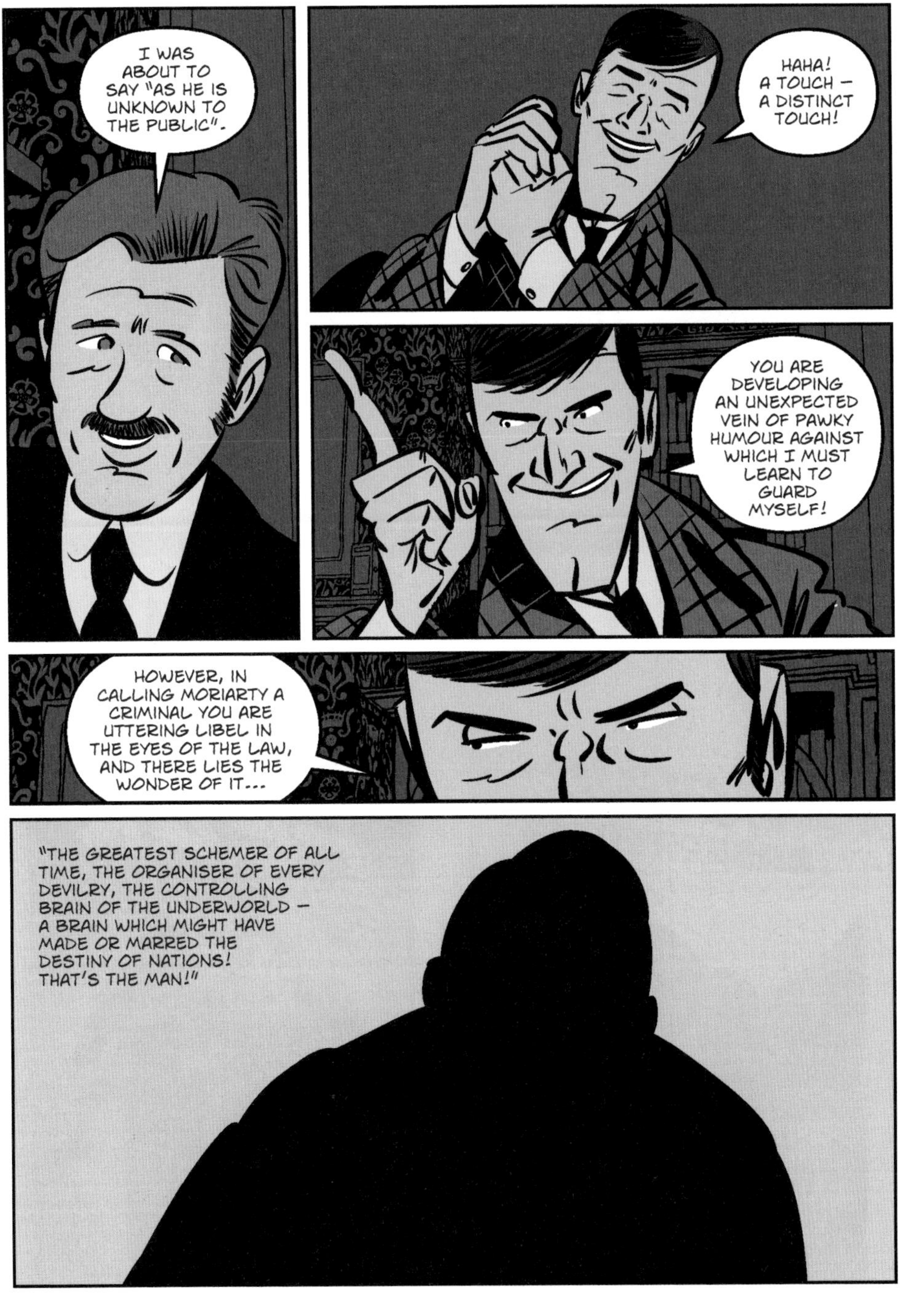
I WAS ABOUT TO SAY "AS HE IS UNKNOWN TO THE PUBLIC".
HAHA! A TOUCH — A DISTINCT TOUCH!
YOU ARE DEVELOPING AN UNEXPECTED VEIN OF PAWKY HUMOUR AGAINST WHICH I MUST LEARN TO GUARD MYSELF!
HOWEVER, IN CALLING MORIARTY A CRIMINAL YOU ARE UTTERING LIBEL IN THE EYES OF THE LAW, AND THERE LIES THE WONDER OF IT...
"THE GREATEST SCHEMER OF ALL TIME, THE ORGANISER OF EVERY DEVILRY, THE CONTROLLING BRAIN OF THE UNDERWORLD — A BRAIN WHICH MIGHT HAVE MADE OR MARRED THE DESTINY OF NATIONS! THAT'S THE MAN!"

Follow the world's only consulting detective...

ISBN 978-1-910593-33-2

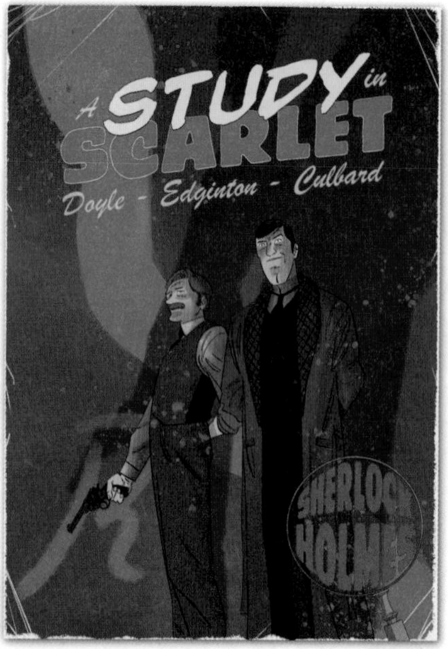
A STUDY in SCARLET
Doyle - Edginton - Culbard
SHERLOCK HOLMES

ISBN 978-1-910593-35-6

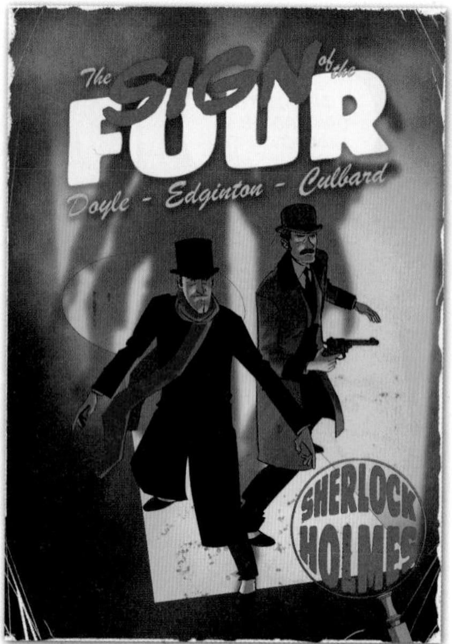
The SIGN of the FOUR
Doyle - Edginton - Culbard
SHERLOCK HOLMES

SHERLOCK HOLMES

ISBN 978-1-910593-32-5

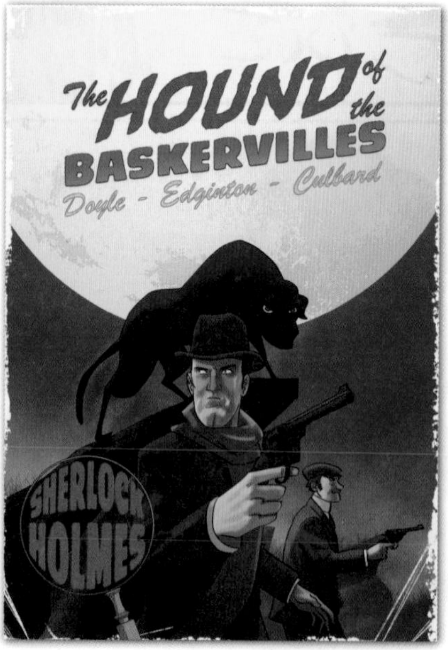
The HOUND of the BASKERVILLES
Doyle - Edginton - Culbard
SHERLOCK HOLMES

ISBN 978-1-910593-34-9

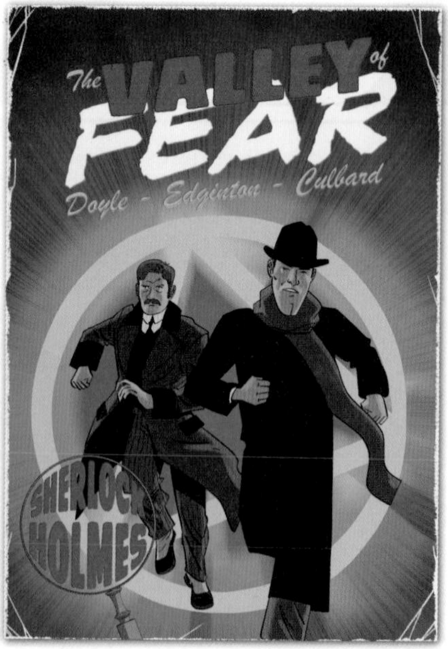
The VALLEY of FEAR
Doyle - Edginton - Culbard
SHERLOCK HOLMES

...on four deadly adventures.